# Words Is a Powerful Thing

# Words Is a Powerful Thing

Twenty Years of Teaching Creative Writing at Douglas County Jail

Brian Daldorph

 University Press of Kansas

Published by the University Press of Kansas (Lawrence, Kansas 66045), which was
organized by the Kansas Board of Regents and is operated and funded by Emporia
State University, Fort Hays State University, Kansas State University, Pittsburg State
University, the University of Kansas, and Wichita State University.

Library of Congress Cataloging-in-Publication Data

Names: Daldorph, Brian, 1958– author.
Title: Words is a powerful thing : twenty years of teaching creative writing at
    Douglas County Jail / Brian John Daldorph.
Description: Lawrence : University Press of Kansas, 2021. | Includes
    bibliographical references.
Identifiers: LCCN 2020044341
    ISBN 9780700632152 (cloth)
    ISBN 9780700632169 (paperback)
    ISBN 9780700632176 (epub)
Subjects: LCSH: Daldorph, Brian, 1958– author. | Creative writing—Study
    and teaching—Kansas—Douglas County. | Prisoners—Education—Kansas—
    Douglas County. | Prisoners' writings, American. | Poets, American—
    20th century—Biography. | English teachers—United States—Biography.
Classification: LCC PS3554.A4149 Z46 2021 | DDC 811/.54 [B]—dc23
LC record available at https://lccn.loc.gov/2020044341.

British Library Cataloguing-in-Publication Data is available.

Printed in the United States of America

10 9 8 7 6 5 4 3 2 1

*To the writers who came to my class in December 2001*
*and kept coming for the next two decades*

# Contents

# Preface

I first entered the Douglas County Jail classroom in Lawrence, Kansas, to teach the creative writing class on Christmas Eve 2001. My last class at the jail for the foreseeable future was in mid-March 2020, right before the coronavirus lockdown; the virus is especially savage in confined communities such as nursing homes and prisons. In August 2020, with the pandemic raging, it's hard to think when my colleagues and I will be allowed back into the jail to resume teaching.

*Words Is a Powerful Thing* is my story of teaching at the jail for the two decades between 2001 and 2020, showing how the lives of all of us involved in the class—but especially how the inmates who came to class week after week—benefitted from what happened every Thursday afternoon in that jail classroom, where for two hours we became a *circle of ink and blood*, writing together, reciting our poems, telling stories, and having a few good laughs. For some of the inmates, as I show in this book, the benefits of the class were long lasting.

Though I've been out of the jail classroom because of the Covid-19 pandemic for longer than at any other time since I started teaching there in 2001, I can still see so clearly the faces of some students, friendly but strained by their circumstances, some of them inside for just a few days or weeks, others looking at long and painful sentences. Most people only ever want to get out of the jail, whereas here I am now wanting to get back in.

As I sit here at my desk at home, I hear in my mind some of the students' words, which I'll keep hearing for as long as I live—passionate expressions that, the first time I heard them, went straight to my heart and stayed there:

> When you arrive, read the sign: "Leave all hopes
> and dreams behind." Forget all you have or had
> in the free world, it no longer matters. It will only
> distract you and you'll become prey to the lions

in this jungle. Trust no one; everyone is out for something
in this cutthroat society.

After so long in here
& so many hours upon days upon weeks locked in a cell,
the more claustrophobic I've become. It's a mental challenge
every time I step through that door & they think I'm
trying to be defiant.

I watch as time slowly chews away on men's
sanity, where confusion reigns supreme.

Soon now the jail awakens to do
its time;
it seems better at that than we.
I think it's because the cold walls
got time down because they know
they will never be free.

For the past two decades, I have been teaching in the US corrections system, which most everyone agrees is not really working for anyone and which compares badly with the jails and prisons of other Western democracies. In *Thinking about Crime: Sense and Sensibility in American Penal Culture* (2004), Michael Tonry states, "The US has a punishment system that no one would knowingly have built from the ground up. It is often unjust, it is unduly severe, it is wasteful, and it does enormous damage to the lives of black Americans."[1] How to change this monster into something that might actually, in a beneficial way, *correct*? There are many calls for change, many ideas for improvement, but at the moment it is the system we have to work in, and I like to think that my twenty-year commitment to a class at a county jail has at least led to some benefits in the lives of the people caught up in "corrections."

I'm thankful to Programs Director Mike Caron at the Douglas County Jail (2001–2015) for not only supporting my colleagues' initial idea for a writing class at the jail but also for supervising me over the fifteen years we worked together. Without him, I would not have had the opportunity for this work, which seemed to be my calling, allowing me to combine my commitment to social justice with my lifelong literary interests, all coming together in that county jail classroom with windows the size of mail slots. Class after class after class at the jail, the weeks, months, years passing. We'd meet *every* week, especially during holiday times, because we realized that inmates most often feel the stress of incarceration when they think of being with their families and friends. There was nothing I enjoyed more on a Thursday afternoon than checking in at the main entrance of the jail, taking the elevator up to the second floor, then walking the corridor to the classroom thinking about who might be in class that week.

When Caron retired in 2015, the class reinvented itself under the co-leadership of Programs Director Sherry Gill, who was determined to make it a positive experience for the inmates she had helped in other ways as a case manager for many years. At the same time, retired business journalist Mike Hartnett began to volunteer on a regular basis. Our teaching team expanded when, for the first time, a former inmate, Antonio Sanchez-Day, was allowed back into the jail as a volunteer. He added a vital element to the class as an instructor with substantial inside knowledge of incarceration. Our teaching team was complete when University of Kansas (KU) graduate student Ayah Wakkad joined us, wanting to find out more about the US justice system to add another perspective to her dissertation work on incarceration in the Middle East.

Two decades of Douglas County Jail classes. I wish I could go back, start over, and hold each of those classes again because, in spite of or as a result of the challenges, I enjoyed them more than any other of my teaching experiences. I've never seen so clearly the significance of making art—in this case, poetry—as a lifeline, a way of surviving in the tough circumstances in which all inmates find themselves. The class validated my belief in making art as a personal and social good, a truly transformational activity.

My jail time has taught me that:

poetry can help to keep someone's head above the dark, cold water, even when confined to a small, stark room for many hours of every day;

poetry is a beautiful gift anyone can receive and make use of, requiring only the simplest tools and a commitment to telling the truth in language;

poetry can bring diverse people together in significant ways, so we do not have to face all our troubles alone;

for those of us trying to come to terms with ourselves and striving for self-improvement, poetry is available to us most any time;

a remarkable body of work, reaching an audience way beyond the one imagined by the writers in the classroom, has come out of a writing class in the county jail of a midwestern college town;

as an inmate once said, "Words is a powerful thing."

I consider my work at Douglas County Jail my "shadow career," alongside my career as an assistant professor and senior lecturer in the English Department at KU. My two careers have often combined, though, because I published poetry and articles about my teaching experience, including my book of poetry *Jail Time* (2008). Each semester, I invite teacher colleagues Sanchez-Day and Hartnett to talk to my university classes about the jail class and about their books to show the students the real-world power of poetry.

I have met many remarkable writers in the classroom at the jail who have illuminated not only the Douglas County Jail but also the world beyond it. The inmates I have worked with have known failure and trouble leading to their incarceration. But sometimes they picked up a pencil, started to write about their dire circumstances, and wrote words that gave them and all of us that most vital thing, hope.

I fail at most everything until my pen unwinds.

Words unveil, through mists of time in my mind.

I may not shine or even get what's mine

but when these words come together, they're one of a kind.

My little mark in the world.

In *Words Is a Powerful Thing*, I have written about notable events and people in the Douglas County Jail writing class during my two decades of teaching there. Most important, though, I believe, are the lines from more than fifty of the student writers included here, their "little mark[s] in the world," written in a dark place, that somehow light up the lives of all of us through the power of poetry.

# Acknowledgments

Thanks are due to

* my team members at Douglas County Correctional Facility over the years 2001–2020: Mike Caron, Sherry Gill, Antonio Sanchez-Day, Mike Hartnett, and Ayah Wakkad. Thanks also to Matt Porubsky and Ryan McCarty, volunteers at the jail, who added their insights to this book.

* all the people who do the hard work very well at Douglas County Jail. There are reasons the jail is considered a model correctional facility.

* my home team, which has supported my shadow career as a jail instructor: my wife, Misae, and my daughters, Brenna and Lucy. I owe considerable thanks to Brenna as a frequent visitor to the class and as a smart editor who helped me when I couldn't see how to make the damn thing any better. Thanks to my sister Christine, who sat in on classes and said that they were the highlights of her visit to Kansas, and to my father, who never expected to be in jail discussing poetry.

* Anna Neill and Kirk Branch for having the guts and vision to start a project that has brought a lot of benefit to many people over the years.

* Pam LeRow at the University of Kansas, for your patience and technical expertise in preparing this manuscript.

* Professor Maryemma Graham, an inspiration to me and to a million others.

* great visitors to the jail, including John and Shannon Musgrave, Bill Bauer, Kevin Rabas, Al Ortolani, Katherine Dinsdale, Arlin Buyert, and Ronda Miller.

* artist Kerry Niemann, for art that tells more than I could say in 10,000 words. How do you do that?

* the editors of *J Journal* at the John Jay College of Criminal Justice, in New York, for permission to reuse material in Chapter 2 from "'What Really

Matters': Nine Years of Teaching a Creative Writing Class at Douglas County Jail, Lawrence, Kansas," *J Journal* 3, no. 1 (2010): 33–45.

* the great editors at the University Press of Kansas with whom I've been lucky enough to work: Kim Hogeland, who read the first raw manuscript and encouraged me; David Congdon, who read many drafts and made them so much better every time; and Kelly Chrisman Jacques, managing editor of production. Couldn't have done this without you. Thanks as well to copyeditor Melanie Stafford.

# Chapter 1

# "Imagination Knows No Cinder Blocks"

## Education Inside the Walls

I breach this cell with every thought I think—

imagination knows no cinder blocks.

> —Vogue Rogue, "The Asylum of Psyche (or Free Cell),"
> *Douglas County Jail Blues*

Writing was water that cleansed the wound and fed the parched root

of my heart.

> —Jimmy Santiago Baca, *Working in the Dark*

*Thursday morning, 11:00 a.m., January 2015, at my desk at home, two hours before I teach the writing class at Douglas County Jail in Lawrence, Kansas.*

I wonder who has signed up for class this week. Some inmates I'll know; some might be returning after a long time away, and I'll be pleased to see them and yet not pleased to see them because meeting someone in jail means, of course, he's in trouble. One inmate back in class last week told me he'd had *big losses*.

Will Shane Crady be back in class with his thick folder of jailhouse poetry a little bulkier with new poems after another week's writing in his cell? Last week in class, he pulled from the folder a new poem, "The Longest Short Walk": "I'm writing this about a walk I've had to make./It's been the most challenging feat I've ever come across." As always, when he read his poetry like it meant so damn much to him, we were right there with him on his poetic walk.

Will Hobo Rick join us again today, with more tales of hopping trains, riding across the continent in winter, staying warm on the floor of the unheated carriage by curling up in his torn sleeping bag? Last week he told us about working on a chain gang down south. Lean, tattooed, hard-eyed, with skin toughened by mean weather, Hobo Rick claims he's seen, in his travels, things no one else has ever seen. He tells us about them in his stories and poems.

Will rapper Jesse James blow us away again, punching away like Eminem with his syncopated lines and rhymes, like his poem last week about playing tic-tac-toe against himself, "and/I don't play fair so I'm always winnen'"?

Will Ishtia Maza be there? He's a Standing Rock Sioux warrior worn down and weary from hard living on the street. But I know he has the office of fire keeper at the annual Haskell Indian Nations University powwow and that fire glints in his eyes when he reads his poetry in class, like his poem "Love," starting, "Omaha wakes up at home with a huge/hangover," or his poem "The Greyhound Trip," about taking a bus to Wichita to see the "frozen two-hearted river with the big/chief in the middle . . . one of my heroes, the Flame Keeper." I look forward to imbibing more of his wisdom.

Michael Harper might be back in class to recite or even sing a cappella perhaps the best-known poem from my two decades of weekly Douglas County Jail classes: "My name is methamphetamine but you can call me speed/I last so much longer than cocaine and I'm so much better than weed." It's the poem all the inmates want to hear when Harper's in class, the poem they tear out of copies of the class anthology, *Douglas County Jail Blues,* in the jail library. For too many of them, it hits close to home.

I hope Jim will be in class again today, an inmate I first worked with more than ten years ago and one of the keenest writers. After last week's class, Jim told me that after his last stint in Douglas County Jail and a long prison sentence, he got out, got married, had a son, and made a good life, but then it all went off the rails again. He used to tell me that he was the best meth cook in the county. Said he cooked meth for his mother to help her ease the awful pain of her arthritis.

Will some young inmate we've never seen before come to class and hit us with the power of his poetry, the cool blast of his rap? Maybe this quiet kid will go on to outwrite Baca, American Book Award winner, king of ex-con poets! The kid's success in class will lift his spirits and the spirits of other inmates, many of them struggling to keep going during more days and weeks of incarceration. The kid's words might disperse some of the fog of depression at the jail.

I've met so many inmates in my decades teaching the class and often wonder where they are now and how many hauled themselves out of trouble. I do know that some of the inmates I've worked with are incarcerated in other jails or serving prison sentences. Some are "on the outs" trying to live their lives with wives and girlfriends watching closely in case they screw up again and with kids they're not sure they can raise any better than they were raised. Some ex-inmates are in other states, trying their fortunes elsewhere. A few of them are dead, and not just the older ones. Their names do not appear on a wall of honor. One inmate I'd gotten to know well, with his frequent appearances in class, was shot and killed in Lawrence, high on meth, after new charges had been filed against him. His murder was on the front page of the *Lawrence Journal-World*. The last poem he wrote in class was for his young daughter. Ghosts, ghosts, but they did leave words behind.

I look at the clock. It's almost time to go. I check my bulky orange plastic jail class folder. A few copies of poems from recent classes in case an inmate who missed a day wants to see his work in print. A plastic twelve-inch ruler and bunch of yellow-and-black-striped Staedtler pencils. My University of Kansas (KU) ID for the front desk. Last week's poems typed up, ready to hand out in today's class. *Ready.*

Half an hour later, inside the Douglas County Jail classroom, I watch the last man in the line of inmates in orange jumpsuits shuffle in, a stocky, owl-faced guy with a shaved head: Antonio Sanchez-Day. He has a distinctive tattoo on his neck that says "Delores" and a beige folder under his arm that he brings every time. He's been coming to class for months now, and he's become one of the most prolific—and best—writers in the class. He sits quietly and extracts from the folder several sheets of paper with neatly written lines on the top page. He sets them on the desk in front of him and bows his head to read through the poem one more time. No doubt he's been working during the week on a new piece he wants to share with us. His life was changed when Programs Director Mike Caron introduced him to Baca's poetry, at a time when Sanchez-Day's wounds needed cleaning and his heart was thirsty, and he thought poetry was about nothing but puppy dogs and balloons. Baca inspired him to write about what happened to him on the streets and showed him it was possible to find a tough language to describe it.

The twelve or so inmates settle into their desks, organized into a loose circle in the center of the jail classroom. They pass around handouts of last week's poems and copies of the class rules. I look around at hard-used faces, "tattered and battered" (as one inmate will later write), even the young guys in the circle. A lot of tattoos, most of them homemade, and the sort of jaded look we most often see here—substance abuse is exhausting, as is incarceration.

But there is a sense of excitement, crackling energy in the air. This is going to be a good class.

Douglas County Jail in Lawrence, Kansas, is one of more than 3,000 jails and almost 2,000 state and federal prisons that make up the huge US corrections system. Estimates vary on the number of inmates in US jails and prisons and on the cost of incarcerating them there, but statistics for the year 2016 set the figure at around 2.2 million inmates. This means that out of every 100,000 Americans, 655 were incarcerated that year at an overall cost of $81 billion a year, though that rises to as much as $182 billion per year when policing and court costs and support by families to incarcerated loved ones are included.[1] Additionally, almost 5 million adults in 2013 were on probation or parole, meaning that almost 7 million Americans were under correctional supervision that year (probation, parole, jail, or prison).[2] Between 1980 and 2010, the number of incarcerated Americans rose from approximately 500,000 to almost 2.5 million, largely because of government-initiated *wars* on crime and drugs, disproportionately affecting minority communities.[3] Though the incarcerated population is under the authority of "departments of correction," many critics argue that little *correcting* is done in correctional facilities. As Baca writes in his foreword to *Undoing Time: American Prisoners in Their Own Words*: "We are all connected to a national madness that absurdly expects prisoners to change for the better as we deep-freeze them in six-by-nine cells and torture them in inhumane environments. We seek to reduce crime while we do everything in our power to create it."[4]

Baca then argues for the worth of inmate writing programs, which can bring about substantial changes for the better—as happened in his own situation. He says that through the redemptive act of writing, inmate writers "announce to the world beyond the walls and bars that a spark of life still burns in them."[5] Through writing, they might become "meaningful human beings in a society that had branded them as nothing more than worthless criminals."[6] I have often seen transformations like this in inmates in my writing class at Douglas County Jail. They have the opportunity in the class—a rare opportunity in their lives, as they often say—to tell their stories, to write about and talk about what matters most to them. They often find it hard to believe that anyone, even their classmates, could be interested in what they say; they're just writing about the bad experiences that have gotten them locked up in jail, with *three hots and a cot* (three meals a day and a bed in a cell). But these poems from their guts, from their bones, from their blood often make a big impact on other inmates and themselves. I don't claim that with the magical powers of language and literature the inmates suddenly acquire new lives and lay to rest all their demons. Their demons are persistent, and inmates often return to jail—and to the class—a few months after they're released. But I do know that many inmates say the class enabled them to get through the hard times of their confinement by giving them something to look forward to every week, two hours of their jail time well spent. In writing, they begin to face up to their troubles rather than succumbing to them. Word by word, word by word, they take steps toward change, glad to be moving in the right direction.

Inmates in the US corrections system, including those I work with at Douglas County Jail, have often struggled in society in general and the education system in particular. Disabilities (particularly mental health disabilities) are common; the number of disabilities in an incarcerated population is considerably higher than in the general population. In her article "Disabled Behind Bars," Rebecca Vallas argues that the widespread closure of state mental hospitals over the past six decades, without public investment in community-based alternatives, has swept people with disabilities—particularly mental health conditions—into the criminal justice system.[7] Vallas states that jails and prisons now house three times as many people with mental health conditions as are cared for in state mental hospitals. According to US Bureau of Justice statistics, inmates in jails and prisons are three or four times as likely to have a disability as are nonincarcerated people. These disabilities have often caused them to fall through the cracks of the US education system.[8] In general, people in US prisons have less education than does the general population. In 2004, 36 percent of inmates in state prisons had less than a high school diploma, compared with 19 percent of the general population. To some extent, incarceration provides opportunities for inmates to catch up on what they have missed in education, one of the main ideas behind inmate instruction.[9] By improving the skills of inmates, supporters argue, education makes inmates more employable and better able to reenter society after their release. Critics of education for the incarcerated often criticize such programs as being "soft" on crime; they call for reduction in educational opportunities for the incarcerated. Congress eliminated Pell Grants for prisoners in 1994, ending public funding for tertiary education in prisons, a move Patrick Alexander calls the "institutionalization of educational deprivation in the contemporary U.S. prison."[10]

Of course, there are substantial barriers to prison education. Classes often contain inmates with large variances in age, educational level, and interest—all problems my teaching colleagues and I have encountered in the Douglas County Jail writing class. Because of security issues, jail and prison administrators are often reluctant to mingle different-security-level inmates in the same class. (In February 2019, after almost twenty years of my class combining medium- and minimum-security-level inmates, the administration at Douglas County Jail decided that the two security levels could no longer be combined in one class.) Inmates often get transferred between correctional facilities and therefore can no longer attend. Often there's limited space in jails and prisons for classes and lack of educational facilities in prison libraries. Yet despite these difficulties, those of us who teach classes for inmates find a level of interest and commitment among our students that outweighs what we find in other places of education. I remember one inmate telling me that after he'd decided to turn his life around, he'd taken every class he could get into in jail and prison, with the hope that he might learn something in each class that he could use for self-improvement. He said he was *hungry* to learn.

There's considerable evidence that education programs in correctional facilities—such as the writing class at Douglas County Jail, for example—reduce the recidivism rate of former inmates. According to the largest-ever meta-analysis of correctional education studies, sponsored by the US Departments of Education and Justice: "Prison inmates who receive general education and vocational training are significantly less likely to return to prison after release and are more likely to find employment than peers who do not receive such opportunities."[11] Researchers found that inmates who participate in education programs are 43 percent less likely to return to prison than those who do not, though there is not yet enough evidence to determine which educational programs perform the best with regard to reduction of recidivism. Reduction of this rate is important because recidivism remains high in the United States; four out of ten inmates return to prison within three years of release.

My involvement with inmate education at Douglas County Jail began in December 2001, when I covered a class for my two colleagues at KU, Kirk Branch and Anna Neill, both young assistant professors at the time. They had started teaching a GED completion class soon after the jail opened in 1999, but by the time I took over in spring 2002, it had morphed into a creative writing class. Neill, who would later become chair of the English Department at KU, said that right from the start, the jail class had a very different energy than did her university students: *totally agree*

> What was really striking and unexpected, perhaps, just because I didn't know what to expect, was how immediate the rewards of teaching were compared to the college environment where often you don't even know what impact you've had. Maybe you'll get a letter from a student ten years later, but probably you won't. The sense of just the visible excitement, the commitment, the passion to the writing, that being so integrated with the students' lives there [at Douglas County Jail], which is so powerful, so that was the most positive thing I noticed immediately.[12]

Over my two decades of teaching the class, I have seen this student excitement, commitment, and passion for writing every single week; no wonder I keep going back. Thousands of inmates have attended the class over the years.

Patrick Alexander believes that inmates such as those in my Douglas County Jail class write as a sort of resistance to their bleak circumstances and dehumanization; for Alexander, inmate writers are the voiceless finding their voices. Drawing on Michel Foucault's *Discipline and Punish* (1975), he writes of the modern prison, with all of its electronic systems of surveillance, as Jeremy Bentham's *panopticon,* in which Bentham conceived of the prison as having the structure and spatial arrangement so that prisoners would be under constant surveillance from a central watchtower. Alexander argues that Bentham's design was for social control of inmates: "Confined people are so fixated on the intensity of this all-seeing panoptic gaze that they anxiously police their behavior as if a guard were actually keeping watch over them in their solitary cells."[13] The prisoners, objectified by this all-seeing gaze, are rendered voiceless. The way to challenge this carceral gaze, according to Alexander, is to recover one's individual voice, as I see week after week as inmates lean over their desks in the classroom to write. "Antipanoptic expressivity" is Alexander's term for inmates' resistance to this objectification through their written language; they are confined people speaking truth to power.[14] Week after week I have seen inmates writing what Alexander calls their "revivifying narratives" as they write, recite, and breach jail walls with every thought they think.

Since December 2001, I have made hundreds of Thursday afternoon journeys to the jail on the edge of town, which one visiting writer said looks more like a corporate headquarters than a penitentiary: "Where's the razor wire? Where are the guard towers? Where are the prison bars?" To this poet, it might have looked like corporate America, but I've heard inmates refer to it as a "misery factory." The Douglas County Correctional Facility (DCCF) was opened on September 11, 1999. The facility holds 186 inmates and operates under the "direct supervision" philosophy, meaning that most inmates are accommodated in open-plan "pods." These pods have broad lobbies with two-tiered rows of cells at each end, unlike the jailhouse look we're familiar with from movies with tall tiers of cells and narrow walkways patrolled by armed guards. The DCCF has approximately 5,500 bookings a year; everyone arrested in Douglas County is initially booked at the jail. Of these bookings, 40 percent are released within forty-eight hours.

Douglas County sheriff's office statistics for August 2, 2018 (a date chosen for a comprehensive survey of jail statistics), give a broad picture of the recent inmate population in terms of the charges against them. Of the 244 persons in custody on that day (those who could not be held at the jail because of insufficient capacity were "farmed out" to other correctional facilities), 14 were charged with murder or attempted murder, 23 with aggravated assault/battery, 19 with possession of opiates and heroin, 20 with driving under the influence (DUI), and 19 with misdemeanor traffic offenses. Other inmates faced charges in between these most and least serious offenses. According to the sheriff's office, "Most inmates have multiple charges. The most serious was selected for category assignment." After working with inmates for almost two decades, I have the sense that addiction often underlies criminal behavior in the Douglas County Jail population, though because of "category assignment" by most serious charge, these sheriff's office statistics cannot be used to confirm my observations about addiction. Most often I do not know the charges faced by inmates in the class, though sometimes I read about their cases in the *Lawrence Journal-World*.

With the swelling of the Douglas County Jail population in recent years leading to the farming out of inmates to other regional jails, there have been calls to expand the jail, including a countywide referendum in May 2018. That initiative was defeated, leading to further public discussion of what can be done to house a growing jail population. In January 2020, the Douglas County Commission voted for a $29.6 million expansion of the jail, adding approximately a hundred more beds to the facility. Opponents of the plan wanted the commission to spend more on alternatives to incarceration. Commissioners argued that the county already funds alternatives, including pretrial release, house arrest, and behavioral health court. In the same week as this Douglas County Commission vote, forty inmates had to be farmed out to other regional facilities. In writing class at the jail, we often hear complaints by inmates (and staff) about this farming out practice. It's unpopular with inmates, who usually prefer Douglas County Jail to other facilities, especially because it's often harder for family members and attorneys to visit other jails. Inmates also appreciate the many educational programs at the jail. Today, more than sixty programs are offered weekly by a staff of five and more than eighty community volunteers. Programs range from religious studies to cognitive behavioral interventions for addressing criminal thinking patterns to creative writing.

In May 2017, a young inmate wrote the phrase "words is a powerful thing" in the writing class at Douglas County Jail, inspiring me to begin finding the words to describe my many years of teaching at the jail and shape them into some sort of coherent narrative, capturing some of the powerful poetic electricity the class generated over nearly two decades. I have included as much inmate poetry as possible (the work of more than fifty inmate writers) because their poems are the rough jewels of this book, whereas my words are the settings that, I hope, show off the jewels' brilliance. For inmates, one of the most debilitating aspects of incarceration is a sense of isolation, feeling like they are cut off from the world. In *Soul on Ice,* Black Panther activist Eldridge Cleaver wrote about the convict's sense of abandonment in his cell: "Why should we have faith in anyone? Even our wives and lovers whose beds we have shared . . . leave us after a while, put us down, cut us clean loose and treat us like they hate us, won't even write us a letter. . . . All society shows the convict its ass and expects him to kiss it."[15] Despite this sense of abandonment—a common theme in the writing of inmates, the incarcerated *are* still a part of society, and it's dangerous and costly to think they're not. Most inmates will be released at some point, and it's to the benefit of all of us that their reentry into society goes well. This book is meant to act as a bridge between the incarcerated and those on the outside, reminding all of us through their poetry that inmates are in so many ways just like us and not "the other," to be shut out from our world, "warehoused" away from society.

Some inmates come to class as an excuse to get out of their pods. Some join the class because they are already invested in writing as poets, storytellers, rappers, or songwriters. Some come to class because they've heard from other inmates that it's worth checking out. In class, I emphasize that everyone can write, *everyone,* if each participant will just commit himself during writing time to getting something down on the page—a story, a thought, an experience, a dream, a wish, a prayer, a vivid description of what was for supper in the jailhouse last night and the effects it had on the inmate's digestive system. They all have meaningful words, and this is their chance to share them with others and listen to what their classmates have to say. I hope they will learn to see the value of writing during their incarceration, I hope their writing will be for them the "revivifying narrative" Alexander describes, and I hope this activity will keep them in touch with their families and friends on the outside and might also help them get in touch with themselves in significant ways. Maybe they will learn what Ken Lamberton learned in prison in Arizona when he was in lockdown, or "prison inside prison," as he calls it: "This place could swallow me alive—a recurring thought I'm having lately. It's not only the physical confinement, but the emotional. How I feel is inconsequential; nothing gets beyond these walls. The mind-numbing routine, worthlessness, loneliness—how I feel about any of this stays locked inside me most of the time, unless I express it as inadequate words put down on paper."[16] "Inadequate" words, perhaps, but invigorating words all the same. Inmates in the writing class at Douglas County Jail often find that writing helps them through the toughest times of their lives as they make the thrilling discovery that "imagination knows no cinder blocks"—that there is a type of freedom available through the power of the written word.

*lovely!*

# Chapter 2

# "What Truly Matters"

## Teaching Creative Writing at Douglas County Jail, Lawrence, Kansas

I first taught the creative writing class at Douglas County Jail on Christmas Eve 2001. I was subbing for my two English Department colleagues at the University of Kansas (KU) who had established the writing program at the jail, Kirk Branch and Anna Neill. In the jail, in a spacious, well-lit classroom with small, rectangular windows with a single bar down the middle, Programs Director Mike Caron gave me a small plastic control box with a red button and told me to hit the button if I needed any help during class. He called it a "panic button" and smiled. I sat in the classroom and waited for him to return with my inmate students. What had I gotten myself into this time?

In the foreword to *Doing Time: 25 Years of Prison Writing*, Sister Helen Prejean writes:

> When I read anything I'm always hoping the writer will take me into realms of experience I wouldn't otherwise have, experiences that push the edges of human life and our ways of doing things, put me up against myself and make me ask: What would I do in this situation, who would I become? Adventure stories are like that. Prison writings are like that. "Come with me," these convict writers say, "I'll take you into my world. Hang on. It's quite a ride."[1]

Like Prejean, I was in late 2001 getting ready to be taken on a wild ride into "realms of experience I wouldn't otherwise have, experiences that push the edges of human life." I'd had substantial teaching experience already by this point in my career: more than ten years as an assistant professor and lecturer in the English Department and teaching appointments in England,

Japan, and Senegal too. I'd taught in the Adolescent Treatment Center in Olathe, Kansas, for two years. Yet, like Prejean, I started teaching at Douglas County Jail as an outsider to jail and prison life. As she writes, "I've never heard the clang of bars behind me as I said good-bye to freedom. Never had all the eyes in the room turn to me, 'fresh meat,' coming in. At the end of each visit I get to walk out. And every time I find myself taking deep gulps of freedom."[2]

At the end of Thursday afternoon class, I too take those deep gulps as soon as I'm out of the jail, leaving behind me inmates back in their pods or cells. Many of them are in deep trouble, not only in Douglas County but also in other jurisdictions. These troubles increase their need to find meaning in their lives through writing; writing might even offer opportunities for salvation. In *Soul on Ice*, Eldridge Cleaver described his response to incarceration: "My pride as a man dissolved and my whole fragile moral structure seemed to collapse, completely shattered." His response to this shattering was one I have seen many times in my years at Douglas County Jail as an instructor: "That is why I started to write. To save myself. I realized that no one could save me but myself."[3] Out of this emotional intensity comes writing of an urgency I rarely see in the calmer waters of a university classroom, though I have found it in the writings of the best-known of ex-con writers, Jimmy Santiago Baca.

In *A Place to Stand*, Baca—one of the most prominent beneficiaries of prison education and a huge influence on incarcerated writers everywhere, including in Douglas County Jail—writes about stealing a book of Romantic poetry from the clerk at the booking desk at Yuma County Jail when he was incarcerated as a young man. He'd felt as a poor, brown-skinned, twenty-one-year-old, illiterate Chicano that books—and poetry—had nothing to do with *his* life:

> I saw the thirty-dollar hardcover price. No matter how much I liked the story, I would never spend money on a book. Guys like me hung out and bullshitted all day. We told stories but they didn't mean much; they were just to pass the time behind a drugstore or on a street corner. I'd never owned a book and had no desire to own one. But still, I did enjoy this one, if for no other reason than it alleviated the boredom of waiting. I hadn't forgotten, though, that I took it to hurt her [the jail clerk] for laughing at the man who could have been my father. To my way of thinking, books had always been used to hurt and inflict pain. Books separated me from people like her and those two detectives, who used

textbooks to perpetrate wanton violence against poor people, and from greedy lawyers, who used lawbooks to twist the truth. There were only two ways to learn things: on the street, fighting to prove you were right, or sharing a fifth of whiskey or a six-pack and hanging out with homies and listening to their stories.[4]

The inmates in the Douglas County Jail writing class are at first often as dismissive as Baca here about the worth of books, of writing. They might attend to get out of their jail pods and to have, perhaps, the chance to catch up with their friends from other pods. They try writing. They dare to read what they've written to other inmates. They like the positive feedback. They return the next week with more stories to tell. Sometimes when they're writing, they find that "time, jail noise, cells, and walls [have] all vanished."[5] In Patrick Alexander's term, they find their words "revivifying."

Douglas County Jail writing class inmates have most often lived harsh, precarious lives, evident in their worn faces as they sit in the class circle and reflected in their writing. They write frequently of substance abuse with an authenticity that indicates they know this subject too well:

> Enough powdered medication flows through me
> 2 feed a sick house of the ill.

> I can still feel the prick, oh man, what a rush,
> like an ice-cold rushing river up my arm.

They write about addiction, how hard it is to break even after release:

> I told the Parole Board that I would
> be a better man
> and I told my cellmate that I was
> afraid of the crackhead that lies within.
> Yeah, I hit the streets and I was
> off and running.
> I tried to fight it, but how could I?
> When I just kept wanting.

I last saw the inmate who wrote about the "crackhead that lies within" in the Lawrence Public Library more than ten years ago. He was on his way back to Chicago, where he had family and hoped to start over. In the class he was a champion who ran the show, reading his powerful lines and encouraging other inmates to reach deeply into themselves to tap into their own poetry. I keep hoping that he's managed to restrain "the crackhead that lies within" and made something of his life. With his mighty words, this poet could shake the classroom floor, walls, and our souls.

In one chilling poem from the class about addiction called "Methamphetamine," Michael Harper wrote that meth will turn you into a "walking skeleton, your teeth will all be gone." There are a number of walking skeletons with bad teeth in every jail class, with that haggard look typical of meth addiction. Inmates know that though meth makes you feel like a god, it's manufactured by the devil. There are poems about the terrors of withdrawal, a common horror facing many new inmates:

> Shakes are not the problem
> Keep some food down would be kind
> Hallucinations are what scare me
> Sometimes they seem so real

Inmates scribble again and again about the misery of incarceration, the guilt, the sleepless nights: "I've been here so long/my misdeeds haunt me in my sleep, damn it's hell." They hear their victims crying. They hear other inmates moaning at night. They write about how often they feel abandoned by people on the outside, even by family and those they considered close friends: "I've learnt that often enough the person who says I'll always/be there is the first one gone." In *Wilderness and Razor Wire*, Ken Lamberton also writes about the inevitable loss of relationships for inmates. According to Lamberton, some accept this inevitability and, from the start of their sentences, cut themselves off from their outside worlds:

> Friends go first. Then girlfriends, wives, children. Two years is about all the time it takes. Parents, who generally feel some responsibility towards their sons, hang on, visiting on weekends and sending along some money. In prison, thirty-five-year-old men may get a monthly allowance from Mom and Dad. For families, I think death would be easier to accept and deal with than a son, dad, or husband in prison. Consider the de-

mands of the long-term terminally ill and bedridden. Prison carries an enormous emotional burden that the whole family is sentenced to for at least as long as the inmate spends behind bars. Possibly longer. At least with death there is an end, and there are survivors.[6]

And inmates write over and over again about feeling like they are going crazy because otherwise they cannot explain the "insanity" of incarceration and the madness of criminal behavior that gets them into trouble again and again:

> Insanity is being locked up away from family and friends.
> Insanity is always coming back to jail for the
> same insane shit I've done over and over.

In writing this book about the positive influence I believe the jail writing class brings to the lives of these inmates, I don't want to underestimate at all the problems they are facing from so many directions. Many inmates are dealing with the ravages of substance abuse. They often struggle with mental illness, especially depression. There's guilt and regret. Broken families. They are often facing substantial jail time, years cut out from their lives, so that they feel "life trickling down toilet. Fearing flush." They feel abandoned. They fear that even when they get out of jail, the "cold dark hand" will pull them down again. In these desperate situations, they turn to writing as perhaps the last small, good thing in reach.

Caron, who retired in 2015, a Vietnam veteran with more than twenty years of work experience in correctional facilities, was involved from the start with the writing program. Caron often sat in on classes and contributed his own writing. Though he believes jail writing programs bring many benefits, he is under no illusion that they are a cure-all for inmates: "I don't believe jail writing programs do a lot to keep offenders from making bad choices or aid significantly in living more functional lives when they return to the community. Learning to write does, however, open an important door for many folks who feel voiceless in the criminal justice system. Most have never experienced the stress relief of getting thoughts and emotions onto paper."[7] He argues that writing can be a new and liberating experience for many inmates who previously had no outlet for their pain and troubles except drugs, alcohol, or violence toward themselves and others: "Writing can be a gateway to a far better kind of medication." He is careful to emphasize, however, that learning to write is only one small step in the right direction and that for many inmates there's much more work to be done if they are to successfully reenter society and build new lives: "Learning to express oneself on paper is no guarantee *stinking thinking,* impulsive bad decision making, will end. That usually requires much harder work and different interventions, but writing classes do contribute, sometimes profoundly, to self-awareness and insights about others. That is no small step in the right direction along the path to a better life."[8] Caron believes that the most immediate benefits of participation in a jail writing class are the pride in writing well and drawing a positive reaction from teachers and peers, especially for many inmates who have not done well in the education system and have only ever gotten attention for disruption. Time and time again, I have seen inmates deeply pleased with themselves for making a contribution to the class that was appreciated by others: *revivifying* for everyone involved. It's possible to see each inmate given a boost by words recited by someone in the class circle. Inmates give each other credit for contributing something of themselves, something that "really matters." Quite often they tell me that they share their writing in the pods too. It feels good to think of them turning to poetry outside of the classroom.

I do not want to idealize the class, however. During my time teaching at the jail there have been three fights in the pods after class, linked to words in class clearly directed against other inmates. On one occasion, an aggressive White inmate, angry with everyone, it seemed, wrote a poem mentioning a "noose," and Black students believed it was a reference to lynching and challenged him on it. A lot of anger in the air. We struggled through the rest of that class. Soon after, an emergency code sent guards rushing to a pod where a fight had broken out involving the students who'd clashed in the classroom. There's a lot of tension in a jail; inmates live close together, and they're around each other all day. Any spark can start a fire that brings the guards. The security camera in the classroom is a recent addition after the first and only fight that actually took place *in* the classroom, though the fight must have been based on some former "beef" because as soon as the inmates saw each other, they charged and started fighting. Someone sounded the alarm and guards burst in, pulled the fighters apart, handcuffed them, and escorted them out. It was like watching a squad of firefighters smother a blaze.

Let me bring you into the Douglas County Jail classroom.[9]

The last day of 2009; nineteen degrees in Lawrence, Kansas; icy patches on the parking lot of Douglas County Jail. I'm here to teach my last writing class of the year. My last two hours of *jail time* (as I call it) for 2009. I teach here every week of the year apart from when I'm out of town. I've found that holiday times are often the hardest times for inmates. They appreciate that the writing class will still take place, and the least it will offer them is a two-hour break outside their pods. Let no one underestimate the harrowing experience of jail for the inmates. Grown men, sometimes middle-aged and old men, must obey rules they often find petty and degrading. Many inmates face complicated cases, not only in Douglas County but also in other jurisdictions. They often feel out of control of their lives, in a sort of limbo in which most all the news is bad. Their cells are small, and in most pods, they have to sleep right next to a metal toilet. Though a sort of gallows humor abounds, it's easy to see the pain underneath it and a sense of profound despair that's familiar to anyone who has had experience in the corrections system, even as a volunteer.

I have at least one student today who was in the class back when I started at the jail. In fact, he jokes with me as I escort him from the work-release pod to the classroom that it's his time of year to be "inside." He says that "on the outs" he has a tent and three sleeping bags but thinks that he's much better off in jail. He says that on the outside he might end up like too many of his friends, drinking a pint of whiskey at night, then found frozen to death down by the river the next morning. This inmate is articulate, well read, witty as hell, and fiercely committed to writing: he often brings a small stack of new poems to class. He signs them "Vogue Rogue."

Writing class size fluctuates. Sometimes there are as many as twenty inmates in the class drawn from three different pods: medium security, minimum security, and work release. Inmates' clothes are color coded: orange jumpsuit for medium, blue jumpsuit for minimum, and white jumpsuit for inmate worker, one of the coveted positions at the jail because it gives the inmate the freedom to walk the hallways unescorted, to earn a little pay, and to earn days off sentences—one day off the sentence for each day worked.

There's always a substantial turnover of students. Inmates are lost to the class when they get out of jail or get transferred to another institution or simply because this week they didn't want to leave their cells. Some students I only ever see one time. I've had quite a number of excellent writers in the class who have only come once or twice. Then there are the students who show up every week for months at a time. These are often the students who might be gone for a year or two years but then return, vowing that this time when they get out of jail, they'll stay out. (They're often referred to in the jail as "frequent fliers.") Several of my "serious" students have asked if they can keep attending class after they're released, wanting to return to jail on Thursday afternoons. The jail authorities have not shared their enthusiasm.[10]

We sit in a circle in the classroom, orange and blue and white jumpsuits together, and races intermingled too, Black, White, Native American, Hispanic, Asian American. The class provides the opportunity for inmates to catch up on what's happening in other pods, so there's quite a lot of chatting, often in whispers, as we hand out poem "packets" (typed up poems from the previous week), pencils, and writing paper.

We always begin with a speech from Caron, who sits in on most writing classes, about what is not allowed. He makes all of these points because of trouble in previous classes about these issues (see Chapter 4 for a full discussion of class rules):

No mention of legal cases.

Nothing written that will "get under the skin" (as Caron says) of anyone else in the class or back in the pod.

No violent lyrics, in particular gangsta rap (as Caron says, nothing about "offing cops" and blowing off kneecaps).

No criticism of the pod officers (he explains that there's a grievance system for that).

He also forbids the use of certain words that are always problematic: *bitch, ho, snitch.* Caron outlaws the N-word because again we have had trouble with this particular word for reasons discussed in Chapter 4. The N-word is still a potent word in most settings, including the jail classroom.

Caron knows these points need to be made every time because we have many impulsive students who are not good at following rules—this has gotten them into trouble in the first place. Also, of course, inmates often feel compelled to test boundaries to see if they can get away with it. Quite often, we have to stop a student from reading a poem that breaks the rules. Just when the student is into the flow of a poem about how tough his gang is or about his prowess as a Romeo, we have to put a stop to it. (When Sherry Gill took over Caron's position as programs director in 2015, she formulated the "Rules of the Class" I write about in Chapter 4, the sheet of rules handed out at the beginning of each class.)

I divide the class into three parts: first, a read-through of the poems from the previous week; second, a "free writing" period; and third, a read-through of poems written this week. I try to get as many students involved as possible.

Over my years of teaching at the jail, I've found that my inmate students tend to be about twice as engaged and responsive as an average university class. I think this is because they have often lost a lot in their lives—families, friends, money, time, homes, jobs, opportunities, and so forth—and they want to make the most of what they do still have. Also, there's a lot of boredom in any institution, especially in jails, so an opportunity like this does allow the inmates to express themselves, to make use of their pent-up energy in creative ways, to see what others have to offer in the way of poetry, to do that essential human business of telling each other stories. I've also found over the years that some inmates are "serious" writers who have located in writing a source of strength, solace, and significance in their lives—these are the inmates such as Shane Crady who bring new work every time. The class is full of raw energy, and sometimes it seems that attention deficit disorder is a requisite. It's still a great class to teach; I'm excited to see what happens every week. I'm not even close to burning out. I'd miss so much if I stayed home on a Thursday afternoon.

When I originally started teaching at the jail, I'd thought that the class might follow the model of a university writing workshop: critiques, portfolios, and so on. I soon found out that was not the way to teach at the jail. I wanted to include as many students as possible rather than try to select an elite group of "serious" writers, so the class turned into a sort of forum with as many students as possible given the opportunity to write and then read their poems to us. This has certainly worked well in the jail setting. The slow, painstaking process of critiquing would not really work in the often rambunctious atmosphere of our jail classroom. Also, because of the inevitable turnover in a jail population, it would be hard to make the sort of commitment to working with a student that's possible in a prison population, for example, when it's likely that the inmate will be incarcerated for a long period. That long-term commitment would make a workshop type of class more viable.

Part 1, the read-through of the poems from the previous week's class: yes, the writing is often raw and unfinished, but many of the poems are far from "simple" and have important things to say not only about jail life but also about human experience in general. If I ever get to thinking that I have heard enough poems that rhyme *cell* and *hell,* then I am wrong. What I've discovered is that there are endless perspectives on jail life and that not even two *cell/hell* poems are alike. I quote here from some of the poems in this week's packet.

> At night I fight with myself alone in
> my cell when there's no one to tell. said I'm
> stuck in this jail ya I'm stuck in this hell
> and these wounds they won't heal got me pop-n
> pills to cope n deal with the pain.

> Feelin' too stuck now, sitten' so long, like who what
> how, where did I go wrong, what's the point of havin' an
> hr out, with no tv, or no phone call, man how long
> do I have stay here, while looking in the mirror, is
> that a gray hair? a game of tic-tac-toe by myself, and
> I don't play fair, so I'm always winnen'.

> Born & Raised
> Confused & Dazed.
> Living in a haze,
> But those were my ways.
> How do you know
> what's right and wrong?
> When you were raised that way
> by your Pops and Mom.
> Hell, I could be in the back of a hearse.
> I got one resolution
> and it's never to come back to this institution.

Poems of loneliness, pain without relief, boredom, broken families, abandonment: this sample is typical of the poetry on the dark side that we see in the class. Does it help to write it out? Sure it does, even if only a little bit. And that little bit might be just enough to help the inmate through another week in jail without any communication from the out-side. Does it help at all to be in class? How else would inmates get to hear lines like this that they can probably relate to very well? "Sometimes I feel like people think I'm dead./Like I'm on another planet./Boys I would have died for, can't seem to find the time to write." That's roughly written, but the thought is complex and trenchant.

If the writer of the poem from last week is in this week's class, then he reads aloud his poem. If he is absent, then someone else reads for him. There are always willing readers. Again, I get the sense that many of the inmate students are keen to put their energy into something positive during their time of incarceration. Many inmates turn to religion, so we often have poems thanking God for His infinite love and mercy:

> When waking up in the morning is a blessing
>
> every day in our lives
>
> because God is blessing us and showering his unconditional love
>
> toward us every day in our daily lives.

The poem above, "Sometimes I Feel Like People Think I'm Dead," is all about the common occurrence of friends turning their backs when some-one has jail time. It's likely enough that the writer would be bitter about these betrayals, but the poem takes a surprising spiritual turn:

> When I hit the
>
> bricks and I see those old smiling
>
> faces, will I smile or turn my back.
>
> I'll probably smile and accept the hugs
>
> because forgiveness is always up above.

The read-through gives the new students a good sense of what is permis-sible and, I always hope, some sense of class boundaries. We have a lot of young inmates of all races who have grown up listening to rap and hip-hop and see the class as the perfect opportunity to emulate their outlaw he-roes. Quite often students will cross the line and start talking about Glocks, bitches, and dope, and we have to cut them off. This is not going to work in a jail setting. In one class, for example, a young Black student stopped reading when he reached the last line of his poem and said, "In the last line

I talk about *bitches and ho's*. That's not allowed, is it?" As another inmate remarked, "I guess you got away with saying it, anyway." There's a constant balancing act for the instructor between letting the inmates tell their stories in their own words and keeping within class—and institutional—limits. I'm constantly patrolling the border, trying to make the right calls. What else would one expect from rule breakers in an institution filled with rules?

When I said at the beginning of one class that students should not write poems like rap lyrics, one student pointed out that in his opinion, country songs are often about violence, so what about them? "Johnny Cash sings, 'I shot a man in Reno, just to watch him die,' so why does Johnny Cash appear in our classroom week after week, glorifying violence?" (see Chapter 8: "'[The] Automatic Connection Between Inmates in Class and Mr. Cash': Johnny Cash's *Hurt*"). He had a good point, and I thanked him and broadened my pool of examples of songs with inappropriate lyrics for a class in a correctional facility.

After the read-through, we spend about twenty to twenty-five minutes free writing. As prompts for writing, I usually write about ten phrases on the board and explain that it often helps in writing if you have something to start with: for example, *miracle worker, small wonder, grains of sand, lifetime*. I often borrow phrases from poems in the packet from the previous week, which adds a sort of continuity to our writing. Most of the students understand this idea and use a chosen phrase as a launch pad for their own poetic flights. I emphasize that students don't have to use these phrases. If they have their own ideas, that's great, and quite a few students come to class with stories in mind to tell.

Some students make the effort to use every phrase, every prompt written on the whiteboard, in what they write. Our best student for this was Big Jae Wae, who would do this week after week during his extended stay in jail, making coherent, energetic poems out of these random phrases. He was so adept at this that sometimes he'd use each of the prompts a second time too. Here's an example from one of his poems, "Miracle Worker." This poem was written in November 2009 during the twenty-five-minute free-writing period. It's unrevised: "I want to be a *miracle worker*/working a *small wonder* in everyone/that crosses my path. Planting small thoughts/no bigger than *grains of sand* in their hearts/or in their heads./A *lifetime* of misery and pain."

Wae was a pillar of the class for more than a year while the legal wheels turned; he was in serious trouble for drug offenses. He's a middle-aged guy who was facing at least ten years of prison time. Yet I have seen him talk down an enraged young jail class student angered that we had halted him in the flow of his rap about street violence. It's easy to look at inmates in the circle like Wae and think about missed opportunities. What could he have done with his talents if he hadn't used them for street crime? He might have been a counselor, attorney, or professional writer, but instead of this, he'd chosen "a lifetime of misery and pain" on the street, a life that he's trying to make better.

I always write with my students. I want to share the creative enterprise, *and* I find that I do some of my best writing when I'm under pressure to write. (All the poems in my book *Jail Time* were written at the jail.) I know that some of the things I write in jail class I could not have written sitting in my own house or in the university library. There's a sort of energy in the air—easy to feel, hard to explain. Each week, I'm hungry for praise after reading my new poem. If I didn't care about that, then it would be time to quit. Most of the students *do* write during this period, welcoming the opportunity to participate. As I write, I can feel the creative energy in the air. It rises, rises, peaks around twenty-two minutes, then fast declines. The whispers start. Some students ask to use the bathroom. Shuffling. Laughing. Time to move to Part 3.

I ask for a volunteer to begin reading. One of the regulars usually volunteers and reads to us, pleased to share with a group of his peers something he made, something he can be proud of something that is no one else's. Another inmate reads, then another, building up momentum, so that when it gets around to 3:00 p.m., we're reluctant to stop. I think of the inmate so turned on by this reading of poems that he'd always say, "Who's got one more? Who's got one more?" But in the end we have to finish, the inmates shuffle back to their pods, and with my stack of new jail poems to type up for next week I leave through the classroom door, the first of seven doors on my way out to "deep gulps of freedom."

This teaching energizes me for my university teaching. In fact, I'm energized for all aspects of my life. I've learned again that poetry can thrive in a jail classroom and make the harsh experience of incarceration manageable at least for two hours every Thursday between 1:00 and 3:00 p.m. in the Douglas County Jail. I think if you're in love with literature, then you realize that this is a raw yet profound literary experience, literature of real urgency and passion written in the blood ink of the heart, writing that can help people in bleak circumstances to hold on and then start taking steps toward improvement—I have seen this again and again.

I have worked hard during my university teaching career to make connections between the campus and the community, teaching at the Lawrence Arts Center, the Senior Center, high schools and junior high schools, and the Olathe Adolescent Treatment Center. I think it's too easy for academics to disconnect from the community and stay "on the hill." But if we do stay in academia, then we miss out on everything members of the broader community can offer us and what we can offer them. I know my life and career would be less for that. Just look at what is being produced in a small writing class in that plain concrete and glass building that you could easily miss on your drive out of Lawrence, Kansas, on K-10 toward Kansas City.

When I return to these words years later, I still find essential truth in them, and nothing that has happened in the decade since I first wrote them has diminished my belief in the good work I'm doing, assisted by inmates and a cast of dedicated coinstructors. When I taught my first class at the jail in December 2001—that seems like another world now—how could I have known that my teaching at Douglas County Jail would turn out to be my most important and soul-satisfying work in my thirty-year teaching career?

How would I have ever known the full truth of the phrase "words is a powerful thing?" I have seen the true power of words to change lives, including mine, for the better, and I am forever thankful for that.

# Chapter 3
# *"Sing Soft, Sing Loud"*
## The Literature of US Jails and Prisons

When I was eighteen, I read Alexander Solzhenitsyn's *One Day in the Life of Ivan Denisovich* (1962), one of the first books I read about incarceration. It began my decades-long odyssey through the literature of incarceration, which became increasingly relevant to me as my shadow career of jail teaching developed after my first class at Douglas County Jail in 2001. Even at eighteen, however, I sensed that this literature had plenty to say to the non-incarcerated: for example, I imagined what I would do in the extreme circumstances of the Russian prison camp depicted in Solzhenitsyn's novel and what that would tell me about my own humanity. Denisovich (Shukhov) is a *zek* (convict) in a Russian "special" camp, a hard-labor camp established in the late 1940s specifically for political prisoners. One image in particular has stayed with me: him smuggling a broken hacksaw blade in his mitten on his way back from the work zone to his camp. An eight-year veteran of the camp, he knows that if he smuggles the blade in, he can "hone it into a nice little knife—shoemaker's or tailor's type, whichever you wanted."[1] With this "earner," he could earn food and increase his chances of survival. I think of this again now that I have worked with inmates for almost two decades and have some idea of how much it means to hold on to whatever might aid survival, poetry in particular. When Shane Crady returned to my creative writing class after two years, he brought with him a thick new stack of poetry and told me that his writing had gotten him through some bad times and that he was keen to share his new writing with us. Looking at the wealth of published prison literature, it seems that many inmates in their cells work toward survival and enlightenment with pencil and page.

In fact, there is zek poetry in Solzhenitsyn's novel. Shukhov visits the sickbay and meets medical orderly Kolya, a former student of literature and now a zek in the camp, dressed in a crisp white gown, sitting at a desk, writing. "Shukhov took off his cap as though to a superior officer. He had the old lag's habit of letting his eyes wander where they shouldn't, and he noticed that Kolya was writing lines of exactly the same length, leaving a margin and starting each one with a capital letter exactly below the beginning of the last. He knew right off, of course, that this wasn't work but something on the side. None of his business though."[2] I think of Douglas County Jail inmates such as Donndilla da Great and Jesse James writing in their cells. We're fortunate when they're willing to share their "on-the-side" writing with us. We often hear from them that they consider their writing a lifeline, as it seems to be for Solzhenitsyn's Kolya.

I learned more about prison literature when poet Jimmy Santiago Baca visited the University of Kansas (KU) in the early 1990s, invited by my colleague and Baca's friend, poet Luci Tapahanso. Baca has certainly been an inspiration to me throughout my years as a writing instructor at Douglas County Jail. When I first met him, though, I didn't realize the influence he'd have on my life and the life of so many others. I admire him for his honesty in depicting the depths to which he descended in the harsh Arizona prison system and how he was able to rise to considerable achievement and fame, always keen to help the forgotten population in our prisons. Baca has been a guide to me throughout my years of jail teaching.

I remember my hour or so in a classroom with Baca at the university. He walked in with Tapahanso, told us he had no interest in giving a standard reading, and instead invited all of us in the classroom—twenty or so students, faculty, and community members—to tell him a story. I'd just read a story about a crew painting the sides of a road bridge, constantly on the lookout for suicides flashing past them after jumping off the bridge, and that's the story I told Baca. After meeting him, I read *Working in the Dark*, his memoir of his discovery of the power of language during his incarceration, and his harnessing of that power to tell his own stories, writing his first words in a Red Chief notebook: "I wrote about it all—about people I had loved or hated, about the brutalities and ecstasies of my life. And, for the first time, the child in me who had witnessed and endured unspeakable terrors cried out not just in impotent despair, but with the power of language."[3] Baca adds, "I could do this all alone; I could do it anywhere. I was no longer a captive of demons eating away at me."[4] Rereading Baca, I think of the dedicated writers I've worked with at Douglas County Jail: Donndilla da Great, Iron Eyes, Michael Harper, and many others writing in their cells;

writing to keep those demons of guilt, depression, grief, and despair at bay; bringing their poems to class to share with others also looking for relief and inspiration. When the poem makes a connection with a listener, the poet often hears heartfelt praise such as, "That's what's up. *There it is.* You tell it like it is. Just like it is." I imagine Baca smiling.

After *Working in the Dark,* I was hungry for more Baca.

The prologue to Baca's memoir *A Place to Stand* (2001) begins, "I was five years old the first time I ever set foot in prison."[5] He and his mother had gone to pick up his father, Damacio, from jail. When later incarcerated himself, Baca learned to read and write in prison and through language found redemption and literary success: "Language gave me a way to keep the chaos of prison at bay and prevent it from devouring me; it was a resource that allowed me to confront and understand my past, even to wring from it some compelling truths, and it opened the way towards a future that was based not on fear or bitterness or apathy but on compassionate involvement and a belief that I belonged."[6] Baca's memoir is the story of the survival of a boy who'd been in orphanages and detention centers and finally in Arizona State Prison in Florence with a five- to ten-year sentence after an FBI agent was shot during a raid on drug dealers that included Baca. He soon figured out that the key was to *survive* prison, to "not let it kill your spirit, crush your heart, or have you wheeled out with your toe tagged."[7] Baca wrote his first poem there, for his ex-girlfriend Theresa. He wrote to pen pal correspondents, thrilling to the sense of connection: "With every word I was gulping fresh air and filling my lungs. I felt I was writing for my life."[8] Baca was able to survive and writes of his release from prison in typically vibrant language: "The big spotlights illuminated the deserted main yard. The captain's black boots crunched on the hard-packed ground. Everything here had weight and substance, intended to silence, imprison, destroy. Yet somehow, I had transmuted the barb-wire thorns' hostile glint into a linguistic light that illuminated a new me. In a very real way, words had broken through the walls and set me free."[9] Baca's "linguistic light," the light of a survivor, has helped to illuminate my understanding of the US correctional system and the people in it. Week after week, I sat in a classroom at Douglas County Jail with inmates prepared to dig deep into themselves and write, at whatever cost, what they believed to be true because however much it costs to do that, it costs more not to do it—as Baca tells us repeatedly. They work in their cells to bring their poems into the light. They, like Baca, have faith in the voices of their hearts: "I believed what I wrote, because I wrote what was true. My words did not come from books or textual formulas, but from a deep faith in the voice of my heart."[10] How many times in Douglas County Jail writing class did we hear that voice of the heart, which excites us?

The longer my tenure at Douglas County Jail, the more I began to explore the vast and growing collection of published writing from jails and prisons in the United States. The Prison Arts Coalition, established in 2008, demonstrates this expanding body of work. The poetry section on its website lists thirty books of prison poetry, including well-known works such as Baca's *Immigrants in Our Own Land and Selected Early Poems* (New Directions, 1990). The eclectic list includes anthologies from Clinton Correctional Facility (New York), Pelican Bay, Colorado Women's Correctional Facility, Guantanamo, Folsom Prison, Bedford Hills, Soledad, and Woodburne Correctional Facility. "Prison poetry" on Amazon includes *Prison Poetry* (ed. D. Jerone, 2014), *Poetry Unbound: Words by and about Women Inmates* (ed. Beth Robinson, 2013), and *Inside Out: Prison, Poetry, and Perseverance* (ed. Richard Jackson, 2014). As Eldridge Cleaver wrote in *Soul on Ice* about his time in Folsom Prison: "There are quite a few guys here who write. Seems that every convict wants to."[11] I first read *Soul on Ice* when I was a graduate student interested in Black American writers. I recently found the book at the back of my bookshelves and read it again with new understanding, which I discuss later in this chapter.

Out of this expanding collection of prison literature, several books have been especially influential for me and help to set *Words Is a Powerful Thing* in the broader context of prison literature. Two anthologies, *The Light from Another Country: Poetry from American Prisons,* edited by Joseph Bruchac, and *Prison Writing in 20th-Century America,* edited by Bruce Franklin, have greatly increased my understanding of the US prison system, as have works by former inmate Ken Lamberton, along with Edward Bunker's memoir *Education of a Felon.* As I have become increasingly interested in prison *education,* I turned to two memoirs by teachers in prisons, Richard Shelton and Judith Tannenbaum. On a visit to the *Brown vs. Board of Education* site in Topeka, Kansas, in 2015, I picked up a copy of Michelle Alexander's trenchant review of the contemporary US prison system, *The New Jim Crow: Mass Incarceration in the Age of Colorblindness* (2010). Alexander's book was a sort of capstone for me, helping me to understand the big picture of the system, pulling together most everything I had learned in the jail classroom and in my readings about incarceration. The books discussed in this chapter suggest the range of prison writing, approaching incarceration from different angles; for me, they were beacons illuminating my journey of discovery.

In my early years at the jail, keen to know more about the prison experience, I turned to one of the best-known anthologies of prison writing, *The Light from Another Country*. In his introduction to the anthology, Shelton claims that even though the US prison system is "not working," writers' workshops in prison *are* working and helping with rehabilitation: "The act of writing creatively and the success and prestige which comes with publication can have a profound effect on the self-image and future behavior of those who are incarcerated."[12] In the brief introductions to their poems included in the anthology, many of the sixty poets featured mention the beneficial effects of writing. For example, George Mosby Jr. claims, "It wasn't until I was imprisoned, eight years ago, that I realized the true value of the art. I mean, poetry pulled me through some mighty bad times . . . gave me voice that could not be suppressed . . . gave me meaning and purpose. In this time dark like night, it's been fine, fine light, my writing."[13] Mosby would not have called his writing "antipanoptic expressivity," and yet his description of his purpose for writing might be used to illustrate Patrick Alexander's notion. In his poem "to night: to judith," Mosby writes about "adding another *painsong* to the collection," this one about the "teasing mirage" of his absent lover.[14] There are many *painsongs* in the hundreds of poems in this anthology—and in the writing I was seeing in the Douglas County Jail classroom.

In his foreword to *The Light from Another Country*, Bruchac notes the long and distinguished history of prison writing, including Miguel de Cervantes and Thomas Malory's *Le Morte d'Arthur*. Bruchac argues prison writers show "how the limitation or loss of personal liberty has resulted in a search for a freedom in another direction—imagination."[15] Bruchac is confident his book is more than a volume of prison poetry. He claims the writers speak to all of us; their "light from another country" provides illumination for everyone:

Every person represented in this collection, whether living or dead, is a success. Out of nothing or less than nothing they have created. art. Though they all share the experience of incarceration, the variety of their voices is surprisingly wide, and their subject matter is more than just prison life. And when they do write about prison life, we may see in that experience a metaphor which goes far beyond the prisons. From the darkest corner of our society, their words come shining. Their light might seem to come from another country, but it is, in fact, an American beacon. It offers illumination to us all.[16]

As in many anthologies of US prison writing, Baca stands out here with vivid, elemental images, bringing alive his desperate experience of incarceration: "When a man is drowning, he does not wonder if the decks are polished enough. He simply survives, or tries to, with what he can. Poetry in prison served as a chunk of driftwood I clung to. I believe that for those in prison, and those out of prison, poetry is more than an art form, a way of expressing feelings and ideas acceptable to society. I believe it is a way of changing and bettering the world we live in. It is a way of fighting back and winning our humanity back."[17] In his poem "It Started," Baca writes about a poetry workshop he attended in jail, showing the few resources required for a workshop and suggesting the substantial positive impact this "epicenter of originality" had on inmate writers:

> A little state-funded barrack
>
> in the desert, in a prison. A poetry workshop,
>
> an epicenter of originality, companionship,
>
> pain, and openness. For some,
>
> the first time in their life writing,
>
> for others, the first time saying openly what they felt,
>
> the first time finding something in themselves,
>
> worthwhile, ugly, and beautiful.[18]

All teachers of writing know the excitement of students "saying openly what they felt," often for the first time. Such expression takes on a special intensity in a jail or prison classroom, as I discovered in my teaching at Douglas County Jail. When incarcerated, poets often have to work hard to find the time and space to write. Included in the Bruchac anthology, poet Leon Baker, incarcerated in Ionia's Riverside Correctional Facility, shared a room with eleven inmates, so he wrote at night in the bathroom stall or chose solitary confinement or segregation (removal from the main prison population, most often for disciplinary reasons) so he could write. In "Getting Back to Work (in Solitary Confinement)," he wrote, "Getting back to work/ with a brand-new poetic rap, pen in hand,/notebook across my lap, and rats running/over my floor."[19]

Diana Bickston wrote in "For Zorro": "A person lives a piece of their own soul in a poem," and in reading Bruchac's collection—and in the Douglas County Jail classroom—I felt that I was sharing in this intense living too.[20] Many of these poets have, as a result of incarceration, lost most everything from their lives: families, friends, jobs, homes, savings, and more. But as poet Raymond Ringo Fernandez says, "When everything else has been taken away, I still have my poems."[21] Many students in the Douglas County Jail writing class could relate to this, holding onto their poems when most everything else had been lost. Time and again they have told me that their poems are what they most want to keep when they're transferred to another facility or when they're released. They vow that they will continue writing, keen to maintain the benefits brought to them by their art.

One of the most insightful writers in *The Light from Another Country* is Mario Petaccia, an insurance salesman until his arrest in 1967 and subsequent incarceration in Florida State Prison, the first time he had been inside a prison. Petaccia wrote in an attempt to resist the "real killer" in prison life: idleness. After his release he became director of Florida State University's poetry series and published widely:

> I did not become serious about writing until 1970 while at Florida State Prison in Raiford, Florida. I did it to survive. The worst part about being in prison is the sitting in a small, one-cot cell with nothing to do but look at the space between your hands. I've seen it drive some men insane, men who were strong; stronger than I was. I've seen men waste away in the cells until they became human skeletons. The real killer in prison is idleness, the sudden emptiness in your life. Someone has pronounced you dead and locked you up in a vault. Only you know you are still alive, and you have to go about proving it.[22]

So the inmates prove they are still alive by doing what so many inmates have done and continue to do. they sit in their cells and write as much as possible, try to write that bad stuff out of themselves and remind themselves of what's good. There's the chance too that someone else will thank them for it or that it might enable them to maintain connections to help keep their souls alive. This is what I was seeing in my Douglas County Jail classroom and even more clearly under the light of Bruchac's anthology. Bruchac's country seemed remarkably similar to my own.

I taught week after week at Douglas County Jail, and I kept reading and exploring, turning next to *Prison Writing in 20th-Century America*. In the foreword, Tom Wicker cites Jack London writing about his incarceration in Erie County Penitentiary: "Oh, we were wolves, believe me—just like the fellows who do business in Wall Street," indicating that the theme of this anthology, as he sees it, is that "what happens inside the walls inevitably suggests the society outside."[23] In his introduction, Franklin claims that he chose works for the anthology because of what they reveal about the modern US prison "and about human beings in the most difficult circumstances," again making an essential connection between inmates and the general population because "difficult circumstances" are well known by those outside the prison system too.[24]

Franklin writes about the Walnut Street Prison, in Philadelphia, established in 1790, a Quaker-inspired "penitentiary" based on belief in reformation of the prisoner. In the anthology, many voices, including Baca's, argue that the modern US prison is much more likely to *make* criminals rather than to reform them. Franklin says the publication of *The Autobiography of Malcolm X* in 1965 began a new epoch in US prison writing, with prisoners seen by some activists as a revolutionary vanguard, tying in with the political upheaval of the 1960s and 1970s.[25] Society reacted to this upheaval with rapid expansion of the prison system, harsh mandatory sentences, "three-strikes" laws, "supermax" penitentiaries, and abandonment of belief in rehabilitation in the 1980s and 1990s.[26] Franklin points out the rapid growth and severe racial bias of the prison system: between 1980 and 1995, the US prison population tripled; by 1994, the incarceration rate was seven times higher for African American males over White males. According to Franklin, recent prison writings rise like their forerunners from the depths of degradation, revealing the "creativity and strength of humanity."[27] In his anthology, Franklin includes extracts from *The Autobiography of Malcolm X* in which the author, in Norfolk Prison Colony School, teaches himself to read and write by copying words out of his dictionary. A prolific inmate writer, Malcolm X estimated that he wrote, while incarcerated, a million words. He read widely too. *The Autobiography of Malcolm X* revolutionized prison writing, according to Franklin, by pushing inmates such as Malcolm X to the forefront of the movement for radical change in the 1960s.

*Prison Writing in 20th-Century America* includes extracts from a book of similar impact to that of Malcolm X. Published nearly two decades later, Jack Henry Abbott's *In the Belly of the Beast* (1981) is a collection of letters he wrote to Norman Mailer while incarcerated. Abbott's book was a literary sensation when first published. After his release, Abbott killed a man in murky circumstances and was incarcerated again. This did not negate the *so true*

impact of his book's revelations about the harsh treatment of people in "correctional" facilities. Abbott was first incarcerated as a nine-year-old, then spent most of his life in detention, including many years in solitary confinement. His book shows the brutality and degradation of the US prison system and the will of the human spirit to survive. Abbott emphasizes that even inmates almost cut off from society are still a part of that society: "We are only a few steps removed from society."[28] Most incarcerated people take those "few steps" back to society after serving their sentences.

Etheridge Knight, another writer included in *Prison Writing in 20th-Century America* who now has considerable acclaim, was born poor in 1931 in Mississippi and served in the US Army in the Korean War. In 1960, Knight was sentenced to ten years in Indiana State Prison for snatching a purse: "I died in Korea from a shrapnel wound, and narcotics resurrected me. I died in 1960 from a prison sentence, and poetry brought me back to life."[29] I have worked with many inmates at Douglas County Jail who have tried replacing the dubious restorative powers of narcotics with the more sustainable powers of poetry. They would most often agree with Knight's assessment.

Patricia McConnel highlights a phenomenon easily recognizable to anyone who has worked in the US correctional system in "Sing Soft, Sing Loud," writing about inmates locking their faces into *jailface* to give themselves a layer of protection from the dangerous forces all around: *jailface*

> I get a good look at her face . . . this chick's face hits me hard. She's got a look people only get when they been down and out a long time, usually they been in and out of jails a lot, and so that's why I call this look *jailface*.
>
> Partly, jailface just happens when you been under everybody's heel too long, but after awhile you learn to do it on purpose so that you never let on that you're scared or feeling pain or worry or sickness. What you do is, you freeze your face so nothin' moves. Your eyebrows don't scrunch together in a frown, your mouth don't twitch or smile or sneer. Freeze ain't exactly the right word 'cause it make[s] it sound like the face goes hard, when actually it goes limp and you don't let it tighten up over nothin' at all, ever. The real mark of jailface, though, is the eyes. They don't never look straight at nobody and they don't even focus half the time. You can't look into the eyes of somebody with jailface 'cause your look bounces off a glassy surface of eyeball that's so hard it would bounce bullets.[30]

Each week when I looked around the circle of the writing class at Douglas County Jail, I saw plenty of jailfaces and perhaps one or two young inmates whose faces had not yet gone limp in this way, whose eyes hadn't glassed over yet. They looked terribly vulnerable.

*Prison Writing in 20th-Century America* comes full circle with Mumia Abu-Jamal, incarcerated under controversial circumstances, writing about the harsh prison system in the same city, Philadelphia, as the Walnut Street Prison established along Quaker lines. It is hard to imagine an outcome more different than the one dreamed of by goodhearted Quakers; Abu-Jamal writes of savagery and riots, the system seeming to corrupt everyone who is any part of it—inmates, guards, visitors, all of us. There is still a vibrant movement to "free Mumia" because many people believe he is a "political prisoner."

Years before I started my volunteer work in the US prison system, I'd come across Bunker as "Mr. Blue" in Quentin Tarentino's movie *Reservoir Dogs* (1992). In a *Guardian* poll rating books about incarceration, Bunker's *Education of a Felon* (2000) was the favorite. I checked it out. What Bunker has going for him more than anything is *voice*: Holden Caulfield meets Jack Kerouac with a few bottles of Charles Bukowski mixed in—a gasoline cocktail. If Bunker really did everything he claimed to have done, then he was a lucky man indeed to have lived into his seventies. It's not the sort of memoir that would compel most readers to check out the writer's claims. Bunker is a storyteller, and if he includes a few of Huck Finn's "stretchers," who cares? This man can tell a story.

Bunker, born in 1933 in Hollywood, California, was in a foster home by the age of five after his alcoholic parents divorced. In *Education of a Felon,* he writes of his urge for instant gratification soon getting him into deep trouble: "If anything is true in a young criminal's mind, it is the need for immediate satisfaction. Truly the place is here, and the time is now. Delayed gratification is contrary to his nature."[31] Bunker makes his way through orphanages and into the dark world of juvenile detention, out and soon back inside after more felonious activities. By the time he's incarcerated in the notorious San Quentin at age seventeen, the youngest inmate there, Bunker has had a *lot* of jail experience: "I'd seemingly spent an inordinate amount of my life meditating in a dungeon. Nearly everyone I knew had done some time or was doing it, whereas the average person had not merely never been arrested but also didn't even *know* anyone who had been in jail, much less state prison."[32] Bunker tells his wild and whirling story, including convictions for bank robbery, drug dealing, extortion, armed robbery, and forgery, in the voice of a poet, as with this description of night noise in San

Quentin: Bunker listens to a soft music program because it "blotted out the coughs and curses and flushing toilets, the rude noise of a dark cell house."[33]

Bunker brings alive the sort of world described in Douglas County Jail inmate Antonio Sanchez-Day's "Penitentiary Protocol": you have to be tough to survive, but being tough is not enough—you have to be smart too. Bunker describes one prison bully who picks on a "fool," sure that he can overpower him. He can, but that's not enough: "The 'fool' brooded for nearly a month and then walked up behind the bully as he sat eating in the mess hall. The knife paralyzed the bully from the neck down. He was a bully no more. The prison adages include: Everybody bleeds; anybody can kill you. Where anyone can get a big knife, good manners are the rule of the day—even if they are accompanied by vulgarity. Think about it."[34] Bunker got me thinking about the notion that bullies and all others best have eyes in the backs of their heads when in the prison jungle.

Bunker crosses paths with a number of notorious criminals and some famous people, including, in a dreamlike sequence, Billie Holliday, strung out, dope sick, and in steep decline:

*bully vs. knife*

We caught Billie Holiday at Jazz City on Hollywood Boulevard near Western. Billie was obviously half-sick from withdrawal, so during the break between sets, when she went to the ladies' room, Sandy followed her. There was no chance to take a fix, but Sandy offered her a toot—and when she sang her next set, her voice was husky and deep and at its unique best. It is phenomenal how fast a little toot of smack will take away the agony of withdrawal and most other kinds of pain. What it cannot take away, it makes meaningless. You may still have a broken arm, but somehow it doesn't matter so much. The same is true for angst and anxiety. Toot instantly wraps up your troubles and throws them out the window. It cancels pain so hidden that you were unaware of its existence until it disappeared.[35] " *toot* of smack "

According to Bunker, most crimes are acts of desperation, often because of addiction to alcohol and drugs. I have seen any number of inmates incarcerated at Douglas County Jail because of their "acts of desperation." Unfortunately, after one act of desperation, too often there will be another and another until, inevitably, the addict is incarcerated again—or dead. According to Bunker, "Of course the single overwhelming cause of desperate crimes is the need for money to buy drugs. Hard times make hard people, and nothing makes anyone harder than heroin addiction or the madness of craving cocaine. . . . The black dog in the white powder consumes the whole soul."[36] Many inmates have been chased into Douglas County Jail by that savage black dog, who barks outside their cells at night.

Bunker illuminates many aspects of prison life we might think we know, such as common attitudes of inmates toward child molesters: a child molester is a "maggot to be reviled, spit upon, and persecuted."[37] What would Bunker have made of Lamberton, a sex offender because of his sexual relationship with his fourteen-year-old student? It's hard to think Bunker would have respected Lamberton for his luminous prose.

Bunker writes about a friend soon to be released who doesn't want to go: "He's got nothing to go out to, knows if he gets in trouble again he might waste the rest of his life in prison."[38] In my twenty-year career at Douglas County Jail, I have seen too many inmates who have "nothing to go out to" and often seem to feel most at home when incarcerated with other inmates they have known for years, who speak their language, often a sort of jailhouse legalese. Inmates often get clean while incarcerated and feel physically better when they're locked up. However, the potential for institutionalization is always high when a system doesn't like to let you go or you don't want to let go of the system. There are many such instructive moments in Bunker's memoir, and I am thankful he used his time to illuminate the dark world of the US prison system for all keen to learn more. To me, he's an adult Caulfield, his voice *cool*, compelling, and dangerous in every line.

Programs Director Mike Caron of Douglas County Jail loaned me books by Lamberton, including *Wilderness and Razor Wire: A Naturalist's Observations from Prison* (2000). Caron said he just had to like Lamberton's work because it's focused on two of Caron's most important interests: the prison system and the natural world. Lamberton successfully yokes these two subjects, which might not seem connected in any obvious way. I was drawn into the harsh world, both emotional and physical, Lamberton describes, especially because of his belief in writing as his best hope for survival.

In fact, Lamberton writes with grace and beauty about his own experience and what he can see of the natural world around him from the confines of his incarceration. Perhaps he could write brilliantly on the outside too—who knows? But on the inside, he has to write to survive, to keep his mind from being ruined by the "catastrophic changes" brought on by incarceration:

Prison can work catastrophic changes and bring your mind to its knees. ... The mind is shaken, whipped, then centrifuged. I notice things on a more profound level. I spend a few hours under a tree or in my cell with pen and paper, and I begin to write words that come from deep inside myself. Sometimes I will dredge up material from some oceanic layer rich in organic sediment, lost ideas that hold an emotional ancientness as if they had pooled up from my genes rather than emerged from my mind.[39]

A writing class brings to the surface emotion often hidden in a prison environment because, as Lamberton argues, inmates most often see any emotion apart from anger and hatred as weakness. An inmate who turns away from emotion is doing "easy time," according to Lamberton, suppressing emotions of sorrow, pain, and fear. But if we repress our emotions in this way, we are hardly human:

In the same way that the prison environment deprives us of touch, we, in turn, deprive ourselves of being wholly human. It is a common reaction to doing time—easy time, it's called. But it's also a coward's way of dealing with prison. In my mind, turning away from emotion, and the reasons behind the emotion, is what is weak.

Many people hide in prison. Its very nature isolates and insulates; it constructs barriers deeper than walls and fences. It makes it easy to slip inside your own comfortable and private cocoon. Easy time. No remorse, no depression, no pain. It's weak. It takes courage to face the pain, to expose yourself to the consequences of your actions and accept them, particularly the consequences that affect your victims, your family, your children.[40]

It is not easy to show emotion in a jail classroom: it makes you vulnerable. It might be seen as "weakness." And yet how much more is lost by trying to repress these feelings? How much is gained when inmates follow Baca's exhortations to "cry," to release that remorse, depression, and pain? I think of Lamberton's courage and strength in holding on to his humanity in the direst of circumstances: a convicted sex offender in a cruel prison system in which sex offenders and snitches are at the bottom of the barrel, common targets of prison violence. I admire him for his strength in turning the bleakest situation into the triumph of survival, leading to the publication of books of grit and wonder that have plenty to tell his readers, even if they, like the US justice system, would judge Lamberton harshly.

As I began work on *Words Is a Powerful Thing* in 2017, I checked out two prominent memoirs of prison educators. In *Crossing the Yard: Thirty Years as a Prison Volunteer* (2007), Shelton says he began his prison workshops in the Arizona prison system in 1970 or 1971: "I have never kept very good records."[41] When he was an assistant professor at the University of Arizona in Tucson, he received a letter from a young man on death row in Arizona State Prison in Florence asking for feedback on his poems. The letter was from the notorious inmate Charles Schmid. Shelton said he got involved with Schmid for all the wrong reasons: he was keen to read the "poetry of a monster." Driving home from his first meeting with Schmid, Shelton felt like he was wrestling with the devil: Should he help a young man who was likely enough a murderer? Shelton decided he would, and this decision lead to his thirty-year shadow career as a creative writing instructor in Arizona's prison system: "Although that choice has led me to more pain than I could have imagined then, it has also enriched and enlarged my life. It has led me through bloody tragedies and terrible disappointments to a better understanding of what it means to be human and even, sometimes, to triumph."[42]

Shelton's book is a detailed account of his admirable commitment to creative writing instruction in the prison system and the workings of the Arizona justice system from the perspective of a dedicated volunteer. I found the book short on descriptions of what happened in the classroom, however, which would seem to me the focus of all of Shelton's activity. I also missed the writings of the inmates themselves. The only poem quoted in the twenty-three-chapter book is a short poem by the author himself. There are, however, many intriguing scenes and stories, such as Shelton's comment that even though he worked in places of desperate violence, there were no fights in any of his prison classes. Strangely enough, there *was* a fight in one of his university classes, and stranger still, the fight was between two guys scrapping over Linda Ronstadt.

There's plenty of editorializing in *Crossing the Yard*, about a prison system that seems to be cruel to everyone caught up in it—not only inmates but also families, guards, administrators, and volunteers such as Shelton. He commits so much time to his work there yet knows that many of the inmates he works with have troubles way beyond what's possible to address in a two-hour workshop. For those of us who work in the US correctional system, it is best to be humble about how little we can achieve, yet we should remain proud of our small successes. Inmates have told me that their writing and the writing class have enabled them to keep going, week by week, and Shelton says inmates have told him the same.

In *Disguised as a Poem: My Years Teaching Poetry at San Quentin* (2000), Judith Tannenbaum writes about serving as poet in residence at San Quentin from 1985 to 1989 through California's Arts-in-Corrections program. Tannenbaum did not feel like she was breaking new ground; she believed she was joining an "existing cultural community": "There has always been art in prison."[43] Tannenbaum described the primary purposes of her job at San Quentin as "to encourage people to speak, and then to listen as well as I can."[44] She added, "After expression and reflection, our mutual task—my students' and mine—has been to put their work out into the world, demand inclusion, and find room at the table."[45]

In her book, Tannenbaum shows that she considers herself an artist, not a social worker or therapist, though like most artists she recognizes that writing can often bring substantial rewards: "Those of us sharing art in other places are not therapists or social workers; we're practicing artists who know from our own personal experience that making art has the power to heal. We operate from a belief that creating is a human birthright given to us all—not only those able to attend art schools or writing workshops."[46] I too think of myself as a "practicing artist" in the jail classroom, not as a social worker or therapist. If the benefits of the class extend beyond the poetry, that to me is a bonus.

Tannenbaum was able to work effectively with the inmates because she did not condemn them as criminals; she realized inmates' crimes are only a *part* of their character. She also felt that the class was of substantial benefit to her: "Although I did not forget that many of these men had caused grave harm to another, for me that single fact did not fully define them. In the cocoon of our classroom, I knew these men as intelligent, enthusiastic, funny, and kind; I liked each man very much. Over the next four years, I would watch how the crucible of prison taught us all—each man and myself—profound and complicated lessons about who we were."[47] Such "profound and complicated lessons" are what we all hope for in participating in any way in the making of art in prison—or anywhere else.

Tannenbaum shared with her class a poem by Turkish political prisoner Nazim Hikmet, "Some Advice to Those Who Will Serve Time in Prison," ending,

> I mean it's not that you can't pass
> ten or fifteen years inside
> and more even—

you can

as long as the jewel

in the left side of your chest doesn't lose its luster.[48]

Her class tried to keep those jewels polished, a key image in her book. Jewels on the left side of the chest were polished by the marvelous poetry by inmates quoted throughout her book, including Spoon's "No Beauty in Cell Bars": "Restless, unable to sleep/Keys, bars, guns being racked/Year after year/Endless echoes/of steel kissing steel."[49]

Tannenbaum worked with a set class of approximately eight regulars during her four years of teaching at San Quentin, including Angel, Coties, Elmo, Gabriel, Glenn, Richard, and Spoon. The writing class at Douglas County Jail has been a different type of teaching experience with no core group of inmates, the class changing every week as inmates get released or move on, and even the stalwarts of the class most often coming to class for only a few months. That's one reason I can't use a straightforward chronological narrative in this book. The class has not been a slowly developing entity, such as Tannenbaum's, for example. For me it has been more like a collection of memorable scenes taking place over an extended period of time. But my experience has been similar to Tannenbaum's in that we have both worked extensively with outstanding students in a place we'd thought would not have much interest in poetry. She writes about her student Elmo:

How can anyone this brilliant and talented be in prison, I wondered for the hundredth time. The way I saw it, Elmo was a big factor in our class's success. Without calling attention to himself, Elmo had helped create an atmosphere in which students felt relaxed and trusting enough to share their work. He was respected for what he knew, and also for the way he said what he knew. He was quick to see what worked and what could be improved in a poem and was able to deliver this information in a way that allowed each poet to listen and respond.[50]

In my early years teaching the class at Douglas County Jail, Donndilla da Great was a similar figure, brilliant at his own poetry and well respected as workshop leader. I sat back and watched him work. Over my years of teaching the class, other class leaders have emerged, including Big Jae Wae, Jesse James, and Sanchez-Day. It's not that they talk all the time; it's that they set the tone of the class in the best possible way. "This class is important to me," they seem to say. "It should be important to you too. Make the most of the opportunity. Do not fuck it up for those of us who care."

In the final chapter of her book, Tannenbaum writes about what happened after her last class at San Quentin: "In the following weeks, every man in the room except Will would be transferred to another state prison. The group we'd created together for close to four years would disappear. But the poems—and the love that they sprang from—would be part of our lives forever."[51] That's what I hope to leave behind after my last class at Douglas County Jail in Lawrence, Kansas: vital poems that will live on after all of us who wrote them have gone. I hope they will continue to give light to readers who open the covers of this book.

In a very different way, Alexander's *The New Jim Crow* brings light to this dark world.[52] She argues that the explosive growth of the US prison system since President Ronald Reagan launched the war on drugs in the early 1980s—prison populations rapidly expanding from 300,000 to more than 2 million—has established a new system of discrimination and exclusion that mostly affects poor communities of color. Alexander sees mass incarceration as the contemporary iteration of slavery and Jim Crow. She argues that the United States now uses the "justice" system to label people of color as criminals:

> Rather than rely on race, we use our criminal justice system to label people of color "criminals" and then engage in all the practices we supposedly left behind. Today it is perfectly legal to discriminate against criminals in nearly all the ways that it was once legal to discriminate against African Americans. Once you're labeled a felon, the old forms of discrimination—employment discrimination, housing discrimination, denial of the right to vote, denial of educational opportunity, denial of food stamps and other public benefits, and exclusion from jury service—are suddenly legal. As a criminal, you have scarcely more rights, and arguably less respect, than a black man living in Alabama at the height of Jim Crow. We have not ended racial caste in America; we have merely redesigned it.[53]

Alexander shows how easy it is for young men of color to get caught up in this system and how hard it is—almost impossible—to extricate themselves when so much of it is stacked against them. How to get a job when the application asks if you have ever been convicted of a crime? How to find housing if you're excluded from public housing as a felon? How to get back into education when, again, there is that box to check, "Have you ever been convicted of a crime?"

Alexander also writes about the system loading up newly released offenders with different agency fees, including probation, child-support enforcement, drug testing, and drug treatment. Another fee, a "poverty penalty," is added when former inmates can't pay. How to get out of what Alexander refers to as this "Debtor's Prison"? As the *New York Times* states, "People caught in this impossible predicament are less likely to seek regular employment, making them even more susceptible to criminal relapse."[54] Alexander gives the best explanation I have found for the rotating door at Douglas County Jail, for the reappearance in class of too many inmates, too often people of color, who had left the class vowing that they'd never be back. "I am all done with this shit," they'd said.

Alexander's book gave me a broader vision of what I see in my jail class, especially the high percentage of minority students (often 50 percent of the class) and the number of recidivists. I can see why Alexander argues that the system of mass incarceration is structured more to sustain itself than to "correct" and reintegrate inmates into society. The war on drugs and the sort of tough-on-crime policies it has spawned seem only to have created a "criminal" *undercaste* (as Alexander calls it), to the detriment of society.

Finally, I want to return to Cleaver's *Soul on Ice,* a book I rediscovered after many years in which I had spent a lot of time working in and trying to understand the US correctional system. I remember being moved by Cleaver's words when I first read *Soul on Ice* as a graduate student in the late 1980s. How much more significant Cleaver's book is to me now when I can understand much better because of all my hours in the Douglas County Jail classroom and because of my extensive reading of the literature of incarceration. Believing that the rape of white women was a political act of rebellion against white authority, Cleaver committed rape and was arrested, tried, and sentenced. In prison he had to reassess that notion of rebellion. I admire his willingness, in "On Becoming," to confront harsh truth in the painful process of self-examination in order to become the "best of which I was capable."[55] I have worked with so many inmates who have tried to do the same in the Douglas County Jail writing class, understanding that it is their best hope of rebuilding the "moral structure" of their lives. All of us might be inspired by Cleaver to face up to the hard truths of our own lives and strive for self-improvement:

I realized that no one could save me but myself. The prison authorities were both uninterested and unable to help me. I had to seek out the truth and unravel the snarled web of my motivations. I had to find out who I am and what I want to be, what type of man I should be, and what I could do to become the best of which I was capable.[56]

Time and again in all the books I have mentioned here, I see inmate writers determined to keep writing because how else can they make sense of their experiences and share them with others; how else can they work on becoming the best of which they are capable? Some of these writers have achieved considerable success such as Cleaver, Baca, Bunker, and, to some extent Lamberton, but I'm sure all these writers would eschew any reward for their work as long as they could keep writing for the personal rewards it brings.

Some inmates learn this vital lesson: *Sing soft, sing loud;* keep singing, and you might survive and begin to make a better life.

# Chapter 4

# No "Snitches," No "N-Word"

## Rules of the Class

When volunteer Mike Hartnett and I arrive in the classroom at Douglas County Jail on a Thursday afternoon just before 1 p.m., a clean, well-lit room with oddly narrow windows and a surveillance camera mounted in one corner (if you know where to look), Programs Director Sherry Gill has set the desks and chairs in a loose circle, with writing paper and copies of class rules on each desk. She also has a bag of pens to distribute (and later retrieve) when the inmates arrive from the medium-security and minimum-security pods. After we have picked up the inmates from their pods and the class members have assembled and greeted their friends from different pods, I begin by reading "The Rules of the Class," explaining that we have to stay within the rules in order to keep the jail administration happy and to have a good class.

The inmates know *all* about rules, and often have, let's say, a rather adversarial relationship with them. I explain that we have adopted these rules in response to troubles in the past, and for the most part I can remember clearly enough the incidents, or series of incidents, that led to the establishment of each rule. Mike Caron, former programs director (2001–2015), emphasized the need for strict rules in our writing class because of the "potentially explosive" situation of a jail setting:

Most of the rules we insisted on were crucial to safety for the inmates, staff, and volunteers. In a jail situation where many are awaiting trial, there are inmates who fear codefendants will testify against them. Others owe or are owed drug debts or have a sister who was abused or led into addiction by someone in the jail. All these and many other scenarios make a writing class potentially explosive if the subject matter is not carefully limited.[1]

The rules are our attempts to carefully limit subject matter in order to head off potential "explosions" yet leave the inmates with sufficient space to write.

Here are the rules, as listed on the sheets all the students have in front of them. As I always say before reciting them, "Some of you have heard these rules many times." I've recited them hundreds of times. But there are new class members who need to hear them and old hands who do not always have the best memories as far as rules and regulations are concerned. The rules are our attempt to strike a balance between giving inmates the opportunity to express their creativity and clearly establishing the parameters of behavior.

1. Do not write about your case.
2. Some profanity is OK in context of poem, but no overt sex/violence.
3. Do not write anything that might be considered offensive by someone else in class or pod.
4. No use of derogatory racial language, including the "N-word."
5. Do not glorify the criminal life.
6. Write as clearly as possible!
7. Do not write to complain about jail guards, jail administration, Lawrence Police Force, judges, etc.
8. No "anti-women" poems about bitches, ho's, etc. Be respectful of women.
9. No use of the word "snitch" or anything to do with that subject matter.
10. Do not make comments or talk to the high school diploma inmates or female inmates who pass through our classroom.

Each rule exists for a reason; it's important from the start to set boundaries. Inmates are most often people who need to be reminded of parameters and seem to appreciate having them in place in the jail classroom. If we can establish them from the start, then we don't have to deal with an inmate writing a poem about a snitch he hates who can be easily identified by everyone else in class, or we don't have to clear up the mess of an inmate writing a poem about his bitch of an ex-wife and what he'd like to do to her (with the likelihood that someone else in the circle knows her and might want to respond). That is *not* the place to go in a jail writing class, and trouble like this has a way of poisoning the atmosphere by getting inmates and instructors worked up and on edge about something that should have been kept out. The class is quite often interrupted by officers who have to pull out an inmate for an attorney visit or some other business, so we cannot, for example, have an inmate ranting about the harsh treatment meted out to inmates at the jail while a guard is in the room. Writing like this would likely find its way to the administration soon enough because any jail is a beehive of whispers and gossip.

I will now describe the significance of each rule and its origin.

## 1. Do Not Write about Your Case

This is sound advice, important to set out from the start. Information is power, and this is especially true in a jail or prison setting. We've all heard news stories in which inmates claim their cellmates told them about crimes committed and the inmates came forward to "snitch" on their cellmates, often for the prize of time off their own sentences. Their "snitching" is convincing because of details gleaned from something their cellmates said or wrote. It's easy to see why inmates *want* to talk about their cases because they are very much on their minds. They know, however, that it is *never* smart to talk about their own cases, especially in jail. We remind them of this right away.

## 2. Some Profanity Is OK in Context of Poem, but No Overt Sex/Violence

A lot of inmates, especially the younger inmates of all races, have likely grown up listening to a lot of rap and often take from it the outlaw vibe, which includes big boasts about all the bad things they've done, all the women they've slapped around, and worse. They're tempted to write like their heroes and be seen as big, bad criminals too. This is not going to work in a jail writing class. When inmates start rapping about Glocks and dope and gangs, we have to stop them. There is *no way* the jail administration will let us provide a platform for poems like this, and it goes against what we're trying to do in any number of ways. We also have inmates writing boasts about their sexual prowess or about how tough they are. Again, this will *not* work in the jail class. Caron makes clear why sexual subject matter must be policed: "Some writers create imaginative and truly interesting work that includes sexual content. Unfortunately, if this is allowed, there are many who will immediately take the opportunity to be more blatant and vulgar, and the race is on to transform the class into Porn 101."[2] We know we're working with guys who have been pushing boundaries, sometimes leaping over them all their lives; we try to keep them from doing that in class. Most inmates recognize the benefit of these limits. It's often said that what the jail provides for many of the inmates are rules for them to work within to get their lives back on track—or on track for the first time. Inmate leaders such as Donndilla da Great or Big Jae Wae realize the benefits of our Thursday hours together and try to make sure inmate students stay within the lines.

Even after my reading of the rules at the beginning of class, some inmates read poems that are clearly "inappropriate," often under the influence of rap and hip-hop. Some try poems about violence and sex that cross the lines. We work with some inmates who have long "careers" of transgression and might well know more about violence than many of their peers outside the criminal justice system and consider it an important topic to write about. We have to explain that although we appreciate their need to write about these subjects, class is not the time or place to do it.

I'm always pleased when an inmate announces that he was planning to read something but then thought it might contravene the rules. These are guys who have not been the most reflective people, tending to act on impulses that have gotten them into trouble. It's a small victory when they hold back from unacceptable behavior. After all, the jail is meant to be a *correctional* facility.

Rules apply to instructors too. In March 2010, Caron had to stop an inmate mid-reading because he was reading a poem about gang violence. The inmate pointed at me, "What about what *he* wrote? Some dude getting thrown out of a car. You didn't say nothing to *him*." I'd read my poem called "Sad Dog" (and I suppose he thought I'd used *dog* as it's used on the street):

> I yell at the stupid dog, "Go away!
> Leave me alone!"
> But that sad dog twitches its ears,
> keeps following me around.
> One day I'm going to load that dog in my car,
> drive all night, pull off the road,
> stop in a field, toss Sadness out the door.

I tried to explain that I was writing metaphorically. My critic was not impressed and saw it as just another example of his persecution by a hostile institution, whereas jail officials, including writing instructors, are allowed to get away with things.

### 3. Do Not Write Anything That Might Be Considered Offensive by Someone Else in Class or Pod

Inmates often have "beefs," some of them from the jail and some of them from the street. The one fight that actually broke out on my watch happened without any words triggering it; one inmate walked into the classroom, saw an inmate already in the room from another pod, crossed the room to him, and started throwing punches. They then grabbed each other and wrestled on the floor before a squad of guards, alerted by alarms, burst in and dragged them apart, handcuffing them and leading them out of the classroom.

Incarceration usually means living close to others who are in unhappy places in their lives, sometimes bumping up against them. It's no wonder there are occasional fights. We do everything possible to stop words from igniting trouble. Words is a powerful thing and can cause a *lot* of damage if weaponized or used carelessly.

### 4. No Use of Derogatory Racial Terms, Including the "N-Word"

This is a difficult realm to police, especially because of the way the "N-word" has been "reclaimed" in some parts of the Black community as "nonoffensive." We acknowledge this, but because of the charged nature of this particular word, we ask inmates not to use it in class. Before we made this one of our rules, we had a lot of Black inmates using the word all the time in what they wrote, claiming it was how they talked on the street, so why not use it in the classroom? When Black inmates used the word, some White guys used it too, claiming it was just as much their word, and this led to unwanted racial tension in the classroom.[3] The word transgresses a lot of boundaries, whatever its intention when it's used, so, far better in these circumstances to ban it, even though, as Caron used to say, "I hate playing censor."

Though this racially loaded word has created the most problems in the class, students of other ethnicities have pointed out that they object to words they feel disparage their own races. Therefore, we say clearly at the beginning of the class: no words that are racially demeaning. Most students are street smart enough to know what we mean and know the words that might be considered offensive. A jail is most always more multiethnic than the society outside it, so perhaps inmates are by necessity more conscious of racial slurs than other segments of society are, having seen the consequences of careless uses of derogatory language.

## 5. Do Not Glorify the Criminal Life

I remember that in my early years at the jail, one student wrote a poem about what a great pimp he was and how he was making *shitloads* of money. When we told him this was not appropriate for the class, he said he was just telling the truth. We hoped he could see that there was a problem with making a claim like this while he was incarcerated. (Likely enough, he was making good use of his imagination in making this claim; his incarceration suggested that he was not overly successful in the criminal world.)

Of course, a lot of rap is based on glorifying the criminal life, bragging about what a bad guy you are, but this is not going to work in a jail writing class. (In fact there is a strong outlaw strain running through a lot of popular music in addition to rap.) In *A Place to Stand*, Jimmy Santiago Baca wrote of being transported to the Arizona State Prison in Florence with fast-talkin' Wedo boasting about every criminal thing he could have done: "This kind of empty braggadocio ran rampant among criminals, and I was looking at 5 long years of listening to it."[4] Douglas County Jail is not the Arizona State Penitentiary in Florence, but we still see plenty of "empty braggadocio" about crimes committed and cops outsmarted by inmates facing jail or prison time. Not a lot of correcting gets done when you're keen to boast about your crimes.

## 6. Write as Clearly as Possible . . .

. . . because after class I type up the poems. I don't like to be bogged down trying to read the scrawled handwriting of inmates. Sometimes I have to apologize to a writer when I made mistakes in typing up his poem: "I'm sorry, I couldn't read your writing." (In a recent example, I typed, "I hate my mess" instead of what the writer had written: "I hit my knees.")

Inmate writers put a lot into their writing, so they want me to get it right when I type it up. The packets given out every week are a type of publication, and it's aggravating for inmate writers, as for all writers, to find typos in their work. When we hand out poem packets to inmates, they often turn immediately to their own poems, just like poets checking out their work in a new anthology just arrived in the mail. Every published writer hopes to avoid the pain of the typo.

## 7. Do Not Write to Complain about Jail Guards, Jail Administration, Lawrence Police Force, Judges, etc.

Caron would say "there are grievance processes for these types of complaints," and the jail writing class should *not* be used to air them. Obviously, there would be considerable blowback if the jail administration and other powers-that-be believed we teachers were stirring up the inmates to complain or providing a forum for them to do so. Caron is emphatic about the need for this policy, especially because of security concerns:

> Another problem concerns criticism of officers and jail policies. If those subjects are allowed in the writing class, they grow like a virulent infection until the class turns into nothing more than a chaotic bitch session with such a cloud of negativity that maintaining order and focus on anything else becomes near impossible. Every jail administration is particularly concerned about such massing of negative energies for obvious security reasons. There are many legitimate reasons to complain about jail conditions, individual officer conduct, and particular policies, but few if any jail administrator is going to sit by while a writing class becomes the main vehicle for instigating resistance inside the institution or promoting potential violence toward any staff, volunteers, or inmates within the walls.[5]

Our purpose as instructors is most certainly *not* to provide a breeding ground for resistance or aggression, and Caron is right in emphasizing the necessity of keeping the classroom infection-free.

## 8. No "Anti-Women" Poems about Bitches, Ho's, etc.

Unless we set down this rule from the start, we will get poems about how bitches will mess you up, how ho's will do what ho's do, and that sort of blatant misogyny. A lot of inmates feel as though they were betrayed by their girlfriends, wives, or lovers or that they have been abandoned by them, and this sometimes leads to their anger bursting out in poems of hate. "No anti-women poems," I say at the beginning of class.

Programs Director Sherry Gill holds the inmates to a higher standard of respect for women than many of them are used to, and it's a vital lesson. She is a wonderful example to them of a strong woman in a position of authority who will not allow poems disrespectful of women and will challenge such writing every time.

Jail class inmates might well be under the influence of the misogyny rampant in rap music. In her *Fresh Air* interview with rapper Jay-Z in 2010, interviewer Terri Gross asked what she calls "the bitch and ho question." She asked why so much of men's rap music is about demanding respect, though it seldom gives respect to women in the lyrics. Jay-Z's answer highlights the emotional immaturity of many rappers, especially when they're starting out. His answer might well apply to some of the students in the jail writing class, who are not always as young as he was at the time:

> A lot of these albums are made when the artists are pretty young, 17, 18 years old, so they've never had any real relationships. In the neighborhoods we're in, we have low self-esteem ourselves, and the women—the girls—they have low self-esteem as well. So these are all dysfunctional relationships at a very young age. The poet is pretty much saying his take on his dealings with girls at that time, he's not really in stable relationships, he's on the road, he's seeing girls who like him because he makes music, they have spent one night together, he gets a phone number then leaves to the next town where he does the same thing over again.[6]

When Gross asked if this applied to Jay-Z when he was younger, he agreed that it did but claimed he has matured since then and pointed out songs on his later albums that show this maturity.

When I talk to inmates and hear and read what they write about, it seems that dysfunctional relationships are as common as crude tattoos in an incarcerated population, so it's to be expected that the negative energy generated by these relationships would find its way into their writing. I hope that as Jay Z claims for himself, they will do better as they mature.[7]

## 9. No Use of the Word "Snitch" or Anything to Do with That Subject Matter

Caron explains why this rule is probably the most important of all in our attempts to keep the lid on the "explosive" elements in any jail class:

> Perhaps the most crucial rule we self-imposed concerns the subject of "snitching." In many ways this is central to prison culture. Anyone who

informs authorities about crimes or rule-breaking is subject to severe retribution and no sympathy from fellow inmates. When anyone writes something, no matter how subtle or blatant, that insinuates or accuses another inmate of cooperating in an investigation, whether of a serious crime that led to their arrest or a rule infraction inside the jail, violence is an almost inevitable outcome. Sometimes it could happen in class, but most often they wait until back in the pod, their living unit.[8]

In *Wilderness and Razor Wire,* Ken Lamberton states that the two groups of inmates most often targeted for violence are sex offenders and snitches. He was the first of those things, and because of that he made absolutely sure not to be the second too even though he could often identify his attackers and could have "snitched" on them. He was fully aware of the price he'd pay for "snitching."

Any mention of snitching has to be kept out of the classroom, even though as a significant aspect of prison culture, it is often on the minds of inmates.

## 10. Do Not Make Comments or Talk to the High School Diploma Inmates or Female Inmates Who Pass Through Our Classroom

For inmates, one of the main attractions of going to class is the opportunity for them to get time out of their pods. After pat-downs by guards, the inmates exit the pods through double doors, then walk the corridor, under escort, to the classroom. Just to get out of the pod clearly brings some relief. If we can't use the main classroom because of disciplinary violations such as inmates in the class communicating with female inmates as they walk through the classroom, for example, then we have to meet in the small classrooms in the pods into which we're packed like elevator riders, and the acoustics are so bad that it really is hard to conduct a class.

But using the main classroom means that in some way the inmates going to and from the high school diploma classroom have to be accommodated. (It's unfortunate that the only exit from the high school diploma class is through the main classroom.) High school diploma students enter and leave that classroom while the writing class is in session. This involves inmates from other pods, including women, crossing the room right next to our circle. Sometimes inmates see girlfriends, ex-girlfriends, wives, or ex-wives for the only time during incarceration, and they're often tempted to communicate. This is against jail rules, so we have to police it. Gill tells the class, "No saying 'I love you,' as your girlfriend walks past." Our students know about rules and for the most part obey them, especially if reminded of them on a regular basis.

Ten rules. If we set out these parameters from the start, we most often avoid disruptions that could spoil the whole class.

In my experience, most inmates follow the rules. A few, looking for confrontations, deliberately transgress, and this most often leads to an early trip back to the pod and suspension from future classes. I remember Shane Crady, when he was first in class, deliberately reading (as he'd tell us later) poems that broke the rules. He said he was angry and needed to confront the system. After a few weeks, he cooled down and started reading poems with just as much power as the earlier poems, though now they stayed within the lines.

A single sheet of paper, ten rules with many years of experience behind each one, and a better class for all of us if we follow these rules.

# Chapter 5

# "Self-Expression, Self-Destruction"

## Creative Writing Class, May 18, 2017

In this chapter, I describe the gritty magic of a single class on May 18, 2017, to show how it might represent what has been happening in the writing program over many years, following up on the class from 2009 highlighted in Chapter 2. I always tell people who show interest in the class that they should sit in for a session. (More than fifty people have taken me up on this offer over the years and joined us as visitors—see Chapter 14.) In this chapter, I will bring you into the Douglas County Jail classroom as if you are one of our visitors.

With the ten or so inmates assembled in a loose circle of desks and writing tables around the center of the classroom, I read through the class rules (see Chapter 4) and look around at rough, jaded faces—even the young guys in class have been around their blocks a *lot* of times. Tattoos, most of them crude. Bad and missing teeth. Hollow cheeks. A yellow-jump-suited inmate from special management walks through the classroom with his teacher, and my class obeys the final rule on the list: let other inmates pass through the classroom without comments or gestures or anything at all.

When we start reading poems from the previous week's class from sheets I've typed up and handed out, there's an array of different types of poetry, from Jim's Whitman-esque "Song of the Universe" to a poem about stealing food during jailtime meals: "Sleight of Hand Pays." Not surprising that the gathering of poems in the packet is as diverse in tone, language, theme, and everything else as the class itself.

It's a very attentive group, all following Jim's words as he reads, one of the guys joking that Jim's a jailhouse philosopher: "It seems I had to come/ to prison to find this freedom from within." I remember him in class more than ten years ago when my dad visited. My plainspoken dad said tersely that he found Jim's poetry "wordy." The final poem in the read-through is Hobo Rick's manifesto, "Self-Expression/Self-Destruction":

> I'm a man of extreme passion, a *hungry* man not quite
>
> sure where my appetite lies, a deeply frustrated man,
>
> striving to project my individuality against a backdrop of
>
> rigid conformity. I exist in a halfworld suspended
>
> between two superstructures, one self-expression and the other
>
> self-destruction. I am strong, but there is a flaw
>
> in my strength and unless I learn to control it the
>
> flaw will prove stronger than my strength and defeat me.

I never like to claim too much for the class, but I would say that it helps Hobo Rick—and others—to choose self-expression over self-destruction, and if it only helps one inmate one time in doing that then I have done plenty. Any poet anywhere, but especially one in a strictly controlled environment such as a jail or prison, would appreciate Hobo Rick's mention of his "striving to project my individuality against a backdrop of/rigid conformity." Walt Whitman would probably like that. (In fact, he would probably like a lot of what happens in the class. Come join us, Old Greybeard! Did you walk on this plot when you visited Lawrence in 1879 to stay with your friend Judge Usher and his handsome sons?) But there again, we *all* have to project our individuality against a backdrop of conformity. It's inevitable for every individual living in society. It's one of the great joys and frustrations of being alive, illuminated for a few moments by Hobo Rick's poem.

For the second part of class, I write phrases on the whiteboard as writing prompts, and after I've read through them, Jesse James says, "And? And?" because as I well know when Jesse James is in class, he sets us the challenge of writing something that includes all the prompts on the board: *was I dreaming, millions of dollars, looking into the sky, a hungry man, my strength, the fire within, my own enemy.* He wants me to explain to the class his "wordplay" challenge: writing a poem that includes every word on the whiteboard. I explain to inmates that it often helps in writing to have a prompt to begin with—I call them sparks to start a fire. You'll see that lines I quote from poems written in this class often include these phrases.

Jesse James is wiry, intense, a boxer fighting his demons with a lot of fights to his name—he packs a punch in his pen. His pugilistic stance reminds me of Barrilee Bannister's, inmate at Coffee Creek Correctional Facility in Oregon, featured by Patrick Alexander: Bannister was cofounder of *Tenacious: Art and Writing from Women in Prison,* a forum for women inmates. She describes her contributions to *Tenacious* in a way that Jesse James might echo: "Writing [for *Tenacious*] is my way to escape the confines of prison and the debilitating ailments of prison life. It's me putting on boxing gloves and stepping into the rin[g] of freedom of speech and opinion."[1] Alexander sees Bannister's writing as an example of the "antipanoptic expressivity" of the inmate resisting the carceral gaze and control, establishing some space through writing in which to preserve her humanity. Jesse James would get that, though "antipanoptic expressivity" is not the term he'd use. He was in my class about ten years ago, and I included five of his poems in *Douglas County Jail Blues.* His poems have passion and rhythm in every staccato line, a sort of bass-heavy music:

> Life is short, but go to jail & it's long
>
> Sleep all day, still time drags on
>
> Drags & drags, that's what it does
>
> as the heart grows cold and you forget what's love.

"This Writtin' Class," scrawled in class on May 28, 2017, shows that Jesse James is still firing off those lines, this time with a tribute to the *Douglas County Jail Blues* anthology:

> Let me tell ya lil somethin' 'bout this writtin' class
>
> Check my name, I been vast for a decade past
>
> I bleed myself in this ink, yea, from me to you
>
> Went so hard I was published in the *County Blue.*

Sometimes I see Jesse James on the street when he's "on the outs," and he raps for me, all the lines memorized, raps that go on and on, language fizzing and whizzing while traffic whooshes past on Tennessee or Massachusetts. Though he's down and out, he keeps it real. Hard to know if his life on the edge feeds his poetry or detracts from it. What would he be writing if he'd stayed within the lines and gone to graduate school? Hard to think he'd burn so hot in a University of Iowa writing workshop. Or would he have *gone so hard* there that now he'd be publishing in the *New Yorker* and speaking at a conference alongside Jimmy Santiago Baca?

For the second part of the class, when we write together, I play the beautiful Native American flute music of R. Carlos Nakai to inspire us as we write. It's the sound of wind blowing over flowers and water and the music of insects and birds, and it helps to take us all to the land of the imagination.

Inmates, heads bowed as if in prayer, begin writing, this week's class as quietly focused as an honors class. It's a thrill to feel creative energy flashing around the circuit of the class. I make use of one of the phrases on the board, *a hungry man*, and because it's Douglas County Jail writing class and we'll show Johnny Cash's video *Hurt* when we finish, and because Cash is the dark angel of our class, I start thinking about him and begin to write. I always participate in this free writing; why would I miss the opportunity for sharing in the key enterprise of our time together? I can't explain why I write things at the jail that I couldn't write outside of it. Something to do with the group experience of writing together or wanting to write a poem well received in class. I've been writing for decades, but I'm still keen to have my work validated by positive feedback, especially by guys who won't take any bullshit. When they say "that's for real" about a poem, they mean it. And when it's about my writing, it's a thrill every time.

### A hungry man

Even close to the end, Johnny Cash was hungry,

hungry to sing one more song,

hungry to live a little bit longer

hungry to hang on to his wife,

who was going to leave him.

Close to death, Johnny Cash was hungry

for the memories of the best times of his life,

hungry to see his brother again,

hungry to raise his kids again,

hungry to take a train ride

to some place he hadn't been before,

hungry to wake in a new city

with the sun through the window on his face.

—Brian Daldorph

Hobo Rick says Cash was a hobo too, and I say, "Yeah, there's that scene in *Hurt* when he jumps up into a freight carriage with his guitar." I think that without realizing it, I'd written a poem that although ostensibly about Cash could be a theme song for hungry inmates, men ravenous for so many things—for freedom, for their families, for the sun and rain, for good food the way they like it, for the chance of living their lives over and not messing up this time—and fearful of losing all those good things and more before their hunger could be satisfied. These rambling men know a lot about hunger.

After our twenty-five minutes of writing, it's time to listen to what we have written: Part 3 of the class. We have a tradition of starting with Mike Hartnett, retired business writer and dedicated volunteer since 2015, who has become an essential part of the class and with his wit, wisdom, and good nature a welcome blessing to us all. Hartnett wrote about his brother-in-law's "good death," something the nuns in his Catholic grade school told him about more than half a century previously. Everyone in the class has known losses and can relate. Many lived in neighborhoods with high casualty rates. Hartnett is as engaging as ever, writing a sort of narrative poetry *in the American grain,* under the influence, perhaps, of his parents, both journalists in their day (his father worked in Chicago for Associated Press):

**A Good Death**

When I was in a Catholic grade school in Chicago

I remember the nuns telling us, "Pray for a good death."

When you're six years old, that's kind of creepy.

Now I understand.


My brother-in-law, Jack, died yesterday. He was 81

with more ailments than I can count

but he was in hospice care at home. He was not in pain.

Three days ago he went to sleep, surrounded by his three daughters,

two granddaughters, his wife of 50 years and his dog Bella.

Two days later his heart . . . finally . . . stopped.

I guess when Jack was a kid

He prayed for a good death.

—Mike Hartnett

As Hartnett reads, guys in the circle are nodding; they have a pretty good idea what a "good death" might look like. Some of them know as much about death as combat veterans do. Hartnett's always self-deprecating about his work and claims he's a business journalist, not a poet, but week after week I read his clear, clipped language, and his insights light up my mind. This week he inspires me to ask myself, "What 'good death' do I want?" Typical that Hartnett's hastily written poem has gotten me to ask myself an essential question.

Next in the group, Kenny tells his story, "The Fire Within," a story of self-destruction to which most all inmates in the group can relate, some more closely than others. They know about fires burning within "on overtime":

**The fire within**

I have this twin, he lives

within. It's the fire down

below, once the fire is lit, boy,

it's on overtime, it gets to be

out of control. My thinking is blurred.

My give-a-damn is broken, I try to control

it, but all I can see is

that one crystal clear shard broken down into the fuel

that makes those flames get bigger & out of control

and then before you know it, I wake up in my 6X6 saying

what the Hell happened. Now they usually bring me

a piece of paper saying what I did.

   —Kenny

Chubby, friendly, soft-spoken, yet passionate, Kenny loves the class and tells us he's never tried writing before. Last week he wrote about getting shot and showed us his bullet scars—the inmate's version of show and tell, I guess. Next up, Chris wrote about his mom: "She's the thing that holds my/spirit together, my rock in this/everyday Life." Jeff wrote not about the fire within but "The Beast within": "He comes at night from within/Once again it is that beast/the one I call SIN." David jokes about his fifteen-year-old son thinking that he, David, is "overly old," ending with the line that makes us all smile: "Oh damn . . . I turned into the grey old man."

Young, slim Ty (who looks no older than a fifteen-year-old son) wrote a sort of prayer asking his God for strength and reads it like he's walking a highwire above a bad part of town: "Father God Lord Jesus Christ can you/Just bless me with the heart to do right/at times I felt my soul start to get weak." Ty ends his poem, "[I] looked in/the sky and thought I seen the Lord's eyes." Did Ty know before this moment that he's a poet? What path will he take through life? He seems so vulnerable and the world he's been sucked into so dangerous. Is there a God in the sky to protect him? Will he be able to make the most of his fragile talents, or will they be crushed within him? Self-expression or self-destruction?

Ken's poem is "My Disease": "Oh how I hate this ache I cannot shake./I know it will be the death of me." But he does have God on his side and not only God but "the right people, meditation, classes & meds" to help the quake to dissipate. He's planning to make use of jail time for his latest attempt at self-improvement. When he gets out, he tells us, he's got better places to go.

Caleb writes about his release date, June 30, just more than a month away, and sketches out his plan for the "new me":

### The 30th of June

Starting from the bottom

with nothing. And rebuilding

myself & my way of life

so that someday soon I'll

have all I've ever wanted.

To be happy with who

I am.

When one inmate asked Programs Director Mike Caron for his best advice to students in the class, Caron said that the most important thing for all of them is to have a plan, to work toward it, and to never get discouraged when things turn against them. Caron had heard too many complaints from hard-done-by inmates that life's not fair, that the justice system is out to screw them, that it's not even worth trying to make it in life. But Caleb, in his poem "The 30th of June," is at least sketching a plan for a "new me."

Caleb will certainly encounter many troubles ahead but how else to make improvements other than by figuring out what's wrong and seeking a way, in words, to get to a better place? In his poem, he formulated his plan.

Sherry Gill, last to read, gives so much week after week to make this a good experience for all of us. She's ex-army tough but compassionate. I've seen her march rowdy troublemakers straight back to the pod; she will *not* allow them to spoil a good experience for the rest of the students. Yet most of the time she's sympathetic to the inmates, knowing that she too, but for the grace of God and her own determination, could be in their situations. We all appreciate her honesty and plainspokenness, her instinct to assist every type of underdog. This week, she wrote about being close to turning sixty. None of the guys in class knew what that felt like, but all inmates know what it is to feel "invisible" as an outsider:

> Geez, aging ain't for sissies
>
> The aches, the pains, the feeling
>
> that you are invisible (gray hair does that)
>
> Sometimes our society makes us feel
>
> like we are in the way of *their* progress.

Three in the class responded to Jesse James's challenge, and I leave it to you, reader, to decide who wins the golden pencil for *wordplay* (as we call it) this week:

### Writing class poem (words on board)

> Still a young buck, yeah, *a hungry man*
>
> livin' off the land, doin' what I can
>
> *Look into the sky,* I can truly see
>
> at times I be creatin' *my own enemy*
>
> When I look into myself, there's a *fire within*
>
> The enemy I created was the seven sins
>
> *Was I dreaming* when I went through *my bad times?*
>
> Found *my strength* by defeating all the worst kinds
>
> 'cause when I look at them *folks gray and old*
>
> I knew what I'd want when my story's told
>
> —Jesse James

**Word play from board**

Now that I am grey and old
as I was looking into the sky
I saw a hungry man or
was I dreaming of my bad times?

Sometimes I am my own enemy
but for the fire within
I stand and feel my strength
The power is still there.

   —Sherry Gill

I'm from a town they call the village.
It's here in Kansas, I get my strength from
the fire within me and I'm my own enemy.
The fire, it's what makes my hunger strong
and it also gives me a bad time. Looking into
the sky I see folks grey and old, and I start
to dream. Damn, the fire has made me grey and old
and then comes my self-destruction.

   —Hobo Rick

After Gill's poem, we have made the rounds of the circle, and she moves rapidly to steer these inmates out and her next class into the classroom. She collects the poems to copy so that I can type them up for next week, so the class can continue, week by week, week by week—for almost twenty years. After our concentration on writing and sharing we loosen up; the inmates stand and shuffle around and talk while Gill makes copies and I play Johnny Cash's *Hurt* DVD, our "theme song": "I hurt myself today/to see if I still feel." Who in this room doesn't know what that is all about?[2]

One of the young guys watching Cash put it all out there for us says, "I haven't seen this for a long time," his eyes sparkling, and I say, "I've seen it a hundred times, and I still like it every time." A few guys look out of the narrow windows at the parking lot, which must seem so close and so far away. Do they dream of a car arriving driven by a friend, girlfriend, or mother, of jumping in—like Cash jumping up onto the freight train—and going home? Then, after a few handshakes, it's time for the procession back up the long, white, clean corridor to the medium-security pod and back to the minimum-security pod. Some inmates, inspired by class, will get back to their cells and begin writing for next week. Others will sleep away some jail time. Some will watch whatever's on TV. I leave the classroom, wondering if I'll ever see some of them again. Where will they be by Thursday afternoon next week?

What have we achieved in the previous two hours? Hartnett jokes with the security guard at the gate that we have "solved the world's problems." I wish. Perhaps we have helped to point a few inmates in the right direction. It's my impression that most of the inmates in class today left it feeling better than when they came in, and this I'm sure we did achieve: that in the grim experience of incarceration, our two hours together provided a little relief for a lot of people carrying heavy burdens. If we helped them to carry their loads a little bit farther down a hard road, then I'm just fine with that.

One inmate in class provided the words to describe it:

### Thursday Words Day

I really like this,
this writing group.
Coming together, creative writing
a lyrical poetic soup.


Each week we sit at the table
We break bread
Come to share our thoughts
Think about what's been read


Click, words and phrases
It's a who's who
The combined ingredients
a vocabulary stew.

      —Drew

A "vocabulary stew," a whole world of stories: Douglas County Jail writing class gives us all—inmates, instructors, and visitors—the chance to tell them and the pleasure and enlightenment of listening to what others have to say. Hard to believe how much we achieve week after week with the simplest tools—paper, pens, pencils—and commitment to writing something that matters.

On the drive home, Harnett's got another story for me. His dad, a reporter based in Chicago for most of his working life, was unemployed during the Great Depression in the 1930s until he got a job with one of Franklin D. Roosevelt's "alphabet agencies" (i.e., Civil Conservation Corps, CCC) and was sent to the University of Chicago for training, where his roommate was a scrawny Texas schoolteacher, Lyndon B. Johnson. I say to him, "Your dad brushed up against history."

Self-expression/self-destruction: most of the time our inmate students stay firmly on the side of the former.

For the rest of the afternoon, I walk a couple of inches off the ground, my head full of the "vocabulary stew" of new and vital poetry written by guys who, for the most part, really didn't know they had it in them until they started writing.

# Chapter 6

# "In This Circle of Ink and Blood/We Are for Awhile, Brothers"

## A Poem a Year: Inmate Poetry 2001–2017

To provide some sense of the scope of the material I have collected over my years of teaching at Douglas County Jail and to indicate the longevity of the class, in this chapter I present one poem from each of the first seventeen years of the class. I have thousands and thousands of poems to choose from, multiple files from all those years; I searched these files to make my selections. I have not attempted to choose the "best" poems from each year but rather poems that have stood out for me and will, I hope, give some idea of the extraordinary talent and range of the writers I've been lucky enough to work with over the years and the stories they have told. As former inmate Antonio Sanchez-Day says in his poem "Think Tank" from his first book, *Taking on Life*, after listing the creative endeavors of some of his fellow inmates: "I have said it before/and I will say it again/some of the most creative minds/are locked in the pen."

I have one regret in choosing these poems.

In my first year of teaching at the jail, I worked with Kelly, an inmate I later got to know quite well because he often returned to the jail over the years (not an unusual story). In one of my early classes, Kelly wrote a remarkable poem about the sounds he heard at night in the jail—the moans, curses, cries, farts, chatter between cells—a beautifully written poem that brought the first night of incarceration alive—a mix of resilience, fear, and despair.

When I was compiling the anthology *Douglas County Jail Blues* in 2008, I looked everywhere for this poem, couldn't find it, and had to give up on including it in the anthology. I thought I might have another chance when I met Kelly on the outside, but he'd lost his poems somewhere along his rocky way (again, a common story; a lot of inmates live itinerant lives and lose things on their journeys—as songwriter Joe Parrish sang, "I don't carry much with me no more"). I had one more chance, I thought, when Mike Caron retired as programs director in 2015 and gave me a big box of poetry packets from the class. Unfortunately, Caron hadn't saved Kelly's poem. (Kelly did contribute to *Douglas County Jail Blues* as the cover artist, a better outlet for his artistic talent than crime.)

I'm pleased to say, though, that I saved plenty of poetry of considerable merit, and I'm delighted to have this opportunity to exhibit the following seventeen poems. I feel like a collector with a huge hoard of folk art I sifted through to find treasures. I struggled with whether to add commentary or let poems stand on their own in this chapter and settled with the compromise of including notes or contextualization to some poems I felt would benefit from them. Others I let stand on their own because I thought they were powerful expressions without my comments.

In this book, I included as many as possible of the true jewels of a long-term project such as this one, the poems of the inmates who have so often lit up the Douglas County Jail classroom with their words. These are words most often written (scrawled!) quickly in the twenty minutes or so of free writing in the classroom, first drafts that could do with a little polishing, but words that should speak to all of us and in one way or another do what all good art does: help us to see a little better the world and ourselves so that we can, as Antonio E. says in his poem here (2017), "take the right steps" along the path.

To choose poems for this chapter, I searched through Douglas County Jail files on my computer from each year since I began working there in 2001, looking for poems that seemed distinctive in language and subject matter. Some of the older files, from 2003, 2004, 2005, and so forth contain many poems and writings I would claim I'd never seen before, though some of the names and poems I do recall. I've tried to choose poems with a broad range of themes. I've tried to select some poems that reflect the jail experience and others that would seem to have no connection to incarceration, for example, "High School Reunion." After all, incarceration is only a part of someone's life experience. Reading through the many poems from the class over two decades, I found material for ten anthologies but had to be extremely selective.

Though poems by inmates often concern the jail experience, most all of them contain themes that all of us can recognize: love, longing, remorse, desire, joy, pain, and more. That's because these poems were all written by human beings experiencing situations and emotions we all have to face, intensified perhaps by their extreme circumstances but recognizable, I would argue, to all of us.

Most of these writers have moved on. Some of them have died. Some of them have relocated. I've lost track of most of them. But in the classroom of Douglas County Jail on a Thursday afternoon with cold rain or bright Kansas sunshine outside visible through the miniature windows, they left their mark, left something behind to touch the hearts and souls of other people. Some of the poems did not have names on them (six were anonymous poems, out of the seventeen included here), which make them in their way even more intriguing because we wonder as we read the poem whose world we are entering for the brief span of the poem.

Most of these poems are first drafts, so they often seem "raw" and contain grammatical errors, which I usually did not correct. I believe the power of the language is evident every time: "Words is a powerful thing!"

So many have written about the dehumanizing aspects of incarceration, striving to reclaim their humanity in what Patrick Alexander terms the "antipanoptic expressivity" of their language. Here are sixteen poets (two poems are by the same poet, Ishtia Maza) who were able to hold on to their humanity through their poetry, and even though they all signed release forms giving permission for me to publish their work, they never, never expected to be communicating with you now.

## 2001

It was probably at least a hundred degrees outside
when I saw him. Hanging in mid-air.
The fibers he'd spun had to be so incredibly strong,
In proportion it was like hanging a Volkswagen
from a piece of twine.
I had to envy him for the simple animal he was,
his intelligence at this point far greater than mine.
He lowered himself from the steel grate
that keeps me in and keeps you safe.
He comes and goes at will.

I wonder if he knows where he is? Surely not,

but as he climbs his homemade rope back up

I detect the hint of a smile on his face.

Yeah, I think he knows.

I wonder if this inmate was aware when he wrote this poem of fourteenth-century Scottish king Robert the Bruce? Robert, hiding out and sick at heart after his defeat by superior English forces, watched the spider in the corner of the cave trying and trying again to spin his web and learned what he must do to beat his enemies. For this he is celebrated in Scottish folklore.

I love the easy way a marvelous simile is brought in, "like hanging a Volkswagen/from a piece of twine." "Be specific," I tell my student writers in workshops at the university, and what's more specific than a Volkswagen?

There's the deftest touch in this poem, the wry presentation of the stereotypical notion that it's necessary to imprison such a dangerous inmate, a menace to society, behind a steel grate "that keeps me in, and keeps you safe." I like the empathy at the end, the "smile on his face." Your friends are where you find them, and if this one has eight legs, well, who's counting? (A recent episode of the podcast *Ear Hustle* from San Quentin Prison focused on inmate "pets," including moths and spiders.)

Ken Lamberton writes of the wild sex drive of the male tarantula, which turns that starved arachnid into "little more than hairy bent spokes and sex drive."[1] "Looking at life from the perspective of a spider can be sobering, particularly the perspective of a lonely, wandering male tarantula," Lamberton writes.[2] However, as the anonymous Douglas County Jail writer acknowledges, the spider in *his* cell seems to be savoring its advantage over its cellmate.

## 2002

### I know a place

I know a place where you can live

and never want to be seen

I know a place where your nightmares

are better than your dreams

I know a place where we can smell Death itself

I know a place where the police even need help

I know a place where one out of five kids gets a chance in life

I know a place where a man's woman bear his child but it's not from
his wife

I know a place where school is escape from the norm

Most kids come late 'cause at home Mom's being scorned

I know a place that will bring tears to the face of a clown

Cabrini Green my home shy-town.

— Donndilla da Great

The last time I saw Donndilla da Great was at least ten years ago, after he'd gotten out of jail and was headed, he told me, back to Chicago. He had seemed liked a caged tiger in the classroom, confined but strong, but outside the jail he seemed tired and uncertain, like he couldn't be sure that he had the strength left to meet the challenges in his own life. Maybe there was more weight to carry than he could bear? He looked like a man who'd had a lot of hard times and knew he had a lot more coming.

Donndilla da Great knew he was traveling back to a place that, sadly, smells of death, where "the police even need help." Donndilla da Great seemed like a powerful man in the classroom of Douglas County Jail as he led the class and kept unruly inmates in check, but how long would his strength last in the dangerous world he was returning to?

I'm so glad I saved something of the best of him before it was time for him to go. I'll probably never know what happened to Donndilla da Great, but I have seen him regal in a county jail classroom, and for me he will always be *Da Great*.

## 2003

### A Mind's Ride

My mind catches spark like a rollercoaster
with electricity

that starts the ride we go faster and
faster as my thought process speeds up inside

This is when the fun starts when you get
on this ride, taken' spins through clouded
thoughts

The next turn you tend to be high off
last week's drugs I done bought

Take another turn and take a straight
away from the lessons I've been taught

Then you go down a hill and feel the
pain from all the battles I've fought

Then you start coming up and fun is
get better till you see the flashing lights
inside glaring off the leather

Now the ride stops, and a question enters
my thoughts are you gonna run or get caught
with this clock

The ride starts back going faster than ever
at that point, that move was the only thing
clever

This part of my ride is called the chase
and fear is all I taste.

The fun starts, it's a wild ride, your head spins faster, faster; what's more thrilling than this trip? But the ride gets wilder and wilder until you've got red and blue lights flashing in your rearview mirror, the sirens filling up your ears.

Then you're back in a cell, your head calm but hurting, trying to write about that wild ride and where, inevitably, it took you.

"My mind catches spark like a rollercoaster/with electricity": the first two lines of this poem make me think of what happens in a jail writing class when it fires up and words start flashing! Catch those sparks!

## 2004

### Within the City Limits

*About Flint, MI. Looking back, 2004*

A concrete jungle

Killers on the prowl

Poor car sales contributing to the decline of this once great city;

People making a quick-fast exodus

to remove themselves from within the city limits

Looking back on this town with a significant amount of pity;

Coming to discover the responsibility of those whose nature

is to introduce loved ones to crack-cocaine;

Destroying the lives of God's children

enough to drive anyone insane;

Harlots and hookers standing on street corners selling their bodies

Possibly altering the lives of men who cherish themselves

on being faithful to their wives;

Bangers killing bangers

using big guns and sharp-edged knives;

That all occurs within the city limits;

Not to mention, it gets you nowhere

trying to use ineffective gimmicks;

The hustle and bustle is cold-blooded if

you're not a part of the elite;

Circumstances force those of the unfortunate

to sell drugs

but in doing so you better be discreet;

within the city limits

infiltrated by thugs and gangsters

compiling an inventory of nightmarish dreams;

in a world of eroding values

where certain conditions are not of the norm

and to me, what does this all mean?

Harlots, hookers, bangers, thugs, and gangsters, already a nightmare city "destroying the lives of God's children" even before the city made a drastic decision about its water supply that led to the poisoning of the poor and brave ones who remained.

How to survive in this concrete jungle where killers prowl, and what the hell are we doing to ourselves in our cracked cities? Our enemies don't need to attack us. They can leave us to our own relentless self-destruction.

## 2005

### Sitting and Waiting

All we do in here is sit and wait

We wait for the time to go to court

We wait for the time to see the judge

We sit and wait every day in here.


Some have more days to sit and wait

We do grow tired of sitting and

waiting. We sit and wait in our cells

waiting for our free time.


Some of us in here are young

bloods, that are sitting and waiting

Most of us though are old enough

to be their Dads or big brothers

Pass on to young bloods
what we know, giving them our
knowledge. Hope that they learn
from our mistakes, not to see them
in here again, growing old sitting
and waiting

We just pass most of our time
either sitting playing cards
some sitting watching TV
Either way, we pass most of
our time, sitting and waiting.

                    —McReynolds

More than a decade later, how many of the young bloods of 2005 turned into old inmates still sitting and waiting for their lives to get better, wondering if it will ever happen? How many young inmates joined them, trying to find ways to make it through all the sitting and waiting?

In my years teaching at Douglas County Jail, I have seen faces getting older and more careworn as inmates sit and wait and waste more of their time in this world, sitting and waiting, sitting and waiting, sometimes sitting and writing to try to come up with something better to do than sit and wait and wait and wait.

In *Disguised as a Poem,* Judith Tannenbaum writes about the production of *Waiting for Godot* at San Quentin.[3] It's hard to think of a more appropriate setting for Samuel Beckett's dark play about waiting and waiting for something that might never arrive, for someone who will never appear.

"Nothing to be done," the first words of Beckett's play: What four words could be more apt for an inmate facing a lot of time? Much better though if he or she can find *something,* as many inmates have done in their cells and in writing classes. It's likely that even cynical Beckett would have seen the worth of that, because somehow he got his own writing done in spite of his despair.

## 2006

**The day my life changed forever**

I remember the day my life
changed forever,
I didn't care about the plane
ride, all my travel was by night.
I arrived in Charleston SC around
midnight.
We was all herded on a bus and
taken across a land bridge, every
body was talkin' and crackin' jokes.
The drill instructors replied, *Shut
up, you maggots!* Everybody laughed
until the bus stopped. Then every
body was herded off the bus onto
a bunch of yellow footprints.
That is where I started that day
that changed my life.
The drill instructor said, *Welcome
to Paris Island, you maggots,
This is the first day of a new life.*

This "new life" turned into the life of incarceration, from Paris Island to Douglas County Jail. The writer, now an inmate, not a recruit, is still a maggot; at least, that's probably what he feels like.

I have worked with many veterans in my years at the jail. I've often heard about guys getting out of the armed forces and running into trouble, often losing their way and slipping into addiction to drugs or alcohol. It seems to happen often enough that we might imagine yellow footprints marking the way.

However, according to a report significantly titled "Defying Stereotypes, Number of Incarcerated Veterans in US Drops," between 2011 and 2012 veterans made up 8 percent of the US jail and prison population, though veterans were less likely overall to be incarcerated than nonveterans.[4]

**2007**

## This too shall pass

As I sit in my cell,
thinking . . . this too shall pass;
oh how I wish
I could speed it up fast.

I had a good dream,
the night before last;
I was in the front lawn,
laying in the grass.

Then my dream suddenly came
to a terrible crash;
when someone said, "If you want breakfast
better move your ass."

Then tomorrow was today
Another day passed
One tiny mark
is my time ending task

All the people who are free
can't even ask
about the slow moving sand
in my hourglass

One day I'll be released
and this time like a flash
I'll drop to my knees
and say, "That too has passed."

   —Michael Harper

Because it will pass, it will, if you can just make one day turn into the next day, however slowly those grains of sand in the year (or ten-year) glass fall.

What else is there to hope for, apart from passing time until your jail time has passed?

Then you're back in jail, and the big clock in your head starts slowly ticking again, and there's more waiting and waiting, always waiting, always waiting.

## 2008

### Bricks as they fall

Sometimes I think I'm gonna lose
my mind because I read your
letters, over and over and over,
and then I'm caught up in the
moments, and the bricks around
my life are like snowflakes
melting, falling, day by day as
my heart opens up to you. Whoever would have thought sitting
behind these walls would be
some of the sweetest days when
it's turning into fall.

—Ishtia Maza

I think of Jimmy Santiago Baca receiving letters in the Arizona State Prison in Florence and the bricks melting like snowflakes because he had that most precious thing for someone serving a sentence—he had hope. Baca had something outside the walls, some connection he could work on and live for, because with hope, just about anything is possible, even sitting and waiting for years in a small cell.

Ken Lamberton writes of the hope he found in watching how the desert saguaro produces fruit even in times of cruel drought. Hope enables him to accept his harsh situation and work to survive it, even though, paradoxically, hope also imprisons him sometimes:

Hope becomes my jailor. Hope is a better security system than all the guards, electric locks, fences and concertina wire, motion detectors, and infrared sensors put together. It's what keeps me going in prison, hope that a petition will be heard, that a new law will open the gates or, if I don't get some early relief, that I will make it through the years to my release—and beyond. I have become a disciple of wildflowers and brittlebushes. I am tortoise, saguaro. I will survive the seasons of heat and frost and storm, and I will survive this drought.[5]

Days can be sweet, even when you're incarcerated inside walls, because you have hope that this drought will end and that love will be waiting for you—as it was for Lamberton when he was released and began rebuilding his life with his family, who had, against the odds, stayed loyal.

Most often I don't know what becomes of the inmates I work with after they leave the classroom and jail. Sometimes I see them around town, or in Dillon's or Target. But I do know what happened to Maza. In the "Deaths" section of the *Lawrence Journal-World* (February 1, 2019), the death of Robert "Bob" Iron Eyes was announced. I knew him as Iron Eyes and Ishtia Maza, and he was one of my favorite writers from my years at the jail. "Guitar Dave," who knew him on the street and in the jail, wrote this Zen haiku for him: "Singular Snowflakes/Ultimately Deliquesce/Into One Water—R.I.P., Iron Eyes."

## 2009

### High school reunion

"My word, Greg, what happened to you?"

"I slipped and fell, why?"

"Well, your face resembles pulled pork and your mustache
is only on one side of your face."

"Oh yeah . . . that. Well, you see, I fell on my wife."

"Your wife? What was she doing?"

"Having sex with my brother."

"Oh . . . I'm sorry I brought it up."

"No, it's OK, it's just I was on peyote,
and he was juggling butcher knives."

"When he was . . . "

"Yeah."

"Well, it was good seeing you, Greg."

—Eli

I love the wit here and the play of language, this quick vivid crazy sketch of raw experience, peyote, and butcher knives! Did this writer make use of his intelligence and wit to thrive in the world, or did he use it up on drug deals?

His face resembling "pulled pork," and that odd surreal touch of a moustache on one side of his face—weird and funny.

Thanks for this, wherever you are, my witty friend. It was good crossing paths with you, Eli.

## 2010

### Hangover

It's just the two of us in the wrestling ring,

and I'm ninety-five pounds in my boots

and trunks, and my hangover's three hundred and five

before he even starts in on breakfast,

shoveling it down like a linebacker,

bacon, sausage, waffles, toast, and cold pizza.

It makes me sick just to watch my hangover eat.

I have to fight this guy.

I really have to fight this guy.

I don't even have a few Tylenol

to throw at him,

and the fight's scheduled to last two days.

This is going to hurt.

How many ninety-five-pound inmates have sat in the class up against the challenges of their lives, each one weighing more than three hundred pounds and tucking into a big breakfast while the inmate watches in misery and fear, thinking, "I have to fight these guys"?

This is going to hurt, and quite apart from not having the usual ammunition of booze or drugs, he doesn't even have a few painkillers to toss at the brutes. It's not pain that will get killed in this fight.

Did this inmate ever have the strength to throw off his troubles?

As you'll see, there's a lot of serious grappling with the dark side in the class, but plenty of times too when we all belly laugh and feel much better. Laughter's often the best weapon against bullies inside and out who are set on doing a lot of damage. Sometimes it's best to laugh when we know "this is going to hurt."

## 2011

### Sacred Ground

As I was on my way to the sacred ground
I could start to smell the burning wood
As I came over the hill, I could see the teepees
and the sweat lodges. And the fires
heating up the rocks for the sweat lodges.
I began to feel good and started to
pray for the dancers. And then in the
blink of eye, I seen an eagle feather float
down, and it smashed among the flowers.
So I prayed and gave thanks and blessed
the sacred feather. As I entered the sunny
dance grounds, I felt a great warmth
come over me, and as I was totally at
peace with all of the universe, I listened
to the drum, the heartbeat of Mother Earth, and
to the singing, to the rhythm of ancient songs.
The drum gave the dancers a beat, giving them
energy to lift their legs higher to become
one with the buffalo and the eagle. As I watched
the dancing and listened to the songs, the drumbeat
bringing me into a near-trance state.
Suddenly the drum was silent. I found
myself listening to the wind. In that silence

I saw a feather tied to a pole, fluttering and
dancing in the wind. It was singing the song
of the wind. At that mystical moment seeing
the lone feather fluttering in the wind, I could
feel the wind speaking with the voice of the
feather. I sensed the immense power of all
ancient spirits of the elders merging with the
silence and speaking through the feather. That
vast power transcends the ages just as the feather
and the wind speak an ageless message to
anyone who will listen for it.

—Ishtia Maza

Thank you for this poem. It has made me appreciate that eagle feather and listen to the song of the wind. How many ageless messages have I ignored because I have not listened for them?

If I had not decided to write this chapter, then this poem of a "vast power [that] transcends the ages" would have been stored in a computer file and likely forgotten. Rereading this poem this morning as I edit and revise, I think my whole project would be worthwhile for this one song of the universe.

Listen to it. Learn. Learn from a wise elder who is still with us in his words.

## 2012

### Circle of Men

I'm one of many.
This circle of men
joined as one by a mighty force
of creative intelligence, wielding
the power of a pen.

All different colors and backgrounds,
stations of life and stories to tell.

In this circle of ink and blood

we are for awhile, brothers.

    —Brad G.

It has been my honor and joy to be one link in this ink-and-blood circle of brothers, to be just one small part of the "mighty force of creative intelligence": may the circle be unbroken. I'm glad that I have had opportunities to bring others into this circle.

The poet's life is often a solitary one, with, of necessity, a lot of writing alone in a room (and editing, as on this fiercely hot day in June in Lawrence, Kansas). Every Thursday afternoon for the past two decades, my writing life has been something more, and I am grateful that I am a part of this ever-changing, yet ever-vital writing community, this circle of creativity. (I am revising this chapter on August 30, 2019, the Friday after a thrilling, inspiring jail class in which one inmate wrote about himself as a moth drawn to flame; another described the motorcycle crash that wrecked his life; and my daughter, sitting in on class, wrote about how the night before we'd looked for the last fireflies of summer by Brook Creek.)

Most inmates who have participated in the class over the years acknowledge at least some benefit gained by sharing in this creative brotherhood, and some are quick to say that their lives have been changed for the better.

"We are for awhile, brothers": I think of the group poems we write if there's a spare ten minutes at the end of class, where we all begin with the same phrase and write at least a line or two to contribute to the collective enterprise (a number of them published as group poems in *Douglas County Jail Blues,* using prompts such as *life is, I've learned that, my opinion is*). Because inmates rapidly come and go, it's likely enough that no two classes have ever had exactly the same group of inmates.

Each class a "circle of ink and blood," separate but also joined with all the other inmate writers over almost two decades in our creative enterprise—and, of course, joined in profound ways with all writers and artists everywhere, especially those incarcerated.

## 2013

### It's the End of the World

It's the end of the world, and he wears a smile.

He can't wait to pull his wagon its last mile.

With his bottle in one hand, his Bible in the next
he's searchin' for a scripture in his well-worn text.
His smile was a mask, his face showed his pain—
underneath his kind demeanor lay much struggle and strain.

He took a pull from his bottle and gazed at my face.
He said he knew my child was gone, gone without a trace
but for those who mourn, God's favor has come.
He passed me his bottle, and I had me some.
It's the end of the world and he wears a smile,
he can't wait to pull his wagon its last mile.

Sittin' on a park bench, wishing life made some sense.
I'd posted all my sighs and I was wishing for some better times.
Then I met this crazy guy with a wagon and a sign
sayin' it's the end of time, he asked me if I had a dime.
His wagon full of balloons and toys, he seemed so full of joy.
Life had lost meaning for me, but there was no way he could see.

I wondered why he wore a smile, so I thought I'd stay and talk awhile.
Why the wagon full of balloons and toys, I wished I could share his
    joy.
I knew he must be crazy, and his thoughts were a little hazy
but after he told me why, I soon began to cry.
He said in God's streets of Gold and Gems his son waits for him
and the wagon full of balloons and toys are for his little boy.

—Ron Bailey

I'm looking out for you on God's highway, Ron Bailey, with your wagon full
of balloons and toys! This poet is a songwriter and guitarist, a busker on
God's streets of gold and gems. I remember that underneath his friendly
demeanor "lay much struggle and strain," the many stresses of outlaw living.

2014

### Addiction

I'm writing this about sickness, or maybe it's
a disease better known as an addiction.
It causes a chain of events that lead to a definite end
of freedom, of life, of happiness, loss in general—
friends, family, possessions, you name it. The first to go is
your looks, or is it your sanity, maybe it's your wealth.
It's hard to say, it all happens so fast, does it really matter
the order in which one falls apart. It's not like
it's an art, the way we tear ourselves apart. Where
do I start? First I'd say we start forgetting to eat,
to wash our feet, then as time starts to pass we
forget to wash our ass. Next you'll be lying on the
floor wishing you had some more. Refusing to answer
the door, then you're out in the street wishing you
had something to eat. And this affliction I realize is
an addiction has caused a disease I'm starting to know
it's a sickness—I hope I die with quickness.

    —Shane Crady

Crady's poem is coarse and revealing, finding the language necessary to describe this extreme experience, the rhythm propelling the poem forward, the rhymes hitting like punches, even that odd feminine rhyme in the last line, *sickness/quickness*. As creative writing teachers, we emphasize to students that they must develop distinctive *voice* in their writing; Crady's poem has *voice* in abundance. It tells the reader, "I, the speaker, know exactly what I'm talking about. I am not bullshitting." Crady knows and helps us as readers to know about addiction. The nodding heads in class when Crady first read the poem aloud for us showed that for the addicts in class, he was telling an ugly truth that needed to be told.

    Our first view of Crady in class was of this stocky, intense, tattooed guy who took his place in the circle bunched over a thick file of his own writing.

He was obviously wound up tight with a lot of bad energy, all too familiar in any place of incarceration. There's plenty to be angry at. The first few times in class, Crady passed on his turn to read but listened, head down, to others. When he did start to read his poems to us, he ran straight into trouble, reading poems with extreme language and themes. We had to tell him to stop reading; he was breaking just about every rule we had in place. I got the sense that he was looking for confrontation to work off some of his anger. He retreated into hurt silence but kept coming back, his manila folder fattening.

Then he started to read poems to us that were both artful in a rough way and thrilling (as in "Addiction"); Crady could make it very real, *too* real, perhaps, in his lines. He also had this reputation in the pod of writing *all* the time, never coming out of his cell in the pod, just writing and writing and writing. It was clear he began to enjoy the positive responses in the class from guys who'd been in bad places like the ones he was describing, telling him, "That's how it is. You got that right."

One time when he was "on the outs," I met him on Sunday afternoon at a reading at Lawrence Arts Center downtown. A bunch of local and Kansas City poets were reading their work, and Crady waited and waited for his turn to read. He introduced me to his daughter, a bored teenager who might have been pleased to be sharing this time with her poet dad but was too cool to show it. Crady fiddled with his poems like any anxious writer about to take the stage for his five minutes of fame at a local poetry reading, most everybody there a poet waiting for his or her own chance to read.

I submitted some of Crady's poems to an editor in Wyoming gathering material for a book about addiction, *Watch My Rising*. She accepted one of his poems and needed him to sign a release form. Crady was out of jail at the time. I had an address for him, and the editor tried and tried to get in touch with him but with no luck, so she contacted me with only a week to go before the printing deadline. If she couldn't get the form signed, she'd have to pull the poem. I know how difficult it is to track down released inmates, who tend to move around a lot, but with a day or two to go the editor sent me the good news that Crady had signed and returned the form. He was proud of his publication in Wyoming, though he found it hard to believe that what he'd written in the classroom at a county jail in Kansas might have significance way beyond that. It was obvious that he was writing primarily for himself, and yet he did like it when we could connect with his poems.

I didn't see Crady for two years after that—not unusual. I lose touch with most inmates when they're out, only to see some of them again when they're back in jail class months or years (or even a decade!) later, often looking the worse for wear, needing some jail time for repair work.

I'm glad that at one point on Crady's troubled journey through the world so far, he was able to make his mark and leave some of his poems in my hands. Want to know what the longest short walk is? Let him explain that to you in his poem:

## 2014

### The longest short walk

I'm writing this about a walk I've had to make.
It's been the most challenging feat I've ever come across.
I don't mean physically, though more than once it almost
became a physical obstacle. It isn't about how hard of a walk it is,
or how hard it is to make the walk. No, this has
been much harder than that. It's been a trying effort
that has been non-stop. And though I've made it time after
time, instead of becoming easier it gets harder & harder
every day. I refer to it as the longest short walk I've
ever been on. It doesn't matter where it starts, that's not the problem.
It's where it ends, inside a room, where once you step in,
you have to close the door. Knowing it doesn't
open when you want it to. It doesn't open until someone
else decides to open it for you. After so long in here
& so many hours upon days upon weeks locked in a cell,
the more claustrophobic I've become. It's a mental challenge
every time I step through that door & they think I'm
trying to be defiant. I guess they just can't begin to
wrap their minds around the reality of what one has
to go through mentally to even do this at all. I'm not
trying to be defiant. I'm just trying to get behind it.

—Shane Crady

Here Crady writes about addiction and incarceration, but I know that I've been on similar "longest short walks" in my life, determined to get through them, not "trying to be defiant"; I was "just trying to get behind it." I too have written my way to a better place, even though I despaired at times, on my own longest short walks. Don't we all know, metaphorically at least, what it's like to be trapped in a situation with the door closed, "knowing it doesn't/open when you want it to"?

I got to know Crady quite well and will remember him, but there are many others who also passed through Douglas County Jail writing class. Scrolling through files of poems from other years, I pass the poems of Derek, Josh, Lo, Kelly, and Nick, most of the names and faces forgotten, though I do remember some of the outstanding writers, especially those who stayed awhile at the jail. But most of these characters, vivid at the time, I'm sure, their writing urgent and unique, have gone who knows where, leaving behind them from their time at Douglas County Jail only their lines buried in files on my computer, most of which I'll never open again and no one else will ever read.

Who will remember their longest short walks?

## 2015

### To my family

To my family I'm setting off in prison, I
miss ya,
I guess this is what it took for me to get
the picture,
They say I got a cold heart but I'm
trying to change,
not wanting my soul lost in eternal flames.
God reach in my mind, unlock the wisdom
I possess,
for the sake of my seeds so they can truly
be blessed.
I know the struggle is real or I wouldn't be
locked in this cell,
on the verge of raisin' Hell and talking

to myself,

but ain't no turning back, this is part of

my destiny,

so give my spirit to God and to the grave

what's left of me.

## 2016

### "Trust no man, even the devil was an angel"

Trust no man, even the devil was an angel. You were

my New—New, my new beginning of a new start, but

in time our love grew further and further apart. At

one time you were my everything, My World, the

blood that flows through my veins. At night when I

lay down and close my eyes in my cell I see

your face, so I put my arms around you and

hold you tight with a warm embrace. Then I wake

up to reality, it was just a dream, but for real,

it all felt so real.

*You got me, I got us.* Those

were the words I last heard from you. Like I

said before, the truth don't hurt, lies do. I believe

in once you start something you should finish it

and also finish what you started. Now I end this

the way I started. Trust no man, even

the devil was an angel.

—James H.

How many angels have we met who turn out to be devils?

Here's a man trying in every way to make this relationship and his life work out, but he finally has to "end this/the way I started." Was he writing about love here, or about freedom, the face he sees when he lies down at night in his cell?

James H., a Black man from the South, had done more time on the inside than on the outside, first incarcerated when he was young man in Texas. And what was that like? I urged him to tell his story, but then he was transferred from Douglas County Jail, and I don't suppose his story will ever be written other than in vivid bursts as in this poem. I'm glad that because of the class, I got to know even this much and that I can pass it on. There's a hard-won truth in his lines that deserves to be heard.

## 2017

I recently got stabbed in the back,
literally in my back, in between some ribs and
into my lung. The burn they say you feel is very
real, but the worst was trying to breathe. It's
like inhaling sand and glass, not too terrible
but still pretty bad. I thought I was going to die,
and actually the nurse at the hospital said I
was lucky to be alive, a few more hours and
I wouldn't be here. So I feel like a change
in my lifestyle is necessary. It takes
some experience like that to make me open
my eyes. That's all bad, but I am taking the right
steps, rehab, spirituality, and a better connection
with friends and family. Today like every day I thank
the Lord for being with me when I needed Him
the most, I mean it could have been a spirit or
whatever you wanna think. I guess for the sake
of wanting something to believe in, a purpose
other than getting high awaits me.

—Antonio E.

Let this poem stand as an example of the sort of brilliant writing we see week after week in Douglas County Jail writing class. I remember Vietnam veteran John Musgrave describing to the inmates during one of his visits to the jail what it felt like to be shot in the chest: "It's like getting hit by a train." Antonio E. makes *his* experience of violence equally vivid.

I have used too many times that cliché "stabbed in the back," but what's it like to be *literally* stabbed in the back? Antonio E. brings me into his harsh experience with the perfect simile: it's like "inhaling sand and glass."

"A purpose/other than getting high awaits me": I hope it does, my friend, and I believe that in writing what you wrote, you were better able to see that purpose and to enable others to see it. I hope you have been able to follow the direction pointed to in your words.

# Chapter 7

# "My Name Is Methamphetamine"

## Douglas County Jail Blues, Volumes 1 and 2

*Douglas County Jail Blues* (2010) was my second book about the jail in two years; in 2008 I'd published a book of my own poems based on my Douglas County Jail experience, *Jail Time* (Original Plus Press). I'd worked on the two books for four or five years, writing, collecting, and editing. I'd had the idea of publishing an inmate anthology for many years; even after a year or so of teaching the class, I knew I'd have plenty of brilliant material to publish. Thomas Zvi Wilson, my friend and fellow poet who visited the class, advised me during my first years of teaching at the jail to get the best inmate writers to sign consent forms agreeing to publication, and I wish I'd taken his advice. The forms would have given me permission to publish poems from that period. But my life was complicated at that time; it was as much as I could do to keep up with my university work and jail teaching as well as raising my two daughters as a single parent. I heard about volunteers at the jail who like what they do there so much that they give more and more of their time to it and can't keep up with other aspects of their lives—most often they burn out as jail volunteers. It's a peculiar kind of addiction to want to work so much at "addiction central."

As with writing this book, when I was starting work on *Douglas County Jail Blues,* I was challenged at first by the sheer *volume* of poetry I'd already assembled after five or six years of teaching at the jail, plenty of it with at least the potential for reaching a wider audience and some of it outstanding. But I'd already lost touch with many of the best writers from these years, so

I couldn't get their permission to publish. Ex-inmates are hard to keep up with; they often find it hard to keep up with themselves.

Over the years, I have gotten to know quite well some of the inmates in class, especially the "frequent fliers" (as they're called by some jail staff), who keep coming back to the jail. We chat before and after class, on our way from the pod to the classroom, and on our way back to the pod after class; I get to know something of their lives. But after they leave the class, I've most always lost touch with them, though I know they might well show up in my class on any Thursday afternoon, or I might see them around town or working at Checkers. My daughter says she likes it when we're walking downtown and some wild-haired, rough-edged, tattooed guy says "Hi" to me and we talk; she's pretty sure he is from the jail class.

I worked with Programs Director Mike Caron at the jail, class coleader at the time, on the anthology. We planned on obtaining permission-to-publish releases from the inmates whose work we'd include. Caron likes to tell the story of a reporter from the *Lawrence Journal-World* who came to the jail soon after it opened in 1999 to write a story about the popular yoga class. The reporter interviewed some of the inmates and asked for permission to use their names, and according to Caron, they jumped at the opportunity, thinking no doubt that any publicity must be good publicity. Caron said they hadn't thought through the consequences of their names appearing in a story about the jail and how it might cause problems when they were applying for jobs after their release, for example. He had considerable experience in the reentry program and knew that the last thing inmates need is added difficulty reintegrating into society. We wanted the writers included in *Douglas County Jail Blues* to know what they were getting into in being part of a jail anthology and suggested that they use pen names.

All twenty-six poets featured in the anthology *Douglas County Jail Blues* signed permission sheets, and in spite of our warnings, most of them chose to use their own names. One of the most prolific and gifted writers we worked with in the early years of the class was Jesse James, back in the class years later in 2017, writing this tribute to the class and anthology:

## 2017

### This Writtin' Class

(dedicated to Brian Daldorph)

I'm commin' out swingin' on this rodeo

'Cause my mind's tuned in like a radio

Deep dark trenches where I found the light

Now my spirit inner stellar like a satellite

Doppler better warn 'bout the commin' storm

'Cause I'm blowin' like a hurricane, that's the norm

Let me tell ya lil somethin' 'bout this writtin' class

Check my name, I been vast for a decade past

I bleed myself in this ink, yea, from me to you

Went so hard I was published in the *County Blue*

For you young's that don't know what I'm talkin' 'bout

*Douglas County Blues* is a book, you should check it out

Triple O.G. Fam, I've earned my clout

'Cause I keep it real when I'm down & out.

—Jesse James


Twenty-six poets published in our 2010 anthology—they "went so hard" they were "published in the *County Blue*." Where are they now, seven years later? I've lost contact with most of them. I know that one of them, Headly, died. I know that a few of them live in the area, and they're still "on the outs"; I occasionally see their postings on Facebook. Then there's Jesse James, back in jail class again in May 2017 with any number of new poems and the wonderful ability to come up with three more in the twenty-plus minutes of in-class writing. We can depend on him to "keep it real" for us. Another volunteer in class said his brain must be wired to think in those hard-hitting couplets; they surge out of his pen like it's a fire hose.

As I read through the poems again in *Douglas County Jail Blues*, I remember some of the poets with whom I worked closely. I remember a few things they did or said and retain in my mind sketches of what they looked like, but most of it has gone forever apart from the lines they wrote. In this chapter, I want to review what's in this anthology and tell the stories I remember about each writer. I'd like to record these stories, which make up a history that will not be told if I don't tell it. I want to showcase poems that have brought their special music (Douglas County Jail blues) to the classroom and beyond over the years, poems that will play on.

As editors, Caron and I arranged the writers alphabetically—there seemed to be no better way to do it—so in this review I'll work my way through the book recalling as much as I can about the individual writers. I also want to show how the themes of these poems are not limited to the themes you might expect in an anthology like this: themes of addiction, incarceration, loss, and so on. Many of these writers would not be recognized as inmates if you read their work outside the context of a jail anthology. My argument here and throughout this book is that *what really mattered* to them when they wrote these poems really matters to us all.

Because the class is a collective enterprise, it's fitting that the anthology begins with a "group poem," each of us in class on this particular day, September 18, 2004, writing a line or more starting with the phrase *I write because*. I included a number of these group poems in *Douglas County Jail Blues* because they catch the communal experience of the class and produce a remarkable record of a unique collaboration on a particular day. In the "I write because" group poem, the tone jumps from one contributor to the next: "I write because I can't get high./Because I am in a cement hell./Because it helps keep me sane." I like the way that the "finished" poem is more than the sum of its parts; it's a small celebration of what's achieved on Thursday afternoon in the classroom at Douglas County Jail, a collaborative effort, everyone in class contributing at least a line or two. (Usually I can get everybody to write at least *something* for the group poem, even if an inmate did not share any other work in class.) I like the way the group poem becomes a sort of composite sketch of a day in the life of Douglas County Jail from the perspectives of inmates. After a five-minute communal writing burst, I go around the class to see what each writer came up with. A lot of tough lines, a few laughs—just like the class itself.

## 2004

### I write because

I write because no one else will write what's in my crazy head . . .

I write because I can't get high.

Because I am in a cement hell.

Because it helps keep me sane.

I write because I get locked down.

I write because it helps me to remember my past.

Because it brings a pretty smile to my kids' faces.

Because it helps me heal some of my past . . .

Because the guards think I'm crazy when I talk to myself.

Because it releases built-up emotion.

I write because I enjoy the silence . . .

I write because I want to catch my dream by the tail

before it runs out of my house.

I write because then I'm not afraid anymore.

I write because stories in my head are on fire, and I have to put them

out before they burn me.

I don't include writers' names when I type up group poems. Here the effort is collective, and I like the way this poem catches the raw energy of the class, the patchwork of cries from the heart: the silliness, reflection, memory, need, passion, loss, disappointment, and more that make up every class. I think all of us know what it's like to chase our elusive dreams, but could we say it any better than this: "I write because I want to catch my dream by the tail/before it runs out of my house"? The inmate who wrote this might now be working in Walmart with another kid on the way and his wife working a shift at Checkers. He might be buried in a potters' field. He might have hitchhiked back to Burlington where he's working in his uncle's paint shop. He might be living in town, happily ever after. Who knows, who knows? I hope he caught his dream by the tail and held on tight. With a couple of lines written in a jail classroom on a Thursday afternoon, he made his mark.

I wanted to start the anthology in this way to show that the group effort in class is more important than the work of any one poet. What better prompt than *I write because,* and how to improve on the first line of the anthology: "I write because no one else will write what's in my crazy head." This is a fitting first line because I emphasize to inmates that *each writer* in class has stories to tell about his own life that no one else can tell. It's one of the founding ideas of the class. The guys most often shrug this off by saying something like, "No one's interested in my shit," but when they start writing about their experiences and receiving good feedback, then they begin to see the value of writing what's in their crazy heads. I tell them that in my twenty-plus years of teaching creative writing workshops, most of the students I've worked with have been able to find the voices they need to write *what really matters* to them. I tell them that if something needs to be written, then there *will* be a way to write it; that's one of the great things about writing. My role as instructor is more about helping students to tell their own stories—in the form of poems, perhaps—rather than instructing them how to do it. All my students were telling stories about their lives long before they sat in a creative writing classroom and will be doing so for a long time afterward. I'm lucky they passed on to me some of their work.

Many claim that writing is therapeutic, and I agree with that. I think of Vietnam veteran John Musgrave, the most regular visiting writer to the class during my time at the jail (see Chapter 14 for his take on his visits to the jail), telling the inmates that for him the writing of his poetry about his harrowing Vietnam War experience has been like vomiting out poison that was killing him. Read Musgrave's "combat poems" in his collection *Notes to the Man Who Shot Me* to see how he has tried to expel the horror. Though I don't see the class as a therapy session—I'm not a trained therapist—I do know well enough the benefits of expelling the dangerous things that are hurting us: "I write because the stories in my head are on fire, and I have to put them out/before they burn me." Or do it for this reason: "I write because I can't get high." Too many inmates know the truth of this—in fact, they're living it in class. Writing might help to ease the pain of withdrawal. Even if it helps only a little bit, it's worth it. They might even learn from Jimmy Santiago Baca that writing is a thousand times more thrilling and intoxicating than drugs and alcohol and benefits the writer rather than damaging him and bringing new troubles to his life. Their poetry will make difficult lives a little easier to live and will enhance the writers' communities, which is why Patrick Alexander in *From Slave Ship to Supermax* refers to writing like this as "revivifying narratives," revivifying not only for the writer but also for the people around him or her, in jail and in the community.

To be honest, I don't remember poet Larry Chapman, from at least a decade ago, who was the first individual poet in the anthology. A lot of faces have filled in the class circle since then. But rereading his work, crudely made yet engaging, I do know his experience well enough, to which any number of Douglas County Jail inmates could relate. Most of them would recognize too well "what's real" about Chapman's depiction of addiction and its devastating effects on the addict and his family (with the cruel irony that the family might, because of trauma, get addicted to antidepressants):

## Early 2000s

### What's Real

I smoke weed so my nerves would chill

but I don't fuck with the hard stuff cuz that shit'll kill

and if the dope doesn't do, the dealers will

cuz they only care about their money, their power, their *Skrill* [money,
    cash]

if you lost your life, how do you think your family would feel

probably suffering from depression and a little ill

then be on a schedule 3 times a day poppin' a pill

and you thought you was cool, doin' it for that thrill

but you been up for weeks, and don't remember your last meal

don't take my word for it, but I'm speakin' what's real.

—Larry Chapman

"Speakin' what's real": that's what the class gives these inmates the space and encouragement to do, unlike the writing class at the Adolescent Treatment Center in Olathe, Kansas, where I worked for two years in the 1990s, in which any reference to drugs or alcohol was banned, so what were a roomful of young drug abusers and addicts supposed to write about? "What's real": many inmates will relate to Chapman's depiction of drug use, "doin' it for that thrill," then having to pay the steep price for it. Where are you now, Larry Chapman? Did you manage to haul yourself out of addiction?

Danegrus Dane wrote in "Stay in Your Room!": "When you're in jail you're constantly/surrounded by grief, anguish, disbelief & anger. I'd rather stay/a stranger." Staying a stranger: that was Danegrus Dane's way of dealing with his jail time. I remember him in class: his sensitivity, his quick wit, his haunted eyes; he knew he was likely to get out, go crazy, and mess up again. He was in and out of jail a few times during my first years there, until he performed what one fellow inmate called a "vanishing act." I saw him many years later in Dillon's grocery store, in the produce section, with a cute toddler son in his cart. We talked briefly, and then he was gone. It's not unusual; inmates I get to know quite well in the jail class move on when they get out. I might well remind them of a place they do not want to go back to, in memory or otherwise.

I'm glad that the "danegrus" killer Danegrus Dane sent to kill himself, "holding that big silenced Desert Eagle/with the laser sights and Teflon-rubber grip" didn't kill him: the killer sent out to kill him was *himself*, the ultimate act of self-destruction. He didn't complete that contract, and I'm proud to have saved Danegrus Dane's poems of dark imagination. Though he didn't want to return to his past when I saw him in the grocery store, I couldn't have been more pleased to see him doing well.

Who was "Deuce"? Where is he now? Did he clean up his life like he always vowed to do? Maybe he has carried on writing lines with this despairing power:

> Feeling as if 1,000 ghosts move through my head,
>
> flowing through this bone palace of a shell
>
> called my body.
>
> Enough powdered medication flows through me
>
> 2 feed a sick house of the ill.

Just to say that when I sit in class week after week, I look around at faces young and getting older and some old already with 1,000 ghosts moving through them, and I, of course, could not put it better than that. So thank you, Deuce, whoever you are and wherever you are now. I hope you got well and stayed well and didn't end up in a "sick house of the ill," your health ravaged by "medications." There was a time when you thought you could do better.

David D. was in the class for a few months during my early years there and should have been in a graduate English seminar. After he'd read one of his poems, I remember one of the tattooed, scarred, worn-down inmates looked at him in disbelief and said, "What the fuck are *you* doing *here*?" *Here* was for guys who'd struggled in their lives, who'd gotten beaten up and couldn't stop beating up on themselves, not for articulate young guys like David D., who looked like he could start up a tech company and sell it to Google for a billion dollars. Never did know what he was doing there, but I do remember his brilliant, often surreal poetry.

### Spies Taste Like Lemons

I know there are spies in my coffee,

spies in my eggs

and spies on my hands

They come out of television
(radioactive)
and ring tones.
They evaporate the rain that collects
on my skin.

Move my eyes when I dream.

I know there are spies in my tastebuds.
They taste like lemons
and smell like onions.

Spies in the floor cleaners
and toothpaste,
the tap water
and soil.

They hide in conversation
and words
and the punchlines
of jokes.
And in this pencil.

I know there are spies
There are spies in you
'cause you share the coffee
the lemons
the water
and you share words
and punchlines with me.

     —David D.

David D. had enough time locked up to know that there are spies every-where in jail, cameras in corridors and elevators so we're under surveillance all the time (as envisioned in Jeremy Bentham's panopticon); plus, in such a small crowded space, everyone's always being watched not only by jail authorities but also by other inmates. Spies in your coffee, spies in the water, spies that taste like lemons? After a short time of incarceration, that would *not* seem like a big stretch. I've gotten quite an insight into what guys go through when they're incarcerated, and I don't know how they do it without going crazy. How to follow all the rules and regulations? How to endure be-ing watched all the time? How to spend so many hours in a tiny cell? How to face up to a long sentence? Do you adapt yourself to it just to get by and become institutionalized? After incarceration, is it even possible to live out-side the four walls? Do you carry them inside you forever? I'm still looking for answers. My friend Antonio Sanchez-Day, thirteen years in "the system," says he always sits with his back to the wall when he's out somewhere, al-ways stays on guard. He's always watching out for predators, finding it hard to remember he's not still in "the jungle." Often wakes thinking he's back inside.

Some of the picks for the anthology were obvious: Donndilla da Great was one of the legends of the class. He'd led the class for a number of months during his incarceration at Douglas County Jail, coinciding with my early classes there, encouraging his fellow writers, keeping the class on track, and contributing his own resonant poetry. When Donndilla da Great was in class, he made my job easy: I sat there and watched his demonstration of what a "Great" class leader could do. Inmates stayed on task when Donn-dilla da Great was in charge; no catching up on street business on his watch. A tall, lithe African American who looked like an ex-athlete who still had plenty of game in him, the quality of his poems and his voice when he re-cited them struck the hearts and minds of us all, including literary rookies who aspired to write like Donndilla da Great:

### Hope

As I sit in my cell

I get stronger and stronger

I walk and I pace my cell

like a caged tiger

but as the unit comes to a lull

I think of hope . . .

I see Sitting Bull, and he told me to
pray for a place for my people
I seen Gandhi, and he told me to
pray for peace.
I seen Shaka, and he told me to
pray for the strength of a warrior
I seen Mother Teresa, and she told me
to pray for the children
I seen this other man, and I felt
his glory but his face was distorted,
but he told me to pray for mankind
Then Malcolm X tap me on the shoulder,
and I asked him why was everyone
telling me to pray when I wanted
hope, and he said, Prayer is hope
and didn't I recognize that when
I seen Jesus. Aw man, I missed Jesus!

      —Donndilla da Great

**Wanting**
I've seen the looks of most of
the staff and guards
I can already see all the inmates'
stares as I walk the yard

I know they shake their heads
and I know the cons are going to
wanna know why I am back.

But I haven't been squandering my life away
I've taken all the lessons you've taught me
and put them to use day by day.

I told the Parole Board that I would
be a better man
And I told my cellmate that I was
afraid of the crackhead that lies within

Yeah, I hit the streets and I was
off and running
I tried to fight it, but how could I?
When I just kept wanting.

—Donndilla da Great

I pray that the spirits of Sitting Bull, Mahatma Gandhi, Malcolm X, Shaka, and Mother Teresa are still looking out for Donndilla da Great, helping him to overcome his *wanting*. I hope he is still *fighting it* because he has so much to offer. I'll probably never know.

Tyrone wrote "The Letter": "Watching/the sun and quick shadows of flying birds play/across the pages of my notebook paper." Years later he was back in class, and I wondered what factors had led this man with such a fine poetic gift to go down the hard road to county jail? When I last saw him in 2017, he was on his way to treatment, determined, like so many others before him, that this time, *this* time he was going to make it, this time for sure. He had a wife to get back to, kids to raise, but it sounded like he had scores to settle too with himself and others, and that didn't sound good. Will he shuffle back into class one day with a shy smile and a poem or two to share, or has he gone forever?

In "3:16 a.m.: The Life I Love to Hate," James wrote about frantically seeking help, calling a treatment center desperate for a bed there: "I dial the/ number, someone familiar picks up and I ask, *Is there a bed/open, PLEASE! I hate this life!*" Did he find that bed? Did he turn his life around? How are you doing now, James—did you leave your demons behind at a treatment center like you said you would? (So many inmates go off to treatment convinced that *this time* they'll rid themselves of their demons.)

Poet-artist (he designed the dedication page of *Douglas County Jail Blues*) Fixico wrote about "trying to keep myself clean." But his devils were tugging at him: "I can still feel the prick, oh man, what a rush./Like an ice cold rushing river up my arm." I remember Fixico's weary face lighting up when other inmates gave him the praise he deserved for his poems. I recognized his joy at finding himself good at something after a life in which he'd struggled to make the best of himself and knew defeat very well indeed. I'd see him downtown when he got out, drifting around. Last time I saw him was on the Kansas River bridge, crossing over to the north side of town, going somewhere, maybe to the tent encampment down by the river or to some other world? Wherever he went after he'd crossed over that time, I didn't see him again.

Another obvious choice for the anthology was Michael Harper, who wrote the best-known poem in the anthology, "Methamphetamine." "Lefty," as he is known, is a musician and songwriter, wound up and wiry, with a flair for writing poetry that gets inside your head like songs with great hooks. He was an electrifying presence in the class, reciting his rhythmic, rhyming poems or singing some lyrics a capella. Whenever he was in class, other inmates wanted to hear "Methamphetamine," and they'd indicate how well they could relate to it with comments such as, "That's what I'm talking about" and "You got that":

## 2007

### Methamphetamine

My name is methamphetamine, but you can call me speed

I last so much longer than cocaine, and I'm so much better than weed

I've had many names over the years, crystal, crank, and Ice

and what I can do to the human brain isn't very nice

I'll make you stay up for days & days and see things that aren't there

I'll turn your wife into a whore, and you won't even care

The more you do, the more you want to go faster and faster and faster

stealing pills, for the cook 'cause he's the puppet master

I'll take away everything you love, then laugh at all your pain

I'll make you hear voices, slowly drive you insane

You'll do anything for me, my personal little pawn

You'll be a walking skeleton, your teeth will all be gone

Don't even try to take me on, 'cause you can never win

But you'll come back, you always do, though you know you're gonna
   lose

Don't try to blame me for your problems, you had the right to choose

When you die, if you think I care, well, you are sadly mistaken

I'll just add your worthless carcass to the others that I've taken

But that's all good, don't ya know, it's all part of my plan

I should come in a baggie that says, "Death for Sale," $100 a gram

Sorry 'bout your luck, but you see I only have one goal

That is to ruin your life and slowly take your soul

So hop aboard my crazy train, I know just what you need

My name is methamphetamine, but you can call me speed.

   —Michael Harper

This is the poem that gets ripped out of copies of *Douglas County Jail Blues* in the jail library. It's a tribute to Harper that inmates need his poem so much they steal it. I wish he'd gotten royalties for all those ripped-out pages.

   Headly would be in class for a few weeks and then, after his release, I'd see him around town, in the grocery store, or walking his dog—a cheerful, friendly guy bopping down the street when he wasn't high or intoxicated. Headly would travel off to Oregon or California or some other distant place to attend free music festivals, wildly indulge himself, then somehow crawl back to Lawrence, where he'd end up in Douglas County Jail, messed up and barely able to function when he first came back to class. He'd be back in jail in a terrible state, desperately in need of some jail time to sober up. But he was always writing and would come to class with new poems. A shy guy we'd have to talk into sharing, he was clearly thrilled by our enthusiastic responses to his poetry.

   My father was a man of much importance

   He stood alone in the world

   most of the time atop a hill

   where he looked out across the prairie

He awaited like no other man I've known

for the return of the buffalo.

In Headly's poem about addiction, "yet again," he wrote of the terrors in his mind; the puking; and what scared him the most, hallucinations, because "sometimes they seem so real." He was in a descending spiral of fall and recovery, fall and recovery, knowing that each time he got well again, "there is one thing for sure/my vodka will not be far away." One time he didn't make it back from the dark lands, and I stood beside his father at Headly's memorial service in South Park in Lawrence, attended by guys he'd known on the street. His father told me that the extensive sores on his son's skin all healed miraculously after his death. His father later collected Headly's poems and self-published them. Headly had made his mark on the world, but how much more could he have done without the demons always dragging him down? Or did those demons inspire him? How else could he have gone so far down in himself to surface with his poems? I hope he realized at the end that he'd left behind something of *much importance.*

Bobby Hickman signed his poem, "At Night in My Cell," "Bobby Hickman 08". Almost ten years since he was incarcerated in a Douglas County Jail cell, he sensed at night all the other poor souls who'd been detained in the cell before him who had left their "marks": "Names, quotes, words of anger. Bits of scripture/all scribed on the walls." Cheerful Hickman called himself the "Asian Creation," though most everybody assumed he was Native American. He told me that when he was asked which tribe he belonged to, he'd say, "Korean!" He was such a good writer that a lot of inmates would ask him to write letters for them to their girlfriends, wives, and families. Where are you now, Hickman? Did you beat the addiction that shackled your bright life? I hope so because you had a lot going for you. I don't suppose I will see you again, but you did leave your mark, in a gesture ("leaving a fragment of my own spirit behind") that would have pleased Walt Whitman:

And so I scribe my name and leave

my mark as all the others have, leaving a fragment of my own

spirit behind to dwell with those who have left theirs as well.

As I sit alone at night in my cell.

How many of us sit in our own "cells" at night wondering if we will leave a "mark"?

The first poet I was really impressed by in the writing class was Gary Holmes, a big man with a veteran of life's face and a lot of tattoos; it was obvious he'd lived the outlaw life and was proud of it (see Chapter 12, "'I Done Good and I Done Bad': Topeka's Bad Man from the Badlands, Gary Holmes"). Holmes wrote "Courtroom Drama": the judge on high with gavel, "Victim's family, sad eyes hurting./Knowing anguish, searing scorching daily/pain." He knew the terrible pain of guilt, and he knew the joy of love told to him by the prophet:

> Then the prophet said: "Listen to your
> heart, tell her to listen to hers. And
> each and every day you'll have genuine
> love, fresh and pure and untouched.
> Love . . . each day of your lives."

When Caron and I looked back at the hundreds and hundreds of inmate writers we'd worked with, we always thought of Holmes. He went off to prison to serve his sentence. He's out now, living in Topeka, and we've corresponded on Facebook. He looks like the proudest grandfather in the world. After more than ten years, I met him again in a gritty McDonalds in Topeka. I told him I wanted to write a chapter about him in this book; we talked for an hour or more, and then he had to go. "You made my day," he said. I encouraged him to start writing poetry again.

I've known Jesse James for more than ten years, and it's an odd thing that I like it when he's back in jail class because when he reads he's brilliant, and everybody knows it. I wonder what he could have made of his gift if he hadn't spent most of his life on the street doing deals. I admire the strength of his spirit, the electricity in his lines, and his resolve to keep fighting. There's always a *shine* about Jesse James, who has his own way of seeing things and his own way of telling them. Life has taken a big toll on him, but he's still fighting, mostly against himself. All of his poetry is written in the form of relentless rhyming couplets:

> 'Cause we only get one shot at this thing we call life
> & I'll live it to the fullest, even if it's in jail cells
> chosen perception state uh mind & what ya go call hell
> but they can only destroy my flesh, not my mind or soul

so I'll live & laugh, in suffering while my life unfolds

another story told, are ya getting it

shit happens, chalk it up, no lookin' back, no regrets.

"Shit happens, chalk it up, no lookin' back, no regrets": thanks for that line, Jesse James, and for so many others. In many ways our lives couldn't be more different, yet our shared love of language and poetry has brought us together for our joint benefit, sometimes outside the library in downtown Lawrence for one of your impromptu rap sessions. "Chalk it up!"

One of the big characters of my jail time: Big Jae Wae, a large Black man with gold-capped teeth, a bald dome, and the build of a retired NFL line-backer, had a *lot* of trouble in his life that he was determined to put behind him by the time I met him. He told me he wanted to do his time, finish it, and be done with it instead of getting jerked around with parole. He knew there was no future in the criminal ways he was doing things, and he wanted a future, unlike the death row inmates he'd write about:

As he lays across the

gurney, his right hand twitches,

for they have not injected the vile

poisons that shall make him

no more, as a reminder that

he should have written at least

to say goodbye.

Wae became the unofficial teacher's aide because he had to keep everyone in line so we could have a good class each time—it was only once a week, so he had to make the most of it. I still get to see Wae's big, golden-toothed smile when I visit the writing workshop at Lansing Prison, in eastern Kansas, where my friend Arlin Buyert teaches. Wae greets me and my family at the regular performances of Lansing's East Hills Choir at Kansas City churches. I always enjoy Wae's mischievous humor—the big guy would get us all laughing, as with his thirteen-word "Good Excuse" for being back in jail:

I only come back
to see if I
can get in
writing class.

In Wae's opinion, it's worth getting arrested to get back to the poetry business. Will there ever be a finer endorsement of the class?

On a cold night at Lansing Prison, Wae told me that he wasn't wearing a coat because he was thinking about his security in a place where he was surrounded by killers and violent criminals. It's always possible at a place like Lansing, he told me, that someone would come at him with a shank, and if he didn't wear a coat, then he could move more quickly to defend himself. That's how Wae has to think after too many years of incarceration, yet he's a core member of the Lansing writing workshop, aspiring to do something more than simply survive his prison time. He can even see the end of it in a few years—he's getting closer and closer to that future he has kept alive during all his jail and prison time, and his poetry has played a big part in his resilience.

Three poems from MB appear in *Douglas County Jail Blues*: "Let Go" (letting go of addiction in order to live a new life); "Livin' on Lithium in Lock-up" ("Can't wait to get on meds & out/of here.... Now I don't care.... Yes/I do. Well sometimes a lot ... but not at/this minute"); and "Forget It," his shot at using all the prompts on the board:

I'm in writing class trying to
use all the words on the board
and *root and stone* seem to be the
most difficult, so now I've got that one
out of the way. Let's see . . . *the wrong
room,* Hell, I'm in the wrong
county. . . . OK, *too cold?* . . . Just
the *opposite.* Ha, there's 2 more. . . .
Wow, I hope this isn't total *rubbish.*
It gets worse. To this day I don't think
I've seen a *black curtain* except

on the Addams Family. (You know, where
Lurch was the doorman.) Well, I'm now
almost through. . . . I think I'll call
this "Forget it" . . . hoping that you do.

But I didn't do what you wrote, MB; I didn't *forget it*: ten years after you wrote this poem, I'm back with it, not remembering you but in contact with you through what you wrote in Douglas County Jail class on a Thursday afternoon when you could have stayed in your cell or watched TV, but you came to class and shared something with us; thanks for that. Don't know where you are now, MB; don't know if you're still with us or if you stumbled over the edge like some of the others, but I'd just like to say that you are not forgotten in spite of your instruction. Any poem mentioning Lurch is more than all right with me.

Making use of the prompt *one by one*, from a Woody Guthrie lyric set to music by Billy Bragg, Standing Rock Sioux warrior Ishtia Maza, battered in body but strong in spirit, wrote a small celebration of our class, a poem published in October 2008 in the *Lawrence Journal-World's* "Poet's Showcase":

One by one our poems are
read.
One by one we feel pride in
what we write.
One by one we put the
words onto paper.
One by one we say the
words out loud.

He ends with the hope that he will get out of jail, go home, and stay out of trouble. I'd see him around Lawrence, most often looking sick and tired. For Maza, as for others in the class, Douglas County Jail was a relatively safe place in a precarious world. His wry poetry was like a small fire on a cold night to warm our spirits. We'd sit by the fire and listen to his jokes and stories. I included two more of his marvelous poems in another chapter.

Sean Reese writes of the "Cold dark hand" grabbing him and pulling him down just when he seems to be doing well in the world:

The cold dark hand
It grabs me
and keeps pulling me
down just when
I think I'm about
to escape from
all my problems the
cold dark hand
pulls me back in.

Every inmate in the jail knows the grip and pull of that "cold dark hand"; it's one of the images I'll always remember from the class. At least after reading Reese's poem, they know to look out for it, know what to call it. I don't know if he read Edgar Allen Poe, but to me there's a lot of Poe in that cold dark hand. I'm sure it does not bring blessings. I think we all know what it is to be pulled by that hand to our darker sides. Reese was in class again in 2018, ten years after writing this poem. Unfortunately, it seems that the *cold dark hand* still has a strong grip on him and keeps pulling him down.

Zach T., a tall, handsome, young guy with the good looks of a college football star and a friendly personality, rolled up the leg of his jail jumpsuit to show us the huge scar on his leg, the result of a swimming accident in Clinton Lake, just outside Lawrence, when he was cut up by a boat's propeller. Zach T. is a smart guy but did some crazy stuff at the lake and got badly hurt. His doctors put him on opiate pain medicine, and he got hooked and kept getting into trouble trying to get what he needed to satisfy his cravings. But satisfy it one time, and you have to satisfy it another time and another, and in the end you start doing risky things to get what you need, get caught, and carve a big chunk of time out of your life in the penitentiary. I knew Zach T. when it seemed he had so many possibilities for a good life. If he survives, he'll get out of prison as a middle-aged man with hardly time to make a life for himself "on the outs." I hope you're still writing in prison, Zach, pacing, mind racing, trying to spit it out. You did it well, and I know it helped you and others in class. You'll need all the help you can get for the hard years of incarceration ahead.

**Mind**

Inside & out. My mind is racing,

Pacing . . . from side to side.

Oh I wish I could just hide.

The pain that grows from within

I wish it would just end.

From the ground to the sky

I just wish I was high.

Are drugs a treasure or do they provide

a false pleasure. I'm prescribed

yet still denied. Can't sleep, I'm

in this shit knee-deep.

My stomach's turning, the food was

inside now it's out. My mind

is Racing, Pacing from side to side.

— Zach T.

Three sonnets, an imitation of Alfred Lord Tennyson's "In Memoriam," and a crazy tale set in 1879 at Lawrence's Bourgeois Pig bar of Fyodor Dostoyevsky, Leo Tolstoy, Paul Gauguin, and Vincent Van Gogh getting hammered together: Vogue Rogue was the most literary of inmates I worked with, who should have been a college professor, not a street musician getting himself arrested in the autumn so he could spend winter in jail and get out at the start of the good weather. I'd see him downtown busking, and one time he played "Sakura" for me and my Japanese fiancée.

When musician Joe Parrish came to class, he let Vogue Rogue play his guitar, and after a cool version of "Knockin' on Heaven's Door," Vogue Rogue joked: "Playing guitar's even better than that other thing," and with his salacious sense of humor there could be no doubt what he was referring to as "that other thing." When I asked him why he wanted to live on the street, he said it made him feel free. The problem was that his son was drawn to the same life of harsh freedom and joined him on the street—and in jail. Out of all this madness, Vogue Rogue crafted beautiful formal poems, along with a series of often indecent haiku tossed into the class to see how far he could push the boundaries. There's something of William Ernest Henley's defiant spirit in "Invictus" in a lot of Vogue Rogue's poetry ("I am the master of my fate:/I am the captain of my soul"):

### The Asylum of Psyche (or Free Cell)

They seek to punish—locking me away;

they only hold the "matter" part of me!

The part of me they cannot hold at bay

is writing this: My Immortal Psyche!

I breach this cell with every thought I think—

imagination knows no cinder blocks!

Their time and space continuum's a chink

which I can filter through—despite their locks!

I've gone to shipwrecks in their deepest seas;

I've climbed Mount Everest in the month of Hell!

I've dated more than one of the Pleiades;

I've seen and done more than I've time to tell!

Yea! All this! Plus! Chagrin and consternation—

how I evade their lame incarceration!

    —Vogue Rogue

That's Vogue Rogue, who had hundreds of poems, but where to keep them? One time he told me about his solitary publication; I don't recall the details of it, but I did help him with his second publication—in the *Lawrence Journal-World's* Christmas Day haiku page. If I didn't see Vogue Rogue in class, then I'd see him soon enough on Massachusetts Street in downtown Lawrence and expected to always see him there. But about five years ago he was gone—I don't know where, and I didn't get to give him the best publication he'll likely ever have, his impressive contribution to *Douglas County Jail Blues*. I think you can understand why I'm so pleased to have gotten at least a few poems from this strange, gifted poet on the page. He'd push the envelope and get us riled up, but there was only one Vogue Rogue in the whole world, and I was lucky enough to meet the gifted trickster who trusted me to be the keeper of his poems.

What do all these poems add up to? They did not bring significant fame to any of the poets here, but they did bring the thought to these writers that they had done at least one good thing in lives often chaotic and close to meltdown. In attending class, in being part of the circle, they were able to help themselves and others to be part of something bigger than themselves and their immediate concerns, and that helped the healing. As Ron Z. wrote:

> As I scribe this poem upon the
>
> wall I hope it will ease the pain & suffering of the
>
> next unfortunate soul inside this shell of solitude with only
>
> his or her own silence to keep them company. And I
>
> pray that this silence is not as loud and cruel as mine.

Pain and suffering, solitude, cruel silence—these might all be recognized as elements of the experience of incarceration, but I'm familiar with all of them too, as we all are, though most of us have not been incarcerated. This ties in with Sister Helen Prejean and her sense of *what really matters:* if art is moving to us, then it's because we sense a shared humanity with the artist even though his or her immediate circumstances might be very different from our own.

Empathy, reaching out to others, self-reflection, facing up to troubles rather than trying to obliterate them with alcohol and drugs—all of these benefits have come from the writing class, as I've been told by inmate writers and as I've seen for myself during my two decades of "jail time." The class can at least turn inmates in the right direction. If they still don't make it after this—and I have seen too many vowing never to return and soon back inside—then at least they've given themselves a chance, a better chance than if they hadn't tried.

The anthology ends with James's "Space Ship." Now I do remember James, a young, slender, wired-up Native American who would write so fast you'd think his hand might overheat and catch fire. If all the class offers is an escape from the harsh reality of incarceration with its endless humiliations and terrible boredom, then what's wrong with that? Maybe we could all take a trip on James's "Space Ship" for time out in a fantastic world of our own creation:

> I'm unavailable. Out of my mind. Out of pocket.
>
> Not on my rocket. Not at home. Not in my room. Not in jail.
>
> Not in a cell. Not at work. Not in the office. Not at the gym.

Not at the game. Not on the block. Not in the neighborhood.

Not in town. Not in the city. Not in that spot. Not

running. Not hiding. I just can't be reached. No letters.

No e-mail. No page. No phone calls. No voicemail. No buzzing.

No alerts. No requests. No photos. No questions. *Yessss*

*ssirrreeeee.* this is my time. My life. My limelight. My

zone. My *my space.* My way. My total control. My highway.

My road. My country. My sun. My moon. My clouds.

My stars. My planets. My earth. Finally I can have

some me time . . . in my space ship.

What's to fear for the incarcerated poet who can create his own earth, stars, planets, and moon and zoom around them in his own spaceship? What's to fear? Isn't he a little prince of his own kingdom? For a few hours in his cell every day, perhaps, and for two hours a week in the writing class at Douglas County Jail, he could be out of his cell and on his road, in his time, under his own control, in his own *my space;* with this time out from the grim experience of incarceration, he just might be able to make it through his shift in the misery factory.

By the time *Douglas County Jail Blues* came together in 2009, I'd already been publishing the journal *Coal City Review* for more than twenty years, so I knew how to work with a book designer (Leah Sewell; her design work is as fine as her poetry) and publication support assistant, the endlessly patient Pam LeRow. I had the good fortune to be given the gift of jail artwork by Kerry Niemann, who, with extreme generosity, gave me permission to use her artwork in any way I wanted. She taught an art class at the jail for a number of years, dedicating an impressive number of hours to her volunteer work. When I look at her sketches of inmates from Douglas County Jail, I can't identify any of them, but I recognize them all in another way because there's that beaten-down resilience and sadness about each portrait, something I see in the faces in our writing circle week after week even though the individual inmates change. Inmate Kelly designed the jail bars on the book cover, with the irony that Douglas County Jail as a modern correctional facility does not have jail bars. But Kelly had been around the prison system and knew plenty about jail bars—his bars look authentic indeed. Caron took the photograph of the slot in the cell door, the "bean-hole," symbolizing that the anthology was intended as a way into what's happening inside the cell.

The book was published in 2010 by Coal City Press, and it has sold well for an independent press publication. Its fourth printing was in February 2018. Most of the reviews, including one by Al Ortolani in *New Letters*, focused on Harper's poem "Methamphetamine" (the poet performs the song in a YouTube video). It's still selling copies as, seven years later, I have begun gathering poems for a new anthology.

How to measure the success of poetry publications that will not appear on the *New York Times* bestseller list? I have seen the thrill of success in the faces of the published poets when I first gave them a copy of the publication and they saw their names in print in a "real" book. "I am a poet. I am a published poet. I have done something wholly good in this world." Modern poets often despair that they have no audience. Though we could only claim for *Douglas County Jail Blues* a small audience, it's hard to think the book could mean more to its writers and readers.

I've been collecting inmate poems since 2011 for what I'm imaginatively calling, at this point, *Douglas County Jail Blues,* Volume 2. So far, I have collected the poetry of thirty poets, including some by poets from the first anthology—Harper, Headly, and Maza. New writers have come through since the first anthology and are included in *Words Is a Powerful Thing*, such as Shane Crady, Antonio Sanchez-Day, and others. Thirty poets with their stories to tell, thankful for the opportunity the class—and the possibility of publication—gives them.

I'd like to finish the chapter by looking ahead to the publication of the second anthology of Douglas County Jail poets, focusing on the poetry and what I know of the lives of two of the poets, KP and Anthony J. I believe I can augment their poetry by telling what I know of their life stories.

In my time at the jail, I've noticed that some inmates try to do their time *with* other inmates. They're the ones who seem to fit in well at the jail, talking with others before, after, and during class, with all the jokes and gossip they need to get through the day. They're the ones who make jail look like an okay place to be; they're with the people they know best, most often the people with whom they've lived their lives. Jail time is what it is; they've lived much worse than in a cell, so they might as well make the best of it. Then there are the inmates who try to do time on their own, the introverts who spend a lot of time in their cells, emerging only for meals, classes, attorney meetings, and so forth. KP was in the latter category, writing in his poem "Food": "I just cry and cry and cry. I tell myself/I can do this. When the day is finally over/I am so relieved, I think, Wow, I made it." He was one of the keenest writers in the class for the few months he was incarcerated, not only writing assiduously in class but also bringing neatly scripted poems to class every week. The small prestige his writing gave him seemed to draw him out of himself. Arriving one week in class, however, he took his copy of the previous week's handout and skimmed through it. I'd omitted one of the poems he'd read the week before; it had violated one or more of the rules of the class. KP was really upset, angry at me for this form of *censorship,* as he called it, and kept raging so much that in the end Programs Director Sherry Gill intervened and said he had to go back to the pod—he was disrupting class. She escorted him, fuming, out of the room. KP was back in class the next week. He apologized to me and took his place, a model student. I can understand his outburst, which likely had little to do with the omission of his poem from the packet and more to do with the misery of incarceration; perhaps he'd had bad news from his attorney. As he wrote in "Mixed Up Massive Change," jail for him was a "place of gnashing teeth . . . a preamble to Hell." Poetry lifted him out of that hell at least some of the time. I've selected four of KP's poems for the next *Douglas County Jail Blues.* In "Open Minds," he sees himself as one of the "walking Frankensteins" of the jail. Incarceration can turn anyone into a monster, or at least make you feel like one, but it does help to give a name to it and write it out so you have a better chance of hanging on to your humanity.

Anthony J. has been around for quite a number of my Douglas County Jail years, out and then back in, struggling, fighting with himself: "The half-ass self-inflicted suffering/that comes & goes unconsciously,/paralyzing my being/& causing unwanted damage." He's always bringing new poems to class, making the most of the opportunity, not speaking until it's his turn to read, hanging on tight to the lifeline of poetry. Anthony J. finds comfort in his poetry "like politicians find comfort in lying:/I guess I like the sound of it too—/it's soothing to my soul/as is BB King when I listen to him sing." Anthony J.'s writing helps him to keep a lid on his anger, always threatening to burst out of its container: "The anger which I feel/deep inside/is enough to get me 40 years,/no parole just 40 flat/in Super Max./No sunshine or yard time/& general population ain't even spoke of." Anthony J. has always been drawn to the edge, tempted to hurl himself over, needing the thrill of it all, "the tingling, the hummin',/the burning, the numbness—/the raw pain it exposes/that I can't get enough of." It has led to his turbo-charged poetry in class over many years and his understanding that his writing might be his best chance of all to keep off the low road. Anthony J. got out at the end of 2018 and asked if we could stay in touch so that I could help him to get his poems published. I received a text or two from him trying to set up a meeting downtown so that I could see what he's been working on. I've not heard from him since then. It's likely the cycle of extreme self-inflicted suffering and intense repair work is happening all over again, playing out the essential drama that matters to all of us, the forces of our demons and angels fighting it out. We're all hoping that our angels come out on top.

In *Working in the Dark*, poet Jimmy Santiago Baca describes how it felt to write his first words in a Red Chief notebook when he was incarcerated on a drug charge. Baca said he felt like he was adrift in a "raging ocean," but when he was writing:

> I felt an island rising beneath my feet like the back of a whale. As more and more words emerged, I could finally rest: I had a place to stand for the first time in my life. The island grew, with each page, into a continent inhabited by people I knew and mapped with the life I lived.
>
> I wrote about it all—about people I had loved or hated, about the brutalities and ecstasies of my life. And, for the first time, the child in me who had witnessed and endured unspeakable terrors cried out not just in impotent despair, but with the power of language.
>
> Suddenly, through language, through writing, my grief and my joy could be shared with anyone who would listen. And I could do this all alone; I could do it anywhere. I was no longer a captive of demons eating away at me, no longer a victim of other people's mockery and loathing, that had made me clench my fist white with rage and grit my teeth to silence. Words now pleaded back with the bleak lucidity of hurt. They were wrong, those others, and now I could say it.[1]

The Douglas County Jail writing class has offered many inmates a place to stand, a rare and much-appreciated experience in their lives. Though incarcerated, they have been able to express themselves with the "bleak lucidity of hurt," and for that invigorating expression, they—and all of us—should be grateful indeed.

# Chapter 8

# "[The] Automatic Connection Between Inmates in Class and Mr. Cash"

## Johnny Cash's *Hurt*

**What Johnny Cash Knew**

The one thing Johnny Cash knew with certainty
was that through all the troubles of his life—
the breakups, divorces, fistfights,
pills, booze, depression, drug busts—
he still had any number of songs to
help him through his dark hours.
The one thing Johnny Cash knew with certainty
was that even near the end when he was just about all
broken down, he still had that last great song, "Hurt,"
and sang it as June slipped off the stage
and kept singing it with what was left of his voice
right up to that last note—
then Johnny shut the piano, turned out the lights.

> —Brian Daldorph

> (Written in Douglas County Jail writing class,
> October 2015, from the prompt *the one thing he
> knew with certainty*)

One of my biggest regrets in life is that I didn't see Johnny Cash when he played at the University of Kansas (KU) in the early 1990s. I could have gotten a Lied Center ticket for $20, but I told a friend who already had a ticket to see this "American legend," as he called Cash, that I really wasn't interested in his type of music. Look at the fool who missed out on seeing the Man in Black up close and never had the chance again. I had no idea at the time how much he'd come to mean to me.

Programs Director Mike Caron and I established Johnny Cash's "Hurt," using the video version filmed in 2002, as the "theme song" of our Douglas County Jail writing class, ending each class with the showing of *Hurt*.[1] It always attracted a small group of inmates in orange, blue, and white jumpsuits to cluster around the television, watching closely because Cash seemed to be speaking to them and for them with beautiful, agonizing honesty: *I hurt myself today/to see if I still feel.* In the video, he's doing what the inmates had been trying to do in class beforehand: address the harsh truths of their lives by creating art, putting their lives on the line, laying them out to see what improvements they could make while they still had time and strength to make them. Cash, frail, old, and sick, was almost out of time.

Caron clearly understands the connection many inmates feel to Cash, whose outlaw persona was partly taken from his hardscrabble life and partly from his lifelong keenness to confront authority (both aspects familiar to Douglas County Jail inmates):

There is little mystery about the popularity of the *Hurt* music video. First, Johnny Cash is very popular with a wider swath of Americans than most "country" singers, and he has an especially long-standing positive reputation among incarcerated populations because he was one of the first artists to perform inside prisons. His Folsom Prison album was so popular that an unedited version with all the cursing and mocking of the rules left in was wildly popular with inmates, too.

Secondly, the Nine Inch Nails cover incorporates drug addiction and lyrics that focus directly on Christian redemption, two subjects that enormous numbers of inmates identify with in intense, emotional ways.

Finally, seeing Cash so obviously near death, knowing that June Carter died before the project was completed, and the visual montage of his life resonates with most viewers but has special meaning and emotional impact on almost anyone who finds himself or herself locked up. That event almost inevitably triggers thoughts inventorying one's life choices and experiences.[2]

Programs Director Sherry Gill was equally emphatic about the significance of Cash in a corrections facility:

> We use *Hurt* in the class because Johnny Cash had a criminal life. . . . I believe he's done some things that he wasn't proud of, and he was for the underdog. . . . Cash was gonna help those prisoners and make them feel like men and human beings, and he did that, and he was really one of the first people who addressed prison or even went in to do anything in a prison because I remember at that time it was unheard of, and for him to sing about that? Criminals, you don't talk about them, you don't do anything, but he dedicated music to them, so for them it was like, "Hey, yeah, we're people too." There was no prison reform then; they probably didn't even have programs then, but he made them feel like men, like human beings, like even if you fucked up, that's okay, there's still more to life.
>
> "Let's have some camaraderie, let's be friends, and I want you-all to know that I'm a fuck up too. And happy to be here."[3]

Antonio Sanchez-Day, former inmate at Douglas County Jail and Kansas Department of Corrections prisons, admitted that though he's no country music fan, he does find plenty to relate to in Cash, in particular to his Man in Black rebel attitude. Most of all, however, he can relate to Cash's *hurt*, in the song "Hurt," of course, but throughout his life and music:

> The traumatic death of his brother paved a road of substance abuse and trauma. Common for most inmates in the class. Including myself. Watching my father flatline in front of me at the age of twelve started me in the cycle of self-destruction. There is an automatic connection between myself, the other inmates in class, and Mr. Cash. The camaraderie of incarceration, which in my opinion adds to the authenticity of his pain. He had been through it like I had. He knows what it is to *Hurt*.[4]

Not only did Cash know what it is to hurt but also he knew what he could do about it, making music that so often seemed rooted in the struggles of his life and in his joys in overcoming them. Of course, many inmates can relate to this.

Cash (1932–2003) grew up poor in the town of Dyess, Arkansas, and had to endure the early death of his brother, Jack, who had planned to be a preacher. As Cash said of his brother:

He was a very mature person for his age, thoughtful and reliable and steady. There was such substance to him—such seriousness, if you like, or even moral weight, such *gravitas*—that when he'd made it known he felt a call from God to be a minister of the Gospel, nobody even thought to question either his sincerity or the legitimacy of his decision.[5]

In a horrific accident on May 12, 1944, Jack's stomach was ripped open by a table saw when he was cutting fenceposts at the high school agriculture shop; he died slowly and agonizingly soon afterward. Cash's daughter Rose-anne Cash recognized the major significance of this childhood trauma in her father's life: "Dad was wounded so profoundly by Jack's death, and by his father's reaction—the blame and recrimination and bitterness. If someone survives that kind of damage, either great evil or great art can come out of it. And my dad had the seed of great art in him."[6] Cash carried the grief of this loss for the rest of his life, and it both inspired and tormented him—he felt sure that God had called home the wrong Cash boy. As he wrote in his autobiography *Cash*,

> Losing Jack was terrible. It was awful at the time, and it's still a big, cold, sad place in my heart and soul. There's no way around grief and loss: you can dodge all you want, but sooner or later you just have to go into it, through it, and hopefully, come out the other side. The world you find there will never be the same as the world you left.[7]

Too many of the inmates we work with know a lot about grief and loss and big, cold, sad places inside and out, and after *dodging* for a long time, some of them are ready to go into it in their writing, go through it, and "hope-fully, come out the other side." According to Cash's daughter Kathy Cash: "Grandpa always kind of blamed Dad for Jack's death. And Dad had this real sad guilt thing about him his whole life. You could just see it in his eyes. You can look at almost any picture and see this dark sadness thing going on. Dad even told me . . . that one time when his daddy had been drinking, he said something like, 'Too bad it wasn't you instead of Jack.'"[8] Guilt, dark-ness, sadness: it's easy to understand why week after week a knot of Douglas County Jail inmates are drawn to the mesmerizing video *Hurt* and the voice of a man who spoke their language about things they know too well.

I'm sure Cash would have appreciated his contributions to the Douglas County Jail classroom. Even before playing his famous shows at Folsom and San Quentin Prisons in the 1960s, Cash felt a special affinity with inmates.

When he was in the US Air Force as a Morse Code operator intercepting Soviet Army transmissions in Germany from 1950 to 1954 (he had never left Arkansas before), far away from family and the woman he loved, he felt as lonely as an inmate. According to Kathy Cash, "He told me the reason he wrote 'Folsom Prison [Blues]' was it captured the loneliness he felt in that room [in the barracks] night after night. He told me, 'I felt terrified sometimes because I knew the door was locked for security reasons and I couldn't get out. It was like being in prison.'"[9]

Cash the songwriter, identifying with the experience of incarceration, turned his terror into art in "Folsom Prison Blues" (helping himself to lyrics from Gordon Jenkins's "Crescent City Blues"), drawing on the inspiration of the country, blues, and folk songs he grew up listening to, songs about "crime and punishment, mayhem and madness, trouble and strife writ large and lurid."[10] Fifty years later, he inspires Douglas County Jail inmates to turn their "trouble and strife" into art. "Crime and punishment, mayhem and murder" are often major players in their dramas too.

Some of Cash's best-known performances were concerts for inmates, beginning with a gig at Huntsville Prison, Texas, in 1957, when Cash was invited to the "rodeo" there after inmates heard his "Folsom Prison Blues." Cash "gladly" agreed to perform and persevered through difficulties: "As soon as we kicked off [the concert] . . . a huge thunderstorm let loose—I mean a *big* one, a real toad strangler—and that cramped our style considerably. Luther's amplifier shorted out, and Marshall's bass came apart in the rain. I kept going, though, with just my guitar, and the prisoners loved that."[11] After this success, Cash was invited to perform at San Quentin too, returning there for several years in a row. He always felt that he could empathize with inmates he performed for at correctional facilities: "Those shows were always really hot—the inmates were excited and enthusiastic, and that got *me* going."[12] Just listen to Cash on the live album recorded at San Quentin: he's on fire as a performer and perfectly at ease chatting with inmates in between songs and winning cheers when he disrespects the prison authorities. Although Cash cultivated an outlaw image, however, he never actually served a prison sentence, though he landed in jail seven times for misdemeanors, each time staying only a single night.[13] His live albums at Folsom (1968) and San Quentin (1969) are two of his best-selling albums, elevating him to the top echelon of the music business. These albums almost always appear close to the top of 100 Best Albums charts, appreciated by a wide variety of music lovers.

When we show the video *Hurt* at the end of writing class, the inmates love Cash for putting himself out there, for showing the clash between images of a young, virile Cash and the almost-broken old man of *Hurt*. They love it that even in his awful health close to the end, he was prepared to put himself on the line and to admit his mistakes, his regrets, the broken things he could never repair. Yet, the four-minute video recalls triumphs too: Cash live at Folsom and San Quentin, Cash and his wife June with their kids, Cash the troubadour hopping on trains with his guitar, Cash living the American life of success and freedom. According to Cash's son John Carter, who worked closely with his father during Cash's last years,

> I believe the thing about Dad that people find so easy to relate to is that he was willing to expose his most cumbersome burdens, his most consuming darknesses. He wasn't afraid to go through the fire and say, "I fell down. I've made mistakes. I'm weak. I *hurt*." But in doing so, he gained some kind of defining strength. Every moment of darkness enabled him to better see the light.[14]

Toward the end of Cash's life, in the late 1990s through his death in September 2003, when he was sick and struggling with addiction as were his wife and son, Cash began to work with producer Rick Rubin to make the final five albums of his long and prolific career. Probably because he was under pressure as a result of an array of troubles, Cash produced in his last five "American" albums some of his best music in decades. According to Robert Hilburn:

> With all this heartache around Cash, music once again became his chief escape and hope, a way to rally against the tensions and pressures—physical, emotional, and financial—in his life. Though he still drew upon his faith, he was finally back to a place where he was looking to music for self-affirmation. Through every concert and every bus ride and every sleepless night, he longed for the day when he would go back to Rubin's living room and sing his heart out.[15]

In a similar way, many inmates over the years have made their way to the Douglas County Jail classroom to write, then recite their hearts out (some of them have sung for us), then write some more. Their bare-bones solo performances are like Cash's, with, according to Rubin, "direct transmission" of words from the heart.[16] When we look at the "darknesses" revealed in the video *Hurt*—old age, sickness, guilt, fear, regret, addiction, betrayal, death—we too are better able to see the light. Many inmates are most certainly drawn to it and see in Cash's performance a model for their own self-expression.

The director of *Hurt*, Mark Romanek, says: "It was that juxtaposition [between video clips of Cash as an old, infirm man and Cash as a young, driven artist] that gave the video its power. It's the shocking contrast of a man in his prime smacked one frame right up against someone who is coming toward the end of his life. It's a shocking dose of everyone's mortality."[17] "Everyone's mortality," but often a little closer for the inmates of Douglas County Jail than for the general population, close as inmates too often are to the edge. I know of quite a few who have tumbled over, none of them nearly as old as Cash at his end.

Romanek said he wasn't sure how he should go about making the *Hurt* video, concerned about Cash's failing health and the shabby, run-down House of Cash Museum in Hendersonville, Tennessee, where part of the video was shot. "I found myself struggling with how to do this," he says:

Do I try to glamorize everything and put a scrim over the lens and use lighting tracks you might do with an aging woman who is vain—or do I show it the way it is? My instinct—because it was Johnny Cash—was that we had to be very truthful and show how he looks because it's wrong—especially for this song—to try to prettify the whole thing. Finally I decided that the only thing to do was to be honest. I realized, "This is Johnny Cash. I should do the bold thing, not the safe thing."[18]

"Do the bold thing, not the safe thing": that's true of the best writing in the Douglas County Jail class. Inmates are not interested in using scrims to soften their images. I think it's this type of direct, unfiltered expression that makes their writing so compelling and has kept me coming back week after week for almost two decades.

I like to include with the packets of poems for class the story behind the *Hurt* video, taken from Hilburn's biography *Johnny Cash: The Life*. Cash was physically in decline when the video was made, barely able to see (Romanek placed a tiny flashing light next to the lens so Cash knew where to look into the camera), and hardly able to sing, but his spirit was still strong even after years of beating up on himself, popping handfuls of amphetamines, and burning himself down. A lot of county jail inmates know too well that type of self-destruction, and they hope, like Cash, to save something from the wreck.

I tell the class that in the compelling final scene in which Cash is wrecking the feast and pouring his wine out on the table, the director had encouraged him to cut loose. It was the final take, so Romanek had told him: "This is the last thing we are going to shoot, so if you want to do something crazy, go for it—if you want to sweep the food off the table, this is the time. Let's be bold."[19] Cash was bold. He didn't have long to live, and June Carter, who came down the stairs to gaze so mournfully at him, had even less time left. Cash is tortured with regret, hurting himself to see if he still feels. He knows he has made mistakes for which he will never be forgiven, never forgive himself. He just about makes it to the end of the song. The piano he closes at the end looks ominously like a coffin.

In fact, after the video was made, there was a lot of discussion in the Cash camp about whether it should be released. Cash looks so bad in it, his sickly face puffed up, his hands like a puppet's hands, his voice only just holding out. Wouldn't it ruin his reputation as the tough Man in Black, the rebel; wouldn't it show too clearly the sad results of his rebellious life? There were a lot of conflicting views in the Cash family about whether to release the video. June was against it. One of the most forceful voices in favor was daughter Roseanne: "Dad showed me the video in his office at the house, and I cried all the way through it. I told him, 'You have to put it out. It's so unflinching and brave and that's what you are.' I was tremendously proud of him. I thought it was enormously courageous. It was a work of art, excruciatingly truthful. I thought, 'How could that be wrong in any way?'"[20]

In the end, it was Cash's choice, and he wanted it released because if there's one thing we find in his work, it's his willingness to speak the hard truths, to turn them into songs. Such a willingness is appreciated by the incarcerated struggling to tell their own truths: if Johnny found a way to do it, they can too.

Most inmates relate to Cash's struggles even if they are not musicians; they relate to someone who has often screwed up essential relationships, who feels that he has not made the most of his life's possibilities despite superficial successes. They discover in class that things can be improved by writing, by putting as much of themselves as possible into their written work and sharing it with others, giving it form, giving it voice.

Every time we play the video at the end of class, one of the inmates will point out that "Hurt" is not Cash's song. It's a Nine Inch Nails song, but what does that matter? Cash makes it his own and gives it to us each Thursday afternoon in Douglas County Jail, right before it's time for inmates to trudge along the brightly lit corridor back to their pods.

Because I associate *Hurt* so much with the writing class, I often return to writing about Cash during our free writing times in class. I see him as a troubadour who lived a life of struggle—even if we might think that a lot of his struggles were self-inflicted. He kept coming back to his songs, which had been there from the beginning with his brother listening to the radio at night in their small house in Dyess. They'd been with him on the tough road of his life, and they were with him at the end, when all he wanted was to live his life of songs again: "If I could start again/I would find a way."

Cash was able to make art in his late illness, inspiring Douglas County Jail inmates to make their own art in their poetry. Even though it might not make them famous like Cash, it might do something even more important than that in helping them to live their fraught lives. Responding to the overwhelming sense of regret he sensed in Cash's *Hurt*, Jesse James wrote in "Tired & Can't Change" (published in *Douglas County Jail Blues*):

> If I could take all back, I'd uh done squashed this shit
>
> 'cause now I'm lookin' back, like man, fuck this shit
>
> ya I'm lookin' forward, tryin' ta see better days
>
> but it's like that shit just puts my mind in a maze.[21]

Also inspired by Cash, I wrote "Cave Man" in response to a story I read about the Man in Black in one of his darkest hours.[22] On pills and wanting to die, he crawled down into Nickajack Cave on the Tennessee River just north of Chattanooga, a literal but also metaphorical cave:

**Cave Man**

When Johnny Cash

got so sad and lonely

he only wanted to die,

he crawled into Nickajack Cave

planning to die there—

nothing left to live for.

Only the pills had kept him going,

handfuls of pills.


He crawled as deep into the earth as he could go

until he was dark and lonely on the outside

as he was inside.

But God told him it wasn't his time yet,

and after how many hours in the dark

he wriggled out of that cave

back into sunlight,

back to the woman who loved him

even though he was lonely and dark.

　　　—Brian Daldorph

　　　(Douglas County Jail writing class, March 2016)

It's strange how often there's some new insight into the *Hurt* video, how it is a dark gift that keeps on giving. In class in June 2017, a young inmate said, "You know why they're called *Nine Inch Nails?* I always wondered; then I found out that that was the size of the nails when Christ was crucified." I don't know if it's true, but it's a good story, and in our classroom, we *love* good stories. Cash always loved a good story too.

As far as Cash's drug use was concerned, a matter often discussed by inmates, James Keach, a friend of Cash's during his early success, put it this way: "John said one pill was too many and a thousand wasn't enough. And so it was like once he got into it, he couldn't stop."[23] Too many times in his life, Cash went tumbling down what he called "that old addictive road."[24] How many jail inmates could tell the same story? How many of them have been inspired by Cash to turn toward creative expression to help them deal with their strife? Cash would no doubt be glad that his best song at the end of his life might encourage some inmates to turn back from going down Addiction Street again, however many friends they know on that street.

The lyrics of "Hurt" carry so much meaning for me in the context of the writing class that I'd like to work my way through the song and write my responses to each of the lines, showing the many levels of meaning that resonate for me in relation to the class. I'll also include comments by inmates who have made deep connections with the song, especially Sanchez-Day, who has been inspired by the song to keep writing, to keep his hold on freedom. Again, I have the sense that the Man in Black would be thrilled by our responses.

When Cash starts singing "I hurt myself today/to see if I still feel," the inmates gathered around the TV know exactly what this means. Every week in class they write poems about the ravages of addiction. These guys know about hurting themselves. Look at their gaunt, wasted faces and bad teeth— they know. Here's how former inmate Sanchez-Day sees it:

> The opening line, "I hurt myself today/to see if I still feel," conjures several feelings common to most in incarceration. Guilt, shame, despair, and a desire for change. The video uses imagery to deliver its message. The image of a young Cash and an unfiltered, unedited older Cash. I believe each inmate is doing their own self-comparison as they view the video. Everyone in the class has hurt themselves, some repeatedly. Hurt their families and loved ones by criminal behavior, some to the point where they would say pain is all they know.[25]

The way Cash sings these first two lines, dragging his tired voice through the simple words, shows that he *knows* about hurting himself, *knows* the price he's paying at last, knows he might not have enough strength to get through this song. Yet his triumph is that even after everything he's been through, as close to the end as he is, he is still able to *feel*—for himself and for all of us—and he does, very bravely, make it through the four minutes of the song.

When Cash sings the next two lines, "I focus on the pain/the only thing that's real," inmates get it; they know that most of the time during incarceration "the only thing that's real" is the pain of it all; it's almost too much to bear, and yet what other option do they have than to bear it? At least if you're in pain, you're feeling *something*, and isn't that better than nothing at all? Are you even human anymore if you feel nothing at all? Best way to spend your jail time? Figure out ways to get through that hurt. Make use of it by fueling art.

In *Hurt*, Cash has not shut down his emotions in order to protect himself. Instead, it seems he has ratcheted up his emotions, and that's perhaps what people love so much about this performance, this song. He makes it clear that *to feel* is still a good thing even close to the end, even when pain is just about all you can feel. Inmates are often inspired by Cash's brave resistance to the *hurt* in his life, including Sanchez-Day, who listened to Cash's song and wrote, "When all you got is pain to feel human, then you accept it. Being judged, belittled, and dehumanized are inevitable in the incarceration experience. If pain is all that is left, it is respected. I chose to convert that pain into a motivator for my poetry."

The next two lines of "Hurt" speak to most inmates too: "The needle tears a hole/the old familiar sting"—the sting of the needle, another hole torn in the skin, sweet relief for hours but at such a price. Inmate Zach T. knows about tearing holes in himself: sometimes he'll roll up the leg of his pants to show the huge scar on his leg from when it was cut up by a boat propeller when he was swimming in Clinton Lake, close to Lawrence, Kansas. He traces his decline to that accident because the pain was so bad that he was loaded up with opiates, and it didn't take much time for him to be hooked and doing what he had to do to get more of what he needed to take the pain away. Looking at him, you can still see the boy he was, but that face is almost covered by the face of a man hardening himself for the long prison sentence ahead. And after he's torn a hole with a needle one time, how to stop? There's always going to be a next time and a time after that. Zach T.'s poem is published in *Douglas County Jail Blues*:

**Opium**

Truly a necessity to me

My brain is in pain

I'm feeling the familiar sting

Itching for one more dose

to repair my mind

make the pain disappear

Each dose brings me closer and closer

but in the end

the pain is still there

and I must start again.

—Zach T.

Cash sings, "Try to kill it all away/but I remember everything"; of course, you "try to kill it all away," and your devils cheer you on, "Yes, yes, this is the way to get rid of the pain and despair, yes, take this little pill, use this needle, smoke this pipe, empty this bottle, and you will feel so much better, you will feel like you can go on!" "Kill it all away," and when that beast inside comes back to life even stronger, you will need to kill it again and again, and you will hardly notice or hardly care that you are killing yourself as you try, and you will *not* forget any of it, you will *never* forget. That's the hardest thing about it: you never forget.

"What have I become/my sweetest friend": with the help of your "sweetest friend" you have become the husband your wife doesn't want anymore, the father your children don't know and don't want to know, the man like your drunk father you vowed you'd never be, the inmate facing a lot of jail time and prison time, a man saying, "No, no, no, no! It cannot happen like this!" Why didn't you see that your "sweetest friend," who made you feel so good, was betraying you, taking away your family? Can you even bear to look in the mirror and see yourself? Sometimes you catch a glimpse of the man you've become with hollow cheeks, messy hair, haunted eyes that look away, thin body—but not a healthy thinness, more like a sick skinniness. Who is this man, who is he?

You grow accustomed to losing people during incarceration: "Everyone I know goes away in the end." Your wife doesn't visit. You think she might be seeing that guy at work she's always talking about, the guy who helps her out. Maybe she'll send one of those "Dear John" letters soon that can shatter a guy. Your mother came to visit once, but that was months ago. You've not received a letter from her for how long? You know that you've shamed her, and how can you live with that? A wise inmate once said that it's better for parents if their son's dead rather than in jail.

Your kids don't come to see you anymore. Anyway, you don't want them to come *here*, of all places, where they see you through glass, and you try to tell them that you love them and will see them soon, though they look like they're not really sure they want that. They look like they just want to get out and go home—without you. All your good friends who promised they'd do the time with you—when was the last time they visited? How many letters have they written?

"Everyone I know goes away in the end": Sanchez-Day felt the sharp edge of this line in thinking about his own experience of incarceration: "During my thirteen years of incarceration, this line rang true. The realization of incarceration is evident. Through time the letters stop coming, visits less frequent, if at all, phone calls are considered a luxury. When you sit in a cell, life moves on without you. It's a cliché, but it's 'out of sight, out of mind.'"[26]

The life you made and lost wasn't much, was it? You'd give it all up to get back the more important things you lost: "You could have it all/my empire of dirt." *Take it, take it!* You thought you were so cool with your fast cars, deals, money, fur coats, and palaces, but it was all made of dirt, take it, take it; you want back your good life that wasn't enough for you. You didn't know how much you had until it was gone. Let some other greedy guy be the emperor of dirt. You're done with that shit, and after you get out of here you are never coming back.

But you know that most likely you'll fuck up again: "I will let you down/I will make you hurt"—you will hurt again the people who mean the most to you. But you keep asking for one more chance, just one more chance: "Baby, Baby, please, please, I'll be so good this time, so good. I've made a new start."

*You* don't even want her to believe you. *You* would not believe what you said. You tell her, "Don't let me hurt you again. Don't let me hurt you." You think you have changed, but you're still the same man, spoiling things again and again. But you want her so much because without her you've got nothing. You want to be a father to your children; you want them to have the father you never had.

"I will let you down/I will make you hurt": for Sanchez-Day, these lines are the stark warning of a destructive and self-destructive man: "If you let me close, I will bring you down also."

"I wear this crown of thorns/upon my liar's chair": you're Christ on the cross, with your crown of thorns, you're hurting so much: "Baby, Baby, take me back, make me feel better, please, please!" But then you say, "Don't believe me, I'm lying to you, lying to me, just like I lied the last time and the time before that, just like I'll lie the next time and the time after that." Where else can a liar sit but on this liar's chair where he is the king of lies on his throne?

And yet didn't Christ wear that crown and die on the cross to redeem you and others like you? "Save me, Jesus, save me, I'm not strong enough to save myself, only you can save me." How to reconcile your deep belief in Jesus with all your sins? You say out loud, "Why did you make it so difficult for me, Lord?"

"Full of broken thoughts/I cannot repair": you're trying to repair your broken thoughts, you're trying to repair them, but as soon as you repair them, they break again and again and again, and who needs a broken man, who needs him? And after so many repairs how to fix the broken things anymore? Wouldn't it make more sense to throw them away?

Sometimes when you write, you can make sense of your broken thoughts; it's almost like they're not broken anymore as you read your poem to the class about the last time you messed up so badly, you're looking at how many years? The guy beside you pats your shoulder, thankful to you for putting into words just how it is for him too. He tells you that it helps, and you're glad that you've managed to help.

Could it be the first step to recovery?

Time stains you; you're getting old; you'll never live your beautiful, dangerous youth again—that's gone: "Beneath the stains of time/the feeling disappears." You're so stained by time that you can hardly feel anything anymore. Stained by sin, stained by lies, stained by the hurt you've caused, staining everything you touch, and how can you feel anything at all through this stained skin, stained black and blue?

Sometimes you prefer to feel pain rather than nothing at all, so you go looking for another needle and a bottle, and your demons keep telling you, "Yes! Yes! Yes!" Then there are times when you want to feel nothing at all as you fall and fall out of this world and into another world or out into cold dark space, where you feel nothing at all, your *feeling disappears.*

Your wife is someone else now, "you are someone else/I am still right here," with her new husband who works at Best Buy, everyone says he's a good guy, and your children love him, they call him *Matt* and think he's more fun than their Dad, who gets mad all the time and goes away for weeks or months. Your wife is someone else, and soon she will bring new life into the world, and if you were a better man you would be happy for her after everything you put her through. How could you even support her anyway when you can't get a job because who will hire you once you tick that box, "Have you been convicted of a crime?" But you are "still right here," still here, waiting for your attorney, hoping to get out of here before you're old and gray and your kids are grown up and gone away.

By the end of the song "Hurt," Cash, who moved mountains, is hanging on with his last strength as he sings the last lines: "You could have it all/my empire of dirt/I will let you down/I will make you hurt/if I could start again/a million miles away/I would keep myself/I would find a way." That's what you want, to start again and to *not* make the bad choices this time because look where they got you, right here on a Thursday afternoon, after writing class, watching Cash spill a tall glass of wine all over his banquet, all over his life because what's to stop him from going a little crazy, what's to live for in his empire of dirt, which is all he's got left? When did Cash ever miss a chance to go crazy?

"A million miles away" is that boy you were who played baseball in high school, and you were so good you had a chance of a college scholarship and, who knows, a chance in the Majors, a shot at it at least if you kept on the same trajectory, but then Travis told you about something that made him feel *so* good, and you tried it, and soon enough it's all you wanted, and you quit school and your nice girlfriend, Kathy, to find it, and then you were all washed up as an athlete, quit the team after Coach Barrows had a talk with you, didn't go to college but helped out your best friend Bono in his home business, which involved peddling pills to high school kids. Now you're looking at *possession with intent* charges and can hardly remember that boy crazy about baseball who stands about a million miles away. But you do remember that last home run you hit when you struck the ball so sweetly and watched it fly up up up and away over the perimeter fence!

What's left, Cash, is to thank you for showing us your hurt, thank you for that, for making it real, for not hiding your shame and your guilt, in fact making art of it, which might give us a chance for better lives before we ruin ourselves like you did in the end, almost blind in your house, your wife close to death, and you with nothing left but good memories a million miles away and this last song, perhaps your best song, the song that for all its pain, and there's lots of that, gives us hope. Sanchez-Day too finds hope in the song in the end. For him, the song works through pain to come to a better place in the end, and perhaps to that best place of all for an incarcerated man, freedom: "As I sit and watch the video, I reflect and relate. I refresh and relive the pain. In the last minute of the song, the piano chord hits harder, and Johnny belts out the chorus. I relive the pain and hurt myself a little. To remember it was real. Only this time I won't go back to my cell. I will walk out a free man."[27]

Even near the beginning of his career, there was an extraordinary bond between Cash and the incarcerated. In *Johnny Cash: A Life*, Hilburn describes Cash playing San Quentin Prison on New Year's Day, 1960. Merle Haggard, at the age of twenty-two, was in the audience, serving a fifteen-year sentence. Haggard was inspired by Cash to change his ways. Haggard remembers Cash looked hungover but on fire: "He ripped down the walls with his music, and he touched us with his songs. For a little while, he'd accomplished the impossible. He had replaced our misery with music. He'd made us forget where we were."[28] According to Sherry Gill, Haggard "got out, married a lovely woman, and had a good life, and it was all because someone made him feel like a man and that there was something more, that it wasn't the end, that a crime, and a criminal, and prison, there's more to it."[29] I think of Cash reaching out to all of us who have known struggle. As Gill says, Cash "knows what it's like to be made to feel like you're nothing or to feel like you're nothing. . . . He could see through that; he could see the need for humanity in those situations."

I think of the group of inmates gathered around the TV in the jail classroom to watch Cash sing his song of raw pain for us, and perhaps Cash will inspire one of the inmates to turn his pain and misery into a song. That inmate will have that song on hand when he has to make it through his next hard night, the morning after, and the rest of his life.

### Cash

As long as he was above ground,
Johnny Cash sang songs and kept singing,
even when he lost his voice somewhere
on the road in a motel room or roadhouse,
he kept singing,
didn't matter if no sound came out—
*he* knew what he was singing.

Always sang for himself anyway
and if anyone else liked his songs,
that was just a bonus.

As long as he was above ground
Johnny Cash kept singing
even when he had no voice at the end
he sang "Hurt"—
there was no better song
to take his pain away.

—Brian Daldorph
(From writing class prompt *as long as he was above ground*)

## Chapter 9

# *Maine Man*

## Mike Caron, Programs Director, Douglas County Jail (2001–2015)

I could begin this chapter about Programs Director Mike Caron, who served at the Douglas County Jail from 2001 to 2015 as the coleader of the creative writing class, in many ways. I've known him for almost twenty years, and we've worked closely together during all that time, so I'm spoiled with choices as far as lead-ins are concerned. I could write about him as a Vietnam War veteran and war historian, as the former programs director at the jail (where the library is named after him because of his endless book-gathering for inmates), as a Native American rights activist, as the proud father of three adult children, as a Cajun chef, or as a local historian—there are so many notable versions. Here's a guy who makes the best use of every moment of his time, often to work on social justice issues. He would be extremely grateful for the gift of a few more lifetimes so he'd have time to do everything he'd like to do and then tell stories about it, like the one about meeting a "gypsy pilot" while hitchhiking and nabbing a seat on a private flight up to Fredericton, New Brunswick, spinning a few stories to pay his way.

In fact, I'd like to start with this poem for Caron by our mutual friend Big Jae Wae, one of the best writers and biggest characters in the Douglas County Jail writing class before he was transferred to prison in Norton (in western Kansas), where one day he received an unexpected visitor. Here's "The Unexpected (for Mike Caron)" by Wae, written on October 29, 2010, and mailed to me for inclusion in the writing class packet:

> Reporting to work
> like any other Sunday

restoring stainless steel

to its full glorious shine

wiping down the line

hesitant to grab the phone

not wanting the joke to be on Jae,

or the ton of trouble that follows:

After all, who receives phone calls

while imprisoned in prison?

The long walk to the building up front,

even longer wait feeling like the butt

of a super joke.

Clad in blue jeans

a T-shirt and three days' growth

his hair disheveled from

the jog across the highway

looking as if he himself

came from under a rock

rather than the snakes he was hunting,

brightening my day

ending the drought of visitors.

This is typical Caron, willing to put himself out to help a guy who's in a hard place but working on doing better—Wae had renounced his criminal life and started over, and Caron was helping him all the way, bringing a sort of positive energy, support, and good humor that can make the difference between an inmate making it or failing. Wae describes on-the-road Caron as "looking as if he himself/came from under a rock"; Wae knows that Caron loves his snake hunting with the Kansas Herpetological Society at least as much as he loves walking his dogs over the Baker Wetlands near his house in Lawrence and drinking beer when his Red Sox are on TV.

Shortly before Caron's retirement from his position as programs director at the jail in May 2015, I brought to creative writing class an article from the *Lawrence Journal-World* (April 28, 2015) titled "Counting Critters," with photographs from the latest Kansas Herpetological Society outing including pictures of a coach whip snake, ring-neck snake, and Great Plains narrow-mouthed toad. The society goes on a "critter count" in rural Kansas three times a year, and Caron is the keenest rock-flipper in the crew and would report on his finds to the class—which we loved. Inmates were always intrigued by the venomous snakes of Kansas, and Caron had all the facts and cool stories about them. (I'd still like to know why on the day we'd scheduled for him to give a report to class on his snake hunting, a snake slithered into my house, the only time it has ever happened. What do snakes know, and how do they know it?)

Poetry had played an important role in Caron's life long before we began to work together in the Douglas County Jail classroom in 2001. While he was living in Cambridge, Massachusetts, in 1966, right after high school, he found by chance a book of World War I poet Wilfred Owen's work in the library of Northeastern University, spent all night reading it, and next morning headed for the US Army recruitment center in Roxbury:

> I was shelving books at a little shop off Trowbridge Square. The clerk and I were Dylan fans, and he told me Bob Dylan had taken his performer name from the Welsh poet Dylan Thomas, whom I had never heard of in 1966. I looked him up in the Northeastern University library and there found the Welsh World War I antiwar poet Wilfred Owen's slim volume. I took it home, along with Thomas's *Deaths and Entrances*.[1] I stayed up all night reading them, then took a walk at sunrise before wandering into the army recruiter station in Roxbury. After explaining to the elated recruiter that I wanted to join up to help guys with "shell shock" (a term not used since Owen's war, but what did I know?), he told me what I needed was an MOS (Military Occupational Specialty) as a neuropsychiatric aidman. I called home to Lewiston, Maine, later that day to tell them I'd enlisted. When Mom answered, she did not let me get in a word before putting my brother David on the phone. He had big news. He just enlisted in the army.[2]

In the jail classroom, Caron would often write about his Vietnam War experiences as a Special Forces medic. (In retirement, he is working on a war memoir.) He wrote about fighting with Montagnard allies, indigenous mountain people persecuted by the Vietnamese. He wrote about the guys he'd fought with in Vietnam, too many of them not making it home. He wrote about the time when, at twenty-two years old, he was appointed senior medic at the Recondo school in Vietnam.[3] The senior medic before him had to leave after he lost friends in battle and lost his wife and two daughters to an accident caused by a drunk driver outside Fort Bragg, North Carolina. When the senior medic was sent back to the United States, Caron took over, as he described in his poem "Senior Medic" (May 7, 2009): "There I was, green to this place, twenty-two years old,/suddenly in charge of a dispensary." Though he had little combat experience and no experience at running programs needed to train Recondo team medics, in typical Caron fashion he got to work and made the best of it.

Caron's understanding of his wartime experience is nuanced indeed. Although he understands why veterans tend to focus on the traumatic elements, he also believes that the more positive aspects, especially the camaraderie, should not be overlooked. He believes his Vietnam experiences have made him better able to relate to the trauma, war related or not, of others, a vital point in his favor when working with the incarcerated, who have often experienced substantial trauma:

> Coming home from war is a bit like life after a divorce. For a lot of vets, the trauma blinds us to the parts of that engagement that enriched our lives. In marriages, it is usually the kids that came from the relationship. In war, it is the deep emotional ties made in the midst of terrifying moments and the feelings of incredible bonds among survivors in the aftermath of heavy combat.
>
> For me, however, Vietnam was so much more than the firefights and awful experience of seeing friends blown to pieces or burned beyond recognition. My memories of that time are not without significant trauma, but they are balanced by a lot of other thoughts that are far more positive. Beyond that duality, however, even the most terrible things that I witnessed stay with me differently than with those who have nightmares and flashbacks. History overflows with such terrors, yet the way most folks think about them is as false and trivial as a Hollywood action flick. Knowing, really knowing, what those moments are in real time and real life is a gift that I do not regret receiving. I think I perceive my father's experience in World War II or the realities of nonwar catastrophes like earthquakes or plagues, any real disasters, in ways that were not within my ability before Vietnam. I am not saying that everyone must directly go through hell to have historical insight, but I do know that the incredible ambiguities that informed my Vietnam experience are central

to who I am today and lie at the heart of why I found that working with inmates had so many similarities to being in Vietnam, and why I am still drawn to that work years after "retirement."

Caron's Vietnam days prepared him for and led him to his subsequent career in corrections, starting in the 1980s as a teacher at the US Disciplinary Barracks in Fort Leavenworth, Kansas. Decades later, in "retirement" in Maine, he is working, as might be expected, in programs assisting inmates and former inmates. He is on the board of directors of the College Guild, based in Brunswick, Maine, a 501(c)3 organization that provides free correspondence classes to about six hundred inmates in several dozen states, and he volunteers on committees at the Restorative Justice Project of the Midcoast in Belfast, Maine. He dreams of building small shacks in the fifty acres of forest he owns by his house in Freedom, Maine, as rural transitional housing for men leaving prison and needing a place to stay. When he talks about this plan during his postretirement visits to Douglas County Jail, inmates always volunteer to stay in Caron's cabins just as soon as they're built. Freedom, Maine: What place could sound better to an inmate?

After the Vietnam War, poetry played its part in bringing Caron to Kansas, where he stayed for four decades. Home from Vietnam, he attended the University of Maine, Portland-Gorham (nicknamed "POGO U"), which later became the University of Southern Maine. His mentor, anthropologist Richard Grossinger, introduced him to poets such as Ed Dorn and Ken Irby, connected to the Lawrence, Kansas, literary scene. He also introduced Caron to the works of James Malin,

> historian of the grasslands and like Olson, a thinker who believed there was something significant in the *local* that most academics dismissed too quickly. Rich Grossinger had inspired my love of geographic inquiry and encouraged me to move to the grasslands since I'd been raised in Maine's maritime-oriented world. He was leaving Portland and had applied to teach at the University of Kansas, which happened to have one of the top ten geography departments in the country at the time. That clinched the deal. I applied and even got an undergraduate "research assistantship." Rich did not get his position in the anthropology department. He did teach at Goddard in Vermont for a few years before moving to California and going into publishing full time. Lawrence grew on me. I stayed for forty-two years.

In the Douglas County Jail classroom, Caron did not abide whiners or disrupters. No "stinkin' thinkin'" on his watch. On the other hand, he'd work tirelessly with guys who knew they'd fallen hard because of their own mistakes and now wanted to do better. Drugs and alcohol were often in the mix of their mistakes. He understood that many inmates had been dealt a poor hand of cards in life. Inmates he worked with often came from backgrounds of incarcerated parents, drug abuse, physical abuse, sometimes sexual abuse in their families, and though Caron was sympathetic, he'd tell inmates that they had to get past the attitude that everything was loaded against them and set goals for themselves, not get discouraged if they couldn't attain them at first. As he wrote in his poem "Stinkin' Thinkin'": "Life is not fair. It is 1% what happens to you and 99% how you decide to react to it." Caron would go a lot of extra miles to help guys in reentry trying to reestablish themselves on the outside after weeks or months or years of incarceration. He'd drive them to state capital Topeka for meetings with administrators, set up job interviews for them, meet them for coffee to talk about whatever was on their minds, set them up with mentors, and treat them as people who *could* make good choices, who didn't have to keep going down the wrong roads leading them to further incarceration. I sat with him and an ex-inmate in a downtown Lawrence café and talked on a Sunday afternoon about what Kelly could do to keep out of jail, with Kelly saying over and over that he hadn't had a fair shake and Caron emphasizing that Kelly's life was in his own hands, that he should take responsibility for his own choices.

I remember telling Caron that it is easy for me as a college lecturer to write recommendation letters for outstanding students, knowing that the vast majority of them will make the most of their opportunities, whereas he was usually helping people trying their best to rebuild their lives even though there was always the chance that when too much trouble piled up on them, they'd turn back to pills, needles, spoons, glass pipes, alcohol, or some combination of these temptations, and they'd be back in jail again. I never saw him disillusioned; he knew that the people he was committed to helping would often fall, and every time they did, he'd help them up again. He is sure of the work he's doing and puts his heart, soul, and good sense into doing it well. He says that the satisfaction is in *doing* the important work more than any "success" that might come from it. Caron knows that with a lifetime's commitment and work, it just might be possible to turn the dial of social justice a degree or so toward fairness.

Caron wouldn't let guys get away with writing what they shouldn't in class; he'd put a stop right away to shenanigans, and if a truculent inmate persisted, he'd be marched back to the pod. Caron was tough, and sometimes the inmates resented him for that, but the majority of them knew he was a great ally, one of the best to have on their side, and that he'd keep helping them as long as he believed that they were making progress.

Outside the jail, Caron was a fighter for social justice in Douglas County, deeply involved with resistance to building the South Lawrence Trafficway, a bypass around the west and south sides of Lawrence first proposed in the 1970s but delayed for almost three decades because of lawsuits by environmental groups and Haskell Indian Nations University. The planned route took the highway through the Haskell Wetlands, sacred land for Native Americans so often railroaded by the power of "developers" with their local government allies. Caron fought them all the way, in alliance with Native American activists.

It's always great to get a storyteller talking, and Caron is a storyteller indeed. One time he started talking about how he'd "hitchhike" at airfields, talking his way onboard private flights taking off from major airports, travelling "real good for free" (as Joni Mitchell sang) all over the country. He talked about leaving base in Fort Bragg in 1968 to see a Mitchell concert in Fayetteville, North Carolina, when she was just starting out and drew an audience of about fifteen. Stories about his fish store and restaurant too—how he'd worked so hard to set it up before it all fell apart because of his junkie chief chef and a college-kid truck driver who crashed the company truck and lost the thousands of dollars of fresh fish he was transporting. He wrote about coming home from Vietnam and, Forrest Gump–like, working on the shrimp boats in the Gulf of Mexico and making gumbo that would please any Cajun gourmet in New Orleans. Lots of good stories—it was just a matter of getting him to talk—and to write in class.

Though he believed in the writing class, he was hardheaded enough not to make too much of it. It would not save souls, he believed. But if it could show inmates that there might be a better way to go than lashing out whenever they are challenged, if it might help them find a few moments of reflection before they make another bad decision they might be paying off for years, then it was worth it. And if it only meant that for a couple of hours a week inmates could have a good time telling each other stories, entertaining and enlightening each other, having a few good belly laughs, releasing just a little bit of pressure from systems about to blow, then that was plenty to achieve, plenty. When Caron comes back to Lawrence to visit, he likes to sit in on class, glad to be a part of the circle again, still believing that there are better lives for the hard-worn men in the class if they can just imagine and reach out for them and do the hard, patient work of self-improvement.

Aware that substance abuse is often at the root of inmates' troubles, Caron had a long career working with inmates under the influence of "Old Devils" (as he called them in one poem), that is, addictions that had a strong grip on them, sometimes a stranglehold. Caron was never under any illusions about the battles they were facing. Many addicts he'd worked with had hauled themselves into sobriety only to reacquaint themselves with Old Devils at the first opportunity. These addicts angered their supporters, who'd believed in them, then felt "suckered again" when they fell. Though devils are sly and know a thousand ways to trick you, Caron never lost hope that the Old Devils could be defeated, even when the same inmate faces—a little older and more careworn each time—showed up again in jail. It *is* possible to "confine" Old Devils if you never stop trying:

> But Old Devils can be confined, it
> is possible, as thousands upon thousands have
> learned, to escape their grip if you get yourself
> back up, get back in the game that was working,
> redouble your efforts, and pay close attention to
> job number one—keeping those Old Devils
> in your sights. Old Devils never die.

I have learned a lot from Caron over the years and shared a lot of great experiences with him. When my father visited, Caron invited him to the jail class. Caron signed as a witness at my wedding, we watched baseball together, I sat in on his lectures about the Wakarusa Wetlands, we worked together in hundreds of classes, and he gave me the chance to teach the jail class and the institutional support I needed. He tried to educate me about jail life so I didn't remain too naïve about goings on there. He allowed me to be the "good cop" in class because he was always willing to play the "bad cop" as he sometimes had to do. I think of my visits to his beloved Haskell Wetlands, the Native American children's graveyard there, the medicine wheel, the ghost dancers, the ceremonies. I think of Caron with his loyal dogs at the wetlands, cherishing the sacred land and all its spirits, especially the tortoise, who, as in Native American myth, carried the world on its back.

In his poem "Magic in the Mud" (October 29, 2010), he wrote about visiting the wetlands with an artist friend:

As we walked out the gate, a large snapping turtle
appeared in our path. It had an
enormous lump of clay on its back. I suppose
it had been hibernating or was buried with some
construction nearby.
We went on south, past the sweat lodges,
and visited the medicine wheel and wetlands
before retracing our steps back to the cars
by the cemetery. The turtle met us not far
from the sweat lodge, a good quarter mile
from where we'd seen it earlier. It still had
that enormous mound of earth stacked on its back.
That was the first, but not the last time
I witnessed turtles hauling big lumps of dirt
on their backs. Many native traditions speak of
Turtle Island, the story of how land came
to be after Mother Earth had been entirely
covered with water. That turtle being
there right when I was deep in conversation about
native children and their struggles against cultural
genocide—having traditions erased—that was magic.

Caron brought this "magic," his snake stories, and more to the Douglas County Jail writing class, week after week, month after month, year after year. In Maine, he has worked with the Penobscot Nation on their four-day ceremony at *Nibezun* (a place of healing, literally translated as "medicine") called Healing Turtle Island, a ceremony attempting to heal the historical trauma of indigenous people, a more recent commitment to social justice.

Over his career in corrections, Caron gave inmates the sense of the many possibilities for their lives and encouragement to pursue their goals.

He told them about a turtle with a lump of clay on its back and explained to them why that was important.

He got us all telling snake stories.[4]

By taking a long detour to go visit an inmate in prison, he broke Wae's visitor "drought" and lifted an inmate's spirits out of the mud of incarceration.

In May–June 2020, Caron recorded a series of personal essays about the Covid-19 pandemic and its impact on US prisons and jails, "Doing Covid Time," for *Listen Up!* on WBFY community radio in Belfast, Maine, drawing on his three decades of experience with the corrections system. Caron used the term *regional distribution centers for Covid-19* to describe the 1,719 state prisons, 100 or so federal prisons, 250 private prisons, and 80 Indian Country tribal jails, most all of them far from big cities, often built in rural communities. Infections spread rapidly in closed communities such as prisons and jails, especially when many inmates have underlying health conditions, often the results of addiction. Caron claims that during the pandemic, jail time might be a death sentence for this vulnerable population. He also discusses so-called compassionate release of older cons close to the ends of their sentences, the majority of them returning to some of the deadliest zip codes in the country, in the poorer areas of big cities such as Chicago and Detroit. To state house protesters claiming that state lockdowns are like prison sentences, Caron recommended that they try doing Covid time in cells "smaller than a lot of walk-in closets," cells often built for one or two inmates but too often housing four. In the series, Caron makes the connection between mass incarceration, coronavirus casualties, and the Black Lives Matter movement on the streets in summer 2020, in that the movement came about because of inequities in society most often negatively affecting minority, and particularly Black, communities. Caron argues that it's not a coincidence that "the epidemic of incarceration struck poor Black communities long before Covid-19 devastated the exact same neighborhoods."

# Chapter 10

# "It Don't Get More Real Than That"

## The Poetry of Antonio Sanchez-Day

I first met Antonio Sanchez-Day in May 2013. I don't remember exactly when because Sanchez-Day, in typical fashion, did not make a big entrance into the Douglas County Jail classroom and did not at first stand out from others in the group of inmates taking their places in the circle of desks and chairs for the class. As I began to get to know him over the subsequent weeks, I sensed the gravity of a man carrying a lot of painful experience; he was careful with his words, a thinker, yet there was a steely gleam of humor too. I noted the watchfulness of someone who has done a lot of time and is used to being on guard, needing to know for his own survival what's going on all around him and what might happen next. After he'd attended several classes, I could see in his face that he'd done some hard living, the sort of thing you see on most every face in class. Shaved head all the way from Easter Island. Scars and tattoos too (including "Delores" on his neck for his mother), but in Douglas County Jail an inmate stands out if he *doesn't* have scars and tattoos. Sanchez-Day seemed to be just one more street soldier fighting in "the war of [his] life," as he'd later explain in the following poem trying to make a little more sense of the struggles of his life:

**Scars and tattoos**

When people see me, they see scars and tattoos,

badges of honor earned in the war of my life.

My body reads like a book, the story of a lost soul . . .

Hear my words and see my spirit, see my

energy, feel my blood and tears.

Over the past five years, I have been reading the book that is Sanchez-Day, which tells the story of a "lost soul" finding himself in words of blood and tears that are meaningful to us all. There are some good jokes in the book too, to help in the hard times.

In class, Sanchez-Day perches on his chair, shuffling through his papers, quiet and alert. We often get two-thirds of the way through a class without hearing from him, but as a teacher, I know that he is taking it all in, that he doesn't miss a gesture or a word. When he speaks, everyone pays attention; we all "hear [his] words and see [his] spirit" ("Scars and Tattoos"). I know that the precarious sense of peace he exudes has been hard won and needs to be constantly defended from demons inside and outside himself.

I don't remember him writing in his first class, or in his first few classes, though he later told me that he did write in every class, plus he'd jot down all the prompts I'd scribble on the board and use them as starting points for writing during the next week in his cell. At first, he seemed to be checking out the class, seeing if there was something in it for him, then he'd join the line of orange jumpsuits heading back to the medium-security pod. I had no idea that he'd emerge as one of our best writers and that his poetry would be widely read outside the jail walls as his publications mount: his poetry and life story in *Lawrence Magazine* (2016), poems in *Coal City Review* and *Watch My Rising: 37 Poems and Stories about Recovery from Addiction* (2016), and his first book, *Taking on Life* (Coal City Review Press, 2019).

Reporter Katherine Dinsdale's article about the Douglas County Jail writing class in *Lawrence Magazine* in fall 2016 includes important background about Sanchez-Day. He was born in Topeka, Kansas, in 1974 to a Potawatomie father and Mexican mother. The family moved to Lawrence when he was seven; his parents separated because of his father's alcoholism. His father died when he was twelve: "That started my anger. At that age I was asking, 'Why God? What God would do this?'"

He grew up as a kid from a broken home, joined a gang in 1992, and tried to prove himself as a "street soldier":

I've been shot at, stabbed, everything you'd expect to happen in that life. I moved my way up in the gang hierarchy. I started as a street soldier, earned my stripes. And then, at age sixteen, I was fighting a rival gang and showing I was "down," and I hit someone with a baseball bat. I almost killed them. Because of the severity of that crime and because gang activity was just becoming a problem in Lawrence, the judge decided to make an example out of me. I got ten years.[1]

Sanchez-Day's story is remarkably similar to that of Jimmy Santiago Baca as told in his autobiography, *A Place to Stand;* Sanchez-Day looks to Baca as his spiritual mentor. Baca, of Chicano and Apache descent, writes in *A Place to Stand* about himself as an outcast young man in Albuquerque keen to prove himself in a gang that had given him a sense of belonging, a gang with "no colors, no rules or rituals, just a bunch of us boys who had already been cast off and who didn't have much else to do but cruise around together and get in trouble. We fought other gangs, white kids mostly, and more and more I would step out and be the point man in any fight situation."[2] Sanchez-Day felt a similar need for belonging that drew him to his gang and a similar need to prove himself by street violence. Gang involvement ended badly for both Baca and Sanchez-Day.

In similar fashion to Baca, who taught himself to read and write while incarcerated, Sanchez-Day turned to serious writing for the first time during his ten-year sentence in the penitentiary, at first exchanging raps with a friend in another cell house. Sanchez-Day also began writing letters to friends, trying to find an outlet for his thoughts and feelings because even among his close associates in "the pen," there was, he said, the machismo of "we're in prison, we're tough. Grown men don't cry." With no one to confide in, he turned to lifting weights as a physical release for his anger and troubles:

> I used to lift weights all the time; that's what I chose to do, lift weights. A lot of guys played handball or basketball, you know, they find a way. Weights to me was physical, but the mental, the mental . . . [writing] helped me mentally. Helped me to get it out because I went into a period of depression. Taking the losses I did while I was on the inside, my daughter, my kids, you know, all that, it was a lot, you know. [Writing] was mainly mentally to get it out, to express myself.[3]

Ten years later, in 2006, he was back on the streets. His mother died, addicted and depressed, so he slid into using methamphetamine, returned to violence, and was soon back in jail. Life on the streets alternated with jail and prison time until in May 2013, in Douglas County Jail, he decided to change his life. Thinking about his cycle of criminal behavior and incarceration, Sanchez-Day recognized, "This has been going on way too long":

> That is the day I made the choice to change. I told myself I was done with that life. About that time, I found out that a lot of the guys were signing

up for a writing class. Most of the time, guys will sign up for just about any program just to get out of their cells. I was no different. I said I would go. I sat in that first class, and I participated. Brian wrote writing prompts on a whiteboard, and I began to think, "Okay, I can write something."

I began to write, and I found that my mind escaped for the time being. For a short amount of time I didn't see the walls or hear the clanging doors or smell the disinfectant odor of the jail. It was just the paper and me alone in the universe. I would carry what I had written back to my cell, and I would work on it more. I began anticipating each class, and it was the highlight of my week. For those two hours, it was as though I was getting out of jail for a time. It wasn't that I was escaping the reality of the situation or the consequences, but I was getting away from the guilt and the shame.

I began writing not to see others' approval but just to get the feelings out. I found the power of the written word.

Now that I reflect on it, it is all part of my testimony and story. It takes courage to read in front of people, especially in the setting of a jail, but hearing others' work has played a big part in helping me change my life patterns. Now I put what I feel and think on paper, and I am in a far better place mentally. Going to prison saved me.

At first the shame and guilt were overwhelming. I was "that guy." But as I make progress, it gets easier. I am humbled that I have the chance to tell my story. I hope it will touch someone else and give them hope as well.

As Sanchez-Day began to bring poems to class week after week and read them for us, we all knew we were hearing something special. He found the language to bring us into brutal experiences, like the time he and a Native American friend, in prison, stood back to back to fight off their enemies. He'd often write about the ravages of addiction and the terrors of incarceration. Sanchez-Day has a way of using language and images that are very much his own yet resonate with all of us, enabling us to understand to some degree the harsh experiences he describes, such as arriving at prison. He wrote this poem, he says, as advice for a young guy about to do his first "bid" of prison time, a cocky guy who thought—or tried to show—that going to prison was no big deal:

### Penitentiary protocol

When you arrive, read the sign: "Leave all hopes

and dreams behind." Forget all you have or had

in the free world, it no longer matters. It will only

distract you, and you'll become prey to the lions

in this jungle. Trust no one; everyone is out for something

in this cut-throat society. Stick with your own kind,

your race and/or your set; your choice. Mind your

own business, keep to yourself, don't gossip like a girl.

Have respect, don't let no one disrespect you. Don't gamble

or run a debt you can't pay. Learn to like the sight

and smell of blood, it surrounds you. Prepare to witness

the evil men do. Find your primal survival instinct;

it could be the difference between life and death.

Finally, make peace with God or your higher power:

You're gonna need it.

In his memoir *Wilderness and Razor Wire,* Ken Lamberton echoes what San-chez-Day describes in this poem. Lamberton writes about his incarceration in the Arizona prison system, in the Cimarron unit, the Tucson complex's high-security unit. Incarcerated in a lockdown facility where gang violence is a way of life, Lamberton was warned that there are only two kinds of in-mates there: predators and prey.[4] Both Lamberton and Sanchez-Day turned to writing to help themselves survive and found to their surprise that their work reached a much wider audience than they'd ever imagined.

From lions in the prison jungle, from evil and the smell of blood, to Chuey the Chihuahua: Sanchez-Day has a lighter side too, writing about his tough little dog with a huge heart and a big personality. Here's another side of Sanchez-Day, a hard-earned chuckle to keep his head up when at times the temptation is to surrender to depression. To counteract the negative forces in his life, he found a true *amigo* in his diminutive compatriot:

## The King of Redbud

He was born in Topeka, and moved to Lawrence
to reside with me on 25th and Redbud Lane. Redbud
has a known reputation among locals for its
criminal activities and its streetwise residents. It
was his type of environment, he had no problem
settling in. His name was "Chuey." He was small
in size and often teased for his resemblance to
a famous TV commercial character. Despite his size,
he had the heart of a lion. Others tested his
courage at times, but he never backed down, he
always held his ground. He was *chingon* ("tough guy"), and that
might be my biased opinion, but he was my best friend.
His loyalty was 100%. We were bound
by an unspoken oath of fidelity. If anything or
anyone approached me, he would jump to my defense.
He never, as the saying goes, "bit the hand that fed him."
He was a ladies' man, and I was introduced
to several women thanks to Chuey. He was an excellent
wingman, or rather, I was his, as I recall. Chuey had
respect for all men, women, and beasts during his
reign on the "Bud" (what we called the block). Viva "El
Chuey," the applehead Chihuahua from Topeka, Kansas.

Courageous at all times, faithful, *chingon*, fighter, and lover: easy to see why
this little lionheart was "King of the Bud" and a street fighter's best friend.

Setting aside the humor, Sanchez-Day shows in his poetry the courage
to look inward at his own afflictions: family troubles, gang culture, street
violence, depression, and addiction. He knows what it is to be deep in the
abyss, knows what it is to try to climb out, word by word by word. He does
not blame others for his suffering; he accepts his responsibilities and knows
that his life's work now is to keep from falling back into the abyss and to
keep others from falling. As he tells inmates in class at the jail where he

once sat as an inmate and now works as a volunteer: "I know I'm only one bad decision away from messing up again." His version of a success story is maintaining freedom and sobriety.

### I have been alone

Looking through the windows of my eyes into my soul

one views an abyss that is dark and cold

motivated by money, in the pursuit of material things

plus my carnal cravings make me a pitiful human being

afflicted by addiction, infected with rage

plagued by an innocence stolen at an early age

misled by false friends, betrayed by their lies

in this life of shit, I'm Lord of the Flies

I'm not playing victim for I know where blame dwells

It sits with me in this concrete cell

seated at the right hand of my throne

because misery loves company and I hate to be alone.

At the end of writing class, when Sanchez-Day handed in his poems so I could copy them for the packet the following week, I was struck by the neatness and care of his handwriting: no errors, nothing crossed out. How had he been able to write so clearly and neatly about experiences that almost tore him to pieces? He told me that each poem was written through a series of drafts, and he would always give me the final draft. Here is a poet who believes in the value of words, careful to get every word right. (His letters to me from prison were also neatly crafted, and when he speaks you get the impression that every word is carefully weighed.) Even when he describes being high on the anticipation of imminent adventures, his lines are meticulously made:

### Into the night

The sun has settled, anchored below the

horizon. Darkness has overcome light, giving

birth to the full moon. I inhale the cool, brisk

air deep into my lungs. I exhale the remnants
of the day's heat that resides within. The moon's
gravitational pull is creating a tidal wave of blood
in my brain. A surge of energy shoots through
my body. It is shortly followed by an intense
rush of adrenaline. I anticipate the adventures
that await. What fate lies out in the dark?
Will I feed my cravings of another euphoric
high? Will I satisfy my desires of the flesh
in another sexual conquest? Will I engage
in battle with enemies that lurk
in the shadows? Will I flirt with death on the
dark side of the moon? Like an owl I am
in my element, and ready to hunt under the cover
of night, and the city is my domain.

When I started to talk with Sanchez-Day before and after class, he explained his situation: he'd served a *lot* of time and had more prison time coming, but he was determined to do better. He'd been down at the bottom and then went deeper: "I didn't know that there was a cellar in my cellar," he told class one time; now he was struggling up the cellar staircase to make something of his life. Writing was the key to it, a much healthier high than anything he'd tried before. Through writing, through his new interest in Native American spirituality and Hispanic literature, he was seeking rebirth:

### The rebirth

I used to have scribbles and scrawls
on signs, bridges, and walls
stating loyalty to a crown
that I'd never let fall
the number one *soldado* ("soldier") on the frontline,
when the Generals call
I used to grit and grind

I used to hustle to get mine
I used to recite gangsta rhymes
I used to clack nines
across enemy lines
Since my rebirth that *vida loca* ("crazy life")
is left behind.
Now I spend my time
crackin' the spines
of poetic novels I find
readin' and writin', elevatin' my mind
Now I'm free inside, despite bein' confined
I used to emulate veterans and OGs
Now I aspire to be of the likes of
Baca, Neruda, Paz, and Ortiz.

Programs Director Mike Caron and I were glad to have Sanchez-Day in the class because just looking at this guy we *knew* and other inmates in the class *knew* that he had not only been around the block more times than most of us but also he'd been incarcerated in that block, and he'd done what he'd had to do to survive and was now striving to come to terms with it. Here he was in class, showing other inmates that they didn't have to keep giving in to temptations—they could fight them and keep fighting them; they could live for their better selves and their families—their better angels might win at least some of the time. They could write to understand their lives and write life plans to aspire to, as Sanchez-Day did:

### An important man

An important man is what I aspire to be. A man
with purpose. A man of significance. An honest man.
A God-fearing man. A devout family man. A hard-
working man. A respectable man. A responsible man.
A sober man. A free man. A wise man. A loved man.
A righteous man.

In fall 2013, Sanchez-Day was transported to the Department of Corrections in El Dorado, Kansas, to serve two more years before his release in October 2015 to Oxford House in Topeka, a nonprofit drug- and alcohol-free halfway house. When he went off to prison, we stayed in touch through letters. He wrote about the terrifying experience of losing his sight in prison, and as he said in his letter to me: "The last place where you want to lose your sight is in prison." His sight was saved in a series of operations. His jail buddies looked after him. He kept writing and sending me poems. Believing that Sanchez-Day is a writer with vital things to say to a broad audience in no way limited to incarcerated men, I began to promote his work in a number of ways. I published some of his poems in *Coal City Review* and nominated two of them for the Pushcart Prize. Caron and I sent a file of his work to Baca. Baca's work had been a staple of our class since the beginning in 2001 because of the way his poetry ranges freely across the spectrum of human experience and often concerns subject matter such as incarceration, addiction, mental illness, the justice system, and so on, subjects of special interest to a class of inmates. Through Sanchez-Day's work, telling a story remarkably similar to Baca's, we all felt an even closer connection with Baca. I sent Sanchez-Day's poems to Lynn Carlson in Wyoming, an editor collecting poems for an anthology, *Watch My Rising: 37 Poems and Stories about Recovery from Addiction* (2016). She included one of Sanchez-Day's best poems, "Taking On Life."

Sanchez-Day's publications are mounting up, and his writing continues. Most times when I meet up with him there's new work, plainspoken and compelling, such as this:

**Worldly possessions**

First are my memories, both the good and the bad,

those of joy and pain. All of which I own, no one can take

them from me. Some I wish to grasp

tightly because they make me happy; others I wish

to be banished for eternity. Nonetheless they are mine.

Second are my scars and tattoos. Both of which tell the story

of my 38 trips around the sun.

Finally are my lifelong "afflictions." The reason I name them so

is because I've been told that these "diseases" were given to me genetically. I am plagued with Alcoholism, Diabetes, and Anger Issues. I have fought a lifelong battle with these and will continue to do so until it's my time to walk on.

An elder once told me, "We own nothing, not even our bodies; we only have the use of our bodies until they wear out.

Objects simply pass through our hands without permanence."

After his release in fall 2015, Sanchez-Day enrolled at Haskell Indian Nations University in Lawrence, with the aim of finishing his associates degree and eventually becoming a counselor. I met him again when a group of us gathered downtown for a photo shoot for an article in *Lawrence Magazine* about the writing class—first time I'd seen him out of a jail jumpsuit. He was looking healthy and at peace, and he said his eyesight was good, "though it gets a bit blurry at times."

In December 2016, following the publication of the *Lawrence Magazine* article, I joined Sanchez-Day, Sherry Gill, and Mike Hartnett at a reading at the Lawrence Public Library, where we read jail writing class poems to a large audience. I thought of Sanchez-Day as a star graduate of our class; he embodied everything we'd been trying to achieve. Whereas Gill, Hartnett, and I could *read* work from inmates, Sanchez-Day had *lived* it and written about it, and he was willing to put himself on the line to share it with us. It felt like a triumph, one of the things I'm most proud of in my years of teaching. I called him "Professor" and meant it.

After the success of the library reading, Sanchez-Day was given permission to return to the jail as a coinstructor of the writing class, something other former inmates had asked for but had not been permitted to do for obvious security reasons. Sanchez-Day, completing one cycle, at least, was back in the class he'd gotten so much from, given so much to—which had changed his life for the better. As coinstructor he was his typical low-key self, just one more face in the circle until he spoke at last with gravitas that just has to be respected. I remember him thanking us and telling the class again that although he knew he'd done well, he was only ever one slip-up away from ruining all his hard work and strong will to get so far. That's the thing with demons: they're like a chronic illness from which you can never escape; you have to fight every moment to keep them at bay. How to fight these demons? You can't fight them with your fists—he'd tried that. You can't fight them by getting drunk or high—he'd tried that too and knew it only made him hurt more when he was sober. But he could write, a simple act of putting pen to paper, sometimes as hard as climbing a cold mountain but often exhilarating too.

The great African American poet Langston Hughes (1901–1963) wrote that because of the suffering of his race and his own painful struggles (especially during his early years in Lawrence, Kansas), his soul had "grown deep like the rivers."[5] I'd say that Sanchez-Day's soul has grown deep too. He knows the evil men do; he knows their angels. I listen to him and appreciate his tough wisdom and his gritty, graceful poetry, which reveals the truth to all of us who have been fortunate enough to be close to its light.

He's still writing, still trying to make sense of himself and the world, still meeting up with himself in strange places:

**In passing**

I had one of those experiences
the other day
the kind where I run into someone
at some random place
engage in a conversation
and cannot remember their name
or who they are


This particular encounter occurred
as I was leaving the library
among the vast aisles of books
a voice called my name
and seemed to echo
in the sombering silence


As the individual approached
I immediately started to
run through the archives in my memory
trying to identify this person
as we greet one another

I try to make a connection
he seems so familiar
I just can't place him

As he speaks
I notice a sense of shame in his eyes
I detect weariness
in his body language
and his loose and tattered clothes
serve as a reflection
of his spirit

He compliments me
on the new direction
I've taken in life
He says I look healthy
and like I am doing well
He wishes me continued success
bids me farewell
and goes on his way

As I walk off
from the encounter
racking my brain
asking myself
who was that?
Where the hell does he know me from?
he appeared so weighed down
with guilt, shame, and regret

and then I realize

who the individual was . . .


it was my old self.

Poem by poem, Sanchez-Day is leaving that old self further and further behind.

Sitting with Sanchez-Day in Wheatfields Café in Lawrence, I asked him if he'd still be writing in ten years' time, and he said he'd certainly be writing then; he has so much more to write. He said that he's hardly written about his mother yet, and she'd had a huge influence on his life; plus, he'll want to write about everything that happens to him in the next ten years, with his life prospects looking up. He's been invited by Baca to a writing retreat in Santa Fe to work on one of his writing projects and finds it hard to believe he's been given this opportunity to work with his spiritual mentor.

I said to Sanchez-Day that one thing I emphasize in my jail writing class is that the inmates are writing for a broader audience than simply for the in-carcerated. They're writing poems full of human emotion that should have meaning for all of us—writing about human relationships, life, traumatic experiences, and hard choices. When you're incarcerated, Sanchez-Day says, "you don't have nothing but time to reflect. You can't help it, it's gonna happen. It's all you've got time for. . . . It's raw, it's pretty much uncensored, sometimes it's gritty and it's dark but to me it don't get more real than that." That type of poetry is for everyone hungry for art that says something im-portant about matters that involve us all.

That's what Sanchez-Day does best: he writes poetry of truth and light that could not be "more real" and is, in its way, for all of us.

## Chapter 11

# "Mainly I Just Want to Help People Because No One Helped Me"

Sherry Gill, Programs Director, Douglas County Jail (2015–)

Sherry Gill, programs director at Douglas County Jail since 2015, was formerly an instructor at Haskell Indian Nations University in Lawrence, Kansas. She has worked with at-risk populations for most of her decades-long career. This kind of commitment was in the family because her mother was the executive director of Independence, Inc., for many years (Independence, Inc., based in Lawrence, promotes the independence of people with disabilities). Gill followed her mother's career path in caring for vulnerable populations, "the last people on the totem pole," as she says. She's a military veteran and says she's very patriotic but wants this to be a great country for *everyone,* including those on the lower end of the social scale. When I've talked to her over the five years or so that I've known her, she often mentions the mantra that has guided her work:

> *Mainly I just want to help people because no one helped me.* So that's kind of been my mission. I do a great deal of work with women concerning domestic violence and abuse. I've been able to get those programs into this facility [Douglas County Jail]. Most of my work is around women; the writing class is one of the few classes that I do have with the men. I see so much cruelty and injustice for these folks, and I kind of feel the inmates are really the last people on the totem pole. I think that our society has neglected them, has put labels on them, and does not see that

these are people, these were children—these were children of trauma. These were children of prejudice, of poverty, of neglect, of not getting what they needed in school. And starting in school and not getting what you need will set you up for a very difficult life.[1]

In her mission to aid inmates with their "difficult" lives, she sometimes finds herself working against institutional disinterest regarding the personal lives of inmates, the voices of authority that say, "I don't have time for your story: *you did the crime, you do the time.*" Although acknowledging that people convicted of crimes must face the appropriate consequences, she says she always tries to take the time to get to know inmates as people—as so much more than inmate numbers—to try to understand why they have taken dark roads and to see how she might help them do better for themselves. She talks passionately about what might *really* make a dent in the size of the incarcerated population in the United States: drug rehabilitation (for more than the standard twenty-eight days), more halfway houses, and an increase in the number of drug counselors. All these measures would counteract addiction, which too often leads to incarceration, in particular the dire effects of the opioid epidemic and meth proliferation in the county and in the state. The opioid death rate in Kansas quadrupled between 2000 and 2016, according to the *Lawrence Journal-World* (March 4, 2018).

After working with Mike Caron for more than fourteen years as coleader of the Douglas County Jail writing class, I was uncertain that the class would continue after his retirement in May 2015. One of the main reasons for my commitment to this teaching was Caron's passionate participation in and advocacy for the class. He made it possible by establishing it as an important part of his jail programs. He contributed to it most weeks, sitting in, writing, telling his stories, and acting as an example inmates could follow. In summer 2015, after Caron's retirement, I was gone from the jail for months because I was in England caring for my dying mother. When I got back to Kansas in September 2015, I contacted Gill at the jail and told her I'd like to start teaching there again. She was enthusiastic indeed, as she always is about programs she believes will benefit inmates in productive ways. Since October 2015 she has been coleading the class, surprising herself at how much she has enjoyed working on her own poetry.

When I first met Gill, she made an immediate impact. I'm used to working with people who keep their life cards well hidden most of the time. They don't reveal much about themselves until, I suppose, they get to know you well enough to trust you with the more important things about their lives.

However, within a few minutes of our first meeting, Gill told me that she was a veteran, a recovering alcoholic, and a proud mother, and I was drawn to her immediately, appreciating her candor. She made me think of those Dylan lines in "All Along the Watchtower" about the need for honesty: "Let us not talk falsely now/the hour is getting late." There's an urgency about Gill because she wants to get moving; she always wants to get to what's important in our lives because "the hour is getting late." I have seen her work as a skilled and sympathetic counselor, valuing life stories people share with her in order to better understand themselves and, with her guidance, to try to make the best choices for their lives.

Gill is tall and strong and colorful, speaks up for what she believes in, tells it like it is, doesn't hide what she thinks should not be hidden, and is an advocate indeed for women's issues. She has worked with many women who have been hurt and then lost control of their lives. When she works with people who are hurting, she knows what it feels like from her own experience. She doesn't judge them. She listens to their stories and gives advice. On her watch, no one indulges in self-pity. She believes that lives, even cracked and badly broken lives, can be repaired, and she works with all her considerable strength to help change those lives. There's an aura of hard-won wisdom about her that she admits, with a smile, is not always appreciated. As she wrote:

### Wisdom

For most of us with gray hair

the young people do not want to listen to us,

they think they know everything,

just like we did when we were young.

In class, Gill is empathetic but also tough; no one gets away with anything. If an inmate causes too much trouble, she pulls him out of the classroom and marches him back to the pod. Most often the inmate will be back the following week, after apologizing. For many inmates, the writing class is not to be missed. I asked her what she thinks inmates get out of it so that they keep coming back:

I think they get to see and hear other people's stories, and they get to share their stories, and maybe they've never been able to share their stories with anyone, or maybe they've been afraid to talk about their lives, and I think this gives them an outlet to have a voice; it gives them a voice. Inside the class they have a voice, and we all listen. We're not a group that's going to be demeaning them or making them feel even worse than they already feel . . . we're not going to do that. We're gonna be open, we're going to believe them, and we're gonna welcome their stories. And we're gonna share our own.

With a ring of male inmates around her, Gill is a powerful representative of the XX half of society. In her writing, in the things she says in class, in the way she won't let inmates write poems degrading women—the sort of bitch/ ho strain of rap is never far away from the class (as discussed in Chapter 4)—she stands up for women, whom, she insists, deserve to be respected.

Time and again, Gill celebrates the benefits of the class. It can help as an outlet for inmates' anger, it can offer the opportunity for inmates to talk about vital issues such as depression, it can help inmates to understand the struggles of others, and it can help to show inmates they are not alone in their adversities. Accompanying inmates back to the pod after a recent class, one of them told her, "Yeah, it was kind of good to get this out," and she said, "Yeah, writing will do that for you, if you write stuff down you can get it out and throw the paper away, but it's a way for you to get a release." She told me, "They have no release here." As she acknowledges, the class is a release for instructors too; we bring with us our own issues and often manage to write them out and ease them in the company of other writers working to do the same. All instructors join inmates when we write together because we believe in what we tell the inmates about the benefits of writing and don't want to miss out on the challenge and pleasure of sharing new work.

Gill is one of our keenest writers, writing about her family, her childhood, her husband (also a veteran), and her daughter or sharing her feelings with us about her hairstyle after a short haircut. I love her clarity of language, her good energy every time, her literary sensibility, her sense of humor, and her willingness to share her poetry with the class, showing that she values the opinions of class members and trusts us with her stories. Some of my favorite Gill poems are about her time in bleak Gillette, Wyoming, where she went with her boyfriend soon after she'd gotten out of the army. She wrote about "whiteouts" and people dying a few feet from their houses because they couldn't see their way home through a blizzard. When she read this poem for us, I believe a number of inmates knew all about dying a few feet from home. It seemed a particularly striking metaphor for a common type of experience among inmates—being close to help but not quite making it.

She is not able to reach everyone, of course. I've seen her clash with some inmates keen to challenge her. She accepts her defeats, which seem only to embolden her and push her to try harder to make the rattletrap system of incarceration and rehabilitation work as well as possible. She just keeps showing up for work in her bright colors, a positive force in the lives of inmates, who are, for the most part, in a bad place, thankful for a pair of strong helping female hands in an institution that is essentially a male bastion.

In July 2018, Gill responded to a poem by Antonio Sanchez-Day about a happy day in Lawrence, Kansas, delighted that he had written a poem celebrating the small delights of freedom: breakfast in the Ladybird Diner, coffee at Java Break, a stroll down Massachusetts Street. She says that she often has to explain to young inmates that she understands how freedom seems *boring*, how criminal life is *exciting*, especially for the adrenalin junkies who often come her way in jail jumpsuits. She tells them that "with boring comes beautiful, comes tender," the quiet joys described by Sanchez-Day. There are other joys too, according to Gill, her voice rising because she believes so passionately in what she's saying:

> That's what I tell people, once you get past your demons or at least get a better grip on them, then you can start seeing the beauty, you can start seeing those tender moments with the pets and the children and the puppies, whatever it is. In those times, you're fucking glad you're alive, and you get tears in your eyes and you're like, "This is what it is. This is worth it."

"Worth it": that's the message I get from this motivator. "Worth it." Worth working on our lives—worth writing about them to help to understand them, celebrate them, and begin making repairs. I've seen her work with hundreds of different inmates, and I admire the way she tries each time to make the most of the person with whom she's in contact. If an inmate's not ready to read his poem out loud, she offers to read it for him, then moves on to the next inmate. She might well offer that first inmate a quiet word of encouragement later, telling him that he's made a good start.

For some of the guys cut off from their families, she is a woman who won't judge; she will be sympathetic as much as possible because she sees in the inmates aspects of her own experience, and she's quite willing to tell us "there but for the grace of God go I." She understands there is only so much she can do for people who are too often in substantial need, but she is not frustrated by this, preferring to focus on what she *can* do:

I can only do what I do. I'm staying here, I'm not gonna leave, and that will be my contribution. I tell people, the women and the men, "Never give up." I say you just can't. You've gotta keep fighting. You've got to put one foot in front of the other, even if you don't feel like it, do it. And people with severe depression, that's what we have to do, we have to put one foot in front of the other, and we have to get out of that fog.

"That fog": in July 2018, in response to the suicides of celebrities Anthony Bourdain and Kate Spade, she wrote about depression: "Feels like you are 'fogged in'/you feel as if there is a weight on you/walking around numb,/ sluggish and heavy-hearted/catatonic in a chair/unable to leave the house or leave your bed." After reading her poem, she told us about depression, how it's impossible to know at first *why* someone's depressed, so we must be sympathetic. All ten inmates gave her their full attention. Here was something they *needed* to know for themselves and for others around them. With depression a common scourge in inmate populations, what she had to tell us was the sort of information that might save lives. The writing class gave her the forum to do so and an attentive audience of inmates under stress, eager to learn important information with significant bearing on their lives.

I'd like to end this chapter on a lighter note with two poems that pulled us away from the darker side, one by Gill and one by Sanchez-Day. Gill has often surprised herself and entertained and enlightened us with the quality of her own writing, as in the class in May 2017 when one of the writing prompts was *my first car*, and she wrote about her Carmen Gia convertible, an old beat-up first car just like most everyone else's wreck of a first car.

### My First Car

I found a Carmen Gia convertible for $200. I bought it.

I paid to have it painted a pale yellow.

I loved that car with the shifter and the top down.

My girlfriends and I would drive all over the Square:

6th Street, Iowa, 23rd, and Mass.

As it got older, my best friend would have to push me

so I could get it started. To this day I remember yelling:

"Faster, Sue, faster!"

I loved the freedom, escaping my home life

and I felt happy for the first time in my life!

What joy it is riding in a convertible

on a nice summer day in River City.

I remember her joy when she recited that line, "Faster, Sue, faster!" as though she was right back in that summer afternoon with her friends, decades ago.

In a poem of thanks to Gill, former inmate Sanchez-Day wrote that he wanted to thank her for keeping the class going, thus providing the opportunity for all of us to "tap into that creativity that we all possess." He continued:

Some have

discovered (myself included) talents, solutions,

even peace of mind through writing.

Most of all I am thankful for Sherry

not only believing in the work I do

but for believing in me as a person and

giving me an opportunity to contribute

back within the very walls where I

discovered my passion for writing.

Sanchez-Day thanks her for giving him the opportunity to develop talents that have led him to substantially improve his life: What could be more of a tribute than that? Such a change doesn't make everything right in a world that's still too often at war with itself, but it does make a small part of it better than it was, and that's plenty for someone like Sanchez-Day, who knows what it is to be in the basement of a basement. Drawn toward extremes herself, Gill is well prepared to help out people close to the edge—the vast majority of the incarcerated.

She lives out her mantra, helping others because no one helped her as a child, and in doing this work she has taken herself and others to brighter places and fights every day to keep from slipping back into the darkness she knows too well.

## Chapter 12

# "I Done Good and I Done Bad"

## Topeka's Bad Man from the Badlands, Gary Holmes

At the end of my June 2018 interview with Gary Holmes, a stand-out character from a cast of thousands in the writing class at Douglas County Jail during my twenty years there, he summed up his joy in writing poetry: "When you've been a monster, when you've been an asshole and a mean son of a bitch and then you write sweet words and get away from all that bitterness . . . " He didn't finish the thought, but I got it anyway: here was a man who has done plenty of bad things in his life of which he is not proud, and yet he knows his better angels too and wrote in the class from 2002 to 2003 some of the best poems in all my tenure there. The guys around him knew it: here was a man with a poetic gift. We all had expectations when it was Holmes's turn to read.

When Programs Director Mike Caron and I began working on the anthology of jail class writing published in 2010 as *Douglas County Jail Blues*, Holmes was one of the first poets we thought of including, even though he'd not been in the class for four or five years. We published three of his poems in the anthology: "Courtroom Drama" (which he considers one of his best), "Was It Really Just a Dream?," and "The Prophet." Where did these poems come from in a man you might expect to have little interest in the arts? According to Holmes: "I think it's like magic, man, it comes so sweet off the end of my tongue, off the end of my pen, you know what I mean, that I'll look at something later on, 'I wrote that?' You know what I mean? I know I wrote it."

So there's this likeable big guy I'm talking to in a gritty McDonalds in downtown Topeka about his poetry and our memories of a class we shared almost fifteen years ago, a friendly sixty-eight-year-old guy with a life of fighting, imprisonment, joys, struggles, drinking, and drugging (though he's been sober now for almost sixteen years), the felon who's done a *lot* of time:

> I did a lot of previous time. I've got thirteen felony convictions. People say, "You say that like you're proud of it," but I'm not proud of it at all, but that's my life; I did a *lot* of years but that's what I chose to do, I made a *lot* of bad choices in my life, you know, I've always said I picked the wrong career. I definitely did. But it is what it is.
>
> There's an old saying that says, "You're not really old until regrets take the place of all your dreams," and there's not a truer thing you can say because you say, "Oh, man, I wish I hadn't done that," you know you can't beat yourself over your head with your life.[1]

During my years of teaching at the jail, certain inmates emerged as class leaders: Donndilla Da Great, Big Jae Wae, Jesse James, Michael Harper. One of these leaders I remember was Holmes, who joined the class in 2002 when he was facing a high-profile trial and the likelihood of serious prison time. It's not that the class leaders talk more than others in class. It's just that their presence is felt, and they help to set the tone of the class. Holmes made it clear in the class that important work was under way, and though it was fine to joke around sometimes, the class had vital business to conduct. He's a big guy with a big presence, so everyone paid attention. When I met with him almost fifteen years later and asked him about the class at that time, he said that it had helped him get through one of the hardest times of his life, and if we canceled the class for whatever reason, he really missed it. When he went to trial in 2003, he got a lot more prison time than expected "'cause they didn't honor the plea agreement." Holmes left the jail after his trial, and I stayed in touch with him when he was in prison in Hutchinson, Kansas. In fact, I sent to him in batches a copy of his manuscript of poems he'd asked me to look after for him.

Holmes was born and raised in Topeka, Kansas; got into trouble early; and at sixteen, in 1971, he was in Hutchinson Reformatory and got his GED. He said that at the time everyone in the reformatory had to take their GED: "Back then you had to get a GED before you was released. People definitely wanted you to get it because they didn't want you to go out into society as dumb as you was when you went in." Holmes said he just couldn't keep away from drugs and alcohol, kept getting into trouble, and ended up in the

Kansas state penitentiary in Lansing, where he started serious writing for the first time.

I asked him if he'd read much when he was in school because when I read his work, I can see considerable literary talent, and that's most often inspired by and developed through early reading. Holmes said his mom had always encouraged him to do well in English and math in particular, but he hadn't taken to reading. He was more influenced by country western music and the songs of some of the best American songwriters of recent years such as Willie Nelson, Kris Kristofferson, and John Prine:

> I love country western music. . . . Willie Nelson and Kris Kristofferson were really the main guys in my life. I'll rattle off stuff that he sung like I know all the words to his songs. I was really interested in Kris Kristofferson and John Prine. John Prine's a badass. "There's a hole in Daddy's arm where all the money goes." "Sam Stone." Them people [the songwriters] sit down and they're on the bus or whatever from town to town, concert to concert, and writing in between that, you know. Course, a lot of them's full of whiskey and full of pills too. They're smoking a lot of weed.

It's easy to see why Holmes would feel a connection with these "highwaymen," larger-than-life country western artists. They live wild, get into trouble, write songs about it, make a lot of money, lose it all, win it back again—a mad ride down the highway. Likely enough they'd sum up their lives at sixty-eight in much the same way Holmes does: "It's been a good life. It really has. Whatever happens now, you know, it happens." What's happening for Holmes at sixty-eight: treatment for serious medical issues, separation but not divorce from the wife he loves, sobriety (with only an occasional lapse), and hopefully plenty more living to do. I ask him if he's done any writing lately, and he says not much, although he recently wrote a poem for his wife. He has her name, Tasha, tattooed on his arm.

Holmes is not the type of writer who talks fondly of a high school English teacher who'd turned him on to literature and drew out his talent, so where did it come from? He tells me this story:

> I think, you know a long time ago when I was back in my twenties, I went to Lansing state penitentiary, and I started writing there. There was what they called the *Concept* magazine. It was a prison magazine about the size of that book there [pointing to *Douglas County Jail Blues*], and it came out once a month, and my partner run *Concept* magazine—they

ran it, the prisoners did. They said, "Gary, if you wanna put a poem in there, man . . . " So I started writing, my very first poem. I still remember it to this day, the very first one I put in there, the main one that I wrote back then.

They put your picture with it, so I would send copies to my family, to different girlfriends, and different family members could have a copy of the book. There's none of them around anymore. It's a long time ago, back in the 1970s. And then I realized that a lot of the girls loved the poetry, you know. I was kind of a mean son of a bitch with a sweet bunch of words and you know they were meaningful words. I've always liked to write true about people, you know, and I found out a long time ago that if you write a poem for a girl and you put her name up at the top of it, you're in!

I asked Holmes if he was like many of the other inmate poets I've worked with: Did he do most of his writing when he was incarcerated? I've found that for many inmates, incarceration is the most peaceful, sober, reflective time of their lives and their best chance for the sort of quiet *alone time* often necessary for serious writing. Plus, they're removed from the temptations they face on the outside. Holmes said this was true, and perhaps his best *ever* writing time was during his incarceration in Douglas County Jail, when I worked with him in 2002. I asked him where the poems came from, and he said that quite honestly, he didn't know. Maybe they were gifts from God because how else could he explain it?

I've always said it had to come from God because I was never that smart on my own—I've always 100% believed that because it will come out of my heart just like that, the real good ones. It was amazing because I knew that it was special. I've heard it so many times. It's not that I'm bigheaded about it, it's just the way it was, man, it's just I love to write and impress people, I love to do that.

He mentioned again his sense of himself as having two sides, the outlaw on one side and the poet on the other, and he seemed amazed that these two polar opposites could be contained in the same body: "It's amazing that you have the bad guy, you know, the bandit, the outlaw, and then you've got the good side of him that talks. I wrote poems about Jesus, I wrote poems about barroom fights, a lot of love poems, and friendship poems. It was a major thing back then." But then in prison he'd worked fifteen-hour days, sixty cents an hour, trying to wear himself out, sending half of his money home for child support. But he did agree with me that as opposed to his tumultuous life on the outside, when he was incarcerated he was able to find the time and peace of mind to write: "Yeah, I'd say I wrote a lot more when I was in than out."

I remember that when I was working with Holmes, I encouraged him to try writing outside of the traditional rhyming forms he preferred. Perhaps because his main inspirations were songs, it was not surprising that he would most often write in rhyme and form. Holmes said it was a challenge to make a rhymed poem work out: "The rhyming thing, you always pushed me away from rhyming. . . . Sometimes it was fun to make it rhyme because you have to pick a certain word to make sense, and the whole stanza, the whole verse, you have to make something that makes sense, and a lot of the time, some of the more interesting ones, you know, didn't rhyme." I was always asking him to do that because I wanted him to use his abilities with language to see what would happen when he didn't restrict himself with rhyme and form. It's significant that the three poems we selected for *Douglas County Jail Blues* are all unrhymed, all of them finding their own forms, because Holmes was always known among his peers as a rhyming poet. In fact, one of his own unrhyming poems is one of his favorites:

I think that one you got there in that book, that "Courtroom Drama," was one of the better ones that I've ever written. That didn't rhyme, you know, and it was very significant in my life because I had to look at things. We was having courtroom drama right then because it was a high-profile case in Douglas County, and it was sad, it was really sad. It was what it was.

Holmes often uses fatalistic phrases such as "it was what it was" and the like. It's a sort of acceptance of things as they are even though he'd like to change them, most often because he'd like to do better. In a way, his poetry has given him the opportunity to make amends, as much as it's possible:

**Courtroom Drama**

Defendant—hateful, vacant loser's eyes,
feeling defeated with mediocre counsel.
Wondering, "Who can save me?"
Life trickling down toilet. Fearing flush.
Hoping with useless hope. Scared bitter.

I asked Holmes how he faced up to a prison term of more than a decade: Didn't he just get overcome with depression? No, he said, you just have to keep moving forward.

It's clear talking to Holmes that he has a lot of regrets, though he balances them with all the blessings of his life—children, grandchildren, family, friends, Topeka, poems. Though he's got challenges ahead, including another round of serious medical treatments, he still has more hopes than regrets.

I ask Holmes if he's saved all his work, knowing that often enough my peripatetic inmate poets leave their stacks of poems behind in some rental property or in a tent by the river or in an ex-girlfriend's house after an argument. Poems fly, fly away, gone with the wind. He says he's lost a lot of poems in fires. He still has a stack of his poems at his wife's house; plus, when he was in Texas he made copies of his poems and sent them to family and friends as booklets, so his poems have been spread around—a sort of literary insurance policy.

Holmes is a natural storyteller and an extrovert (in fact, he told me that his wife does not approve of his extrovert character and wishes he could stay more focused on her and her kids). When he was in Hutchinson (which he, like most inmates, refers to as "Hutch"), he said that when I sent him poems from his manuscript he asked the librarian to make copies of the poems for him so he could send them out to friends and family. He said she told him she'd make copies for him only if she could make copies for herself too because she enjoyed his poems so much. Large smile from Holmes when he tells this story. It's just one more example of how damn much an inmate's poetry means to him, what a huge kick he gets out of genuine praise, and how that makes hanging on just a little easier. A guy doing time needs all the help he can get, and praise for his poems lifts a bit of the weight.

I'd been talking to Holmes for about an hour, an intense hour because he's full of life stories, advice, and life lessons. He stands uncomfortably—he's had substantial repair work done on one foot with eight bones shattered after a fall from a tree. He says he's off to give some money to his grandson. We agree to meet again after I've written something, and as a last word to Holmes, I encourage him to write something new. Then he's gone, leaving me with our conversation to write up and a thousand thoughts.

I'd just met the self-titled "Bad Man from the Badlands," a man with a lot of prison time and felonies but who can write remarkably well:

### The Prophet

The prophet. The one who delivers divine
messages. The one who foretells the future.
Then the prophet said: "Listen to your
heart, tell her to listen to hers. And
each and every day you'll have genuine
love, fresh and pure and untouched.
Love . . . each day of your lives."

Holmes said thanks for meeting him, then added:

This here puts me in the mood to write. Now we're talking, I feel like
writing. You know what I mean? That's good. Because I'm never around
people who write.
I'm just such an idiot at times, and at other times I'm so smart. It's just
if you take a human being, and you've dealt with guys in the program
for almost two decades now, you've met some real gen-u-ine idiots, and
you've met some real smart talented people.

But what I often see in my classes at Douglas County Jail are inmates both
smart and "idiotic," talented guys with a self-destructive side to them that
screws them up too often, and that's why they're at Douglas County Jail and
not in a doctor's office in a white coat helping someone like Holmes with
his latest medical trouble (because some of them have the brains for that!).

Had I met with the Bad Man or with a gifted poet and raconteur? The
most intriguing thing is that I'd sat in McDonalds on 11th and Southwest
Kansas in Topeka, Kansas, and met with both at the same time, then watched
the big man hobble across the parking lot to his truck.

I drove off with a chapter to write, "The Bad Man from the Badlands,"
about an outlaw who will always stand out for me from all the inmate writers I've worked with over the years, a substantial *bad* presence in the classroom and in my memory forever, the inmate who asked me at the beginning
of one class if my girlfriend had found her son who'd gone missing because
he'd remembered, in spite of having much else to think about, what I'd written about the week before.

## Chapter 13

# "It Really Is a Form of Counseling, in a Sense"

## Mike Hartnett

Mike Hartnett, volunteer instructor and coleader of the Douglas County Jail creative writing class since fall 2015, loves a good story and regrets that his parents, both journalists, never wrote again after they retired. "They had fascinating stories. I kick myself that I didn't sit there with a tape recorder and get these things down. My mother was a flapper in the Roaring 20s, doing the Charleston and drinking bathtub gin at speakeasies; why didn't I write that down?"[1] His father worked for the Associated Press (AP) in Chicago between 1944 and 1969, covering, among many other things, the Democratic National Convention in 1968 (for which he was issued, by AP, a football helmet to protect his head in riots), and the trial of Jimmy Hoffa in 1962. As for Hartnett's own story, he described it in a short biographical essay about his early life: "I was born in Milwaukee, grew up in Chicago, graduated from the University of Illinois in Champaign, married Barbara the next day, and we moved to Peoria the day after that. I taught speech and English at a public high school. Barbara taught at local grade schools. We both took graduate courses at Illinois State University."

Hartnett's participation in the Douglas County Jail writing class, beginning in fall 2015 when he joined the class as a volunteer after his retirement as a business journalist, has enabled him to write stories that, he says, he'd been thinking about for years without writing them down: "I have found myself, with writing prompts, writing things that I never would have written otherwise, remembering things that I never would have thought of otherwise." An example of this is the following untitled poem written in class on January 26, 2017:

I first got a hint of the pain a parent feels
over the death of a child when we were eating dinner
with a classmate of Barb's and her husband.

The restaurant was crowded, the tables close together.
Eventually Jane and her husband told us how their ten-year-old
son was killed by a car while riding his bike.

Jane became more agitated as she told her story
and even more agitated when she talked about the funeral
and what some of the well-wishers said.
The worst, she said, was the woman who had never had a child die
who said, "I know how you feel."

Jane pounded her fist on the table and shouted:
"SHE DOES NOT KNOW HOW I FEEL.
SHE DOES NOT KNOW!!!"

There wasn't a sound in the crowded restaurant.

This poem, the recollection of an emotionally charged incident from many years ago, would likely not have been written but for some prompt on the class whiteboard that day, plus the creatively stimulating environment of the jail classroom, where we're all inspired to write stories to share. The poem itself, building to that passionate exclamation, is about an outburst of emotion, the sort of outburst often behind some of the best writing by inmates (and instructors). Certain memories do tend to fire up powerful emotion, as they did in Hartnett's untitled poem. We all grip our pencils or pens and try to find the language to express them.

Though Hartnett's first experience of a jail was when he was sixty-nine years old as a volunteer at Douglas County Jail, he'd had substantial experience with the criminal justice system before then, especially forty years earlier in the mid-1970s when he was a counselor at Lincoln College in Lincoln, Illinois, experience that has in many significant ways shaped his life. A student at the college, Russell Smrekar, murdered four witnesses to his petty crimes, and Hartnett, as counselor, found himself near the center of this notorious crime because he knew both the murderer and one of his victims, Michael Mansfield, a student at Lincoln College. One of Hartnett's main reasons for volunteering at Douglas County Jail was because he hoped it would enable him to turn back to a book he left unfinished for about thirty-five years about the four murders.[2] He often writes about these murders in class, as he did in this poem on June 1, 2017, showing that he's still trying to come to terms with that traumatic time of his life. The prompt that day was *what's left*.

### The Missing Piece

My murder case, forty years old, and the killer
has died in prison. What's left?

The detective still working on the case and
I think there's plenty left: an accomplice.
We don't see how the killer did some of the things alone.

If we're right, is the accomplice still out there,
or has he/she died? What has he/she done with
his/her life? Guilt? More crimes? Repentance?

Will the detective and I ever learn the answers?
We're both haunted by this.

Seven questions in a poem of ten lines. This shows how Hartnett is still struggling to come to terms with his experience, still yearning for the answers that will make sense of it all. His constant preoccupation with these events from forty years ago reminds me of how many veterans cannot escape from traumatic events during their military service, even after years have passed, and how many inmates are haunted by their crimes. Some experiences strike us so deeply that they change us forever and raise painful issues that will likely never be resolved: in this, Hartnett and the inmates he sits with are one, a major reason for his rapport with writers in the class.

Hartnett always hoped that in retirement he'd be able to go back to the book he'd drafted decades earlier about the Smrekar case. He'd written it over a period of months in the 1970s, getting up at 5 a.m. to write every day before going to work. After he'd written as much as he could—approximately two hundred manuscript pages—he'd put it away for almost thirty-five years. He wasn't sure if life got in the way of him finishing the book or if he deliberately put life in the way to avoid the painful memory. When he talks about the experience, about his book, it's clear that there's still a lot of pain and that he's still, as he says in the poem above, "haunted." He'd encouraged Mansfield to testify against Smrekar; the murderer later confessed to killing Mansfield, though his body has never been found. When Hartnett heard about the writing class at the jail from a writer in the Kansas Authors' Club—I've given a number of presentations to the club over the years—he got in contact with me, and I invited him to sit in on the class. He has been coming to class ever since.

Hartnett's a tall, rangy guy with a deliberate manner and easygoing nature, likeable from the start. If he taught at a college, he'd be a popular professor with jokes up his sleeves to keep his classes engaged. He's not a grandstander; he sits and listens carefully, loves to hear a good story, and loves to tell one too. People gravitate toward him because he's empathetic and good company. After his first class at the jail, he said he loved it and would be back the next week. Since then he hasn't missed unless he's been out of town. He's one-quarter of our great teaching team of the last few years: Hartnett, Sherry Gill, Antonio Sanchez-Day, and me. (In spring 2020, a fifth member joined, English graduate student Ayah Wakkad, who is writing a dissertation on prisons in the Middle East.) During the writing section of class, when Hartnett and Gill have finished writing, I'm always torn between listening to another Hartnett story or trying to finish up my own writing. Hartnett likes to say that he enjoys his Kansas Authors' Club meetings: he listens to a writer read a poem about sunrise or a flock of birds or sunlight on the river, and it's a fine poem, but it doesn't stay with him. What he likes are the poems he hears in the jail class, in which the inmates are often putting themselves on the line by writing about the misery and stress of incarceration, looking deep within and to higher powers to get them through. He has a point: there just seems to be more at stake in the poems written in the jail classroom compared with works produced by writing groups in other locations, even when inmates are not writing specifically about their incarceration. Perhaps it's because the jail experience produces the huge pressure necessary to form precious stones.

After several weeks of sitting in on the class, Hartnett started talking to the inmates about his own writing project: his book about the Lincoln murders. He thanked the class for inspiring him to turn back to this unfinished business, and he told them the story behind the book. He wrote about the murders in a short essay on June 11, 2017:

A couple of years into our tenure in Lincoln, the dormitories had a number of burglaries. The dorm directors and I were convinced they were committed by a freshman, Russ Smrekar, who was from Joliet, Ilinois, about 100 miles north of Lincoln. We could never prove he was the culprit, however.

Early the following fall, there was another burglary, and this time we caught another student, Mike Mansfield, with some record albums that had been stolen from a girl's dorm room. Mike was a good student and very quiet. I was convinced Mike wasn't the burglar and convinced him if he told the truth, I would recommend that he not be expelled from school and not be charged with theft by the police. He told us that Smrekar would steal items from dorm rooms, then give them to him (Mansfield) to hold for him.

We expelled Smrekar and turned the evidence over to the police. Mike Mansfield was put on academic probation. Three days later we read in the paper that Smrekar was caught stealing three pieces of meat from a local grocery store. There were three witnesses.

The semester ended, and Mike did not return for the spring semester. We eventually learned he was missing from his home in Rolling Meadows, a Chicago suburb. He received a call the afternoon of New Year's Eve, told his family he'd be gone about an hour, and has never been seen again.

Weeks later, Ruth Martin, a witness in the shoplifting case, disappeared. Police found blood on the floor of her garage and her car abandoned in a Holiday Inn parking lot in Bloomington, Illinois, about thirty miles north of Lincoln. There was blood in the trunk.

Later, the police station was broken into, and the records from the dorm burglary were stolen, so the state's attorney, who now had no evidence and no witness, dropped the burglary charge.

Later still, a witness—an employee at the grocery store—and his pregnant wife were shotgunned to death in their living room. Smrekar was charged with those two murders.

I was very involved with the police, testified at the grand jury hearing, was under death threats, etc.

Smrekar was convicted of the two murders and sentenced to life in prison. Thirty-some years later, when he was dying in prison, he admitted to killing Mike Mansfield and Ruth Martin.

Each time Hartnett has told this story to a class, he has gotten their full attention—inmates can relate to so many aspects of a story about serious crime and the judicial process. They're intrigued by the mysteries of the case, such as the missing bodies of two of the witnesses.

Because the college was never the same for him after the killings, Hartnett and his wife left Lincoln soon after and settled in Peoria, Illinois, where his wife taught psychology at Illinois Central College and Hartnett began working for an arts-and-crafts trade publication. Even though they'd moved away from Lincoln and the murderer had been convicted and sentenced, Hartnett could not let go of the case. He was searching for some way to make sense of it and was considering writing a book to tell his side of the story. But how to write it? Then by chance a friend gave him a copy of a novel by *New Yorker* fiction editor William Maxwell, *So Long, See You Tomorrow*, providing him with an idea about how he might write his own book. He wrote about this experience in a personal essay:

> We moved to Peoria, and I immersed myself in this new profession but still carried the story of the murders and the guilt of my encouraging Mike Mansfield to testify.
>
> One day at a party, a friend took me aside and gave me a book, *So Long, See You Tomorrow*, by William Maxwell. My friend said it was one of the best things he'd ever read, and it takes place in Lincoln.
>
> I read it and was blown away by the quality of the writing and the similarities to my case: the narrator is on the periphery of a murder case in Lincoln and comes away feeling guilty.
>
> That's me!
>
> I then learned that William Maxwell was the fiction editor of the *New Yorker*, and I wrote a fan letter to him complimenting him on his book and gave him a short synopsis of my story. I never expected an answer, but a few days later, there was a letter from him.
>
> He thought my story was horrific, and I should write it—and to visit him the next time I was in New York. We exchanged a few letters, and

then I was going to be in New York to cover a trade show. He invited me to his apartment on the Upper East Side.

He greeted me at the door in pajamas and bathrobe. He said he wasn't feeling well, and could we talk in his bedroom so he could lie down? I offered to return some other time, but he insisted.

We talked for three hours, and he convinced me that my story should be first person, not third person. "Anybody with the time and money could go to Lincoln, interview everyone, and write a story, but nobody could write your story but you."

The conversation was one of the highlights of my life. Mr. Maxwell edited most of the great American writers of the second half of the twentieth century, he's sick in bed, and he takes the time to encourage an assistant editor of a trade magazine in Peoria.

I returned home, raring to go. For about a year I woke up early each weekday morning and wrote until I went to work.

[Then] I put the manuscript aside—for thirty-five years.

Hartnett worked as a trade magazine editor for sixteen years before quitting to start an online newsletter about the arts-and-crafts industry. After seventeen more years, he retired and moved to Lawrence in 2012.

Hartnett told his story about the Lincoln murders to the Douglas County Jail writing class, and of course his talk of high crimes, grand jury trials, a confession, the sentencing, death threats, and so on were fascinating to the inmates. Most of them were incarcerated for low-level crimes, often drug related, but they were interested in anything to do with criminal justice and had their own opinions about his case. In fact, inmates would often ask him for an update, especially when there were, to his surprise, new developments. He sent me a link to a Chicago area TV station's story about a police operation in Rolling Meadows. Forty years after the Lincoln murders, police units swooped in on a house owned by a relative of Smrekar: dramatic scenes of a squad in Hazmat suits digging up the yard looking for traces of one of the missing bodies. Nothing was found. Hartnett told the class about a call in 2017 from a police detective in Illinois telling him about "significant developments" in the case. He waited and waited for a follow-up call but has heard nothing since. He now reckons that some questions about the case will never be answered.

Hartnett has an important story to tell not only *in* his book but also *about* his book: why he wrote it in the first place, why he couldn't finish it for decades, why he came back to it. I've heard him speak to my college students too, and they are intrigued by his story, most of them well able to relate to violent incidents on a college campus, a rogue student, police on campus, the trial, and so forth. What interests me in particular is the way Hartnett's story has similarities to the stories we hear week after week in the class with inmates relating their troubles, their dealings with the criminal justice system, how they're struggling to make their way through the system, longing to be done with it, and "on the outs" living their own lives. Hartnett has been able to return to his book to confront that hard time in his life because he's seen inmates willing to do the same thing, only they are most often perpetrators rather than witnesses. They too must sometimes feel that their lives took a certain dark turn because of one seemingly random act of violence.

Hartnett must have kissed the Blarney Stone along with his Irish forebears because he's a repository of great stories, like the story of his feisty mother getting one over on a fussy nurse who asked, disapprovingly, how long she'd smoked: "Seventy-seven years!" his mother said. After each jail class, inmates seek him out to follow up on something he said in class. I remember Hartnett whispering "it could have been me" when one of the inmates told his story about a wretched family life that turned him toward crime.

Week after week in class, Hartnett writes stories or fragments of stories about things he's experienced or read about or seen, turned into short narratives with messages to them, honest writing from which we can all learn. I think of his story about his dad being called out to a fire at Our Lady of Angels elementary school in Chicago in December 1958. His dad saw children hanging on to ledges and windowsills before falling to their deaths. Ninety-two children and three nuns were killed in the fire. His father came home that night and didn't say a word. He got a bottle from the liquor cabinet and drank himself into oblivion.

Most of all I think about Hartnett wrestling with traumatic experience and trying to find some way of dealing with it, finding support and common ground with so many inmates who are, in their own way, doing just about the same thing. Hartnett knows that the repercussions of terrible events often resound down the years, and if you look at his good-natured but haunted face, then you know that some things never get better, you just get better at dealing with trauma because you have to—and the inmates we work with know exactly what that is all about.

When I asked Hartnett in an interview what he would like to leave behind him after his last class at the jail, he answered with typical humility and generosity: "For some of these guys, nobody's ever particularly cared what they had to say. I hope it gives them some self-confidence [to have us listen]. I think the class gives them something to look forward to during the week." We talked about the last words of one class member who wrote a long poem thanking everyone in the workshop for what they'd given to him in their writing in the class. He was soon to face a tough trial likely to result in conviction and prison time, so he thought it likely that he wouldn't see any of us again.

Hartnett mentioned a couple of guys in class with speech impediments and commented on the camaraderie of the class: "Nobody makes fun of them." He recalled four guys in class who had broken down and cried: "Nobody made fun of them. People were perfectly respectful. That's one reason why I really like these guys." Hartnett talks to them, lets them talk, and listens closely. As he says, marking a cycle in his life that connects his first career ambition with the work he's doing so well in retirement in Douglas County Jail: "It really is a form of counseling, in a sense." When I asked him about how he has managed to establish a rapport with Douglas County Jail inmates, most of whom are several generations younger than him, he says, "The younger guys remind me of the Lincoln College students. If they hadn't gotten involved in drugs or whatever they got involved in, they could certainly be Lincoln College students." In this way he connects present and past with the hope that by writing he can turn the bad events of his life into something he can live with, something we can all learn from so that we can carry on with our often-challenging lives.

In 2019 Hartnett's memoir about the Lincoln murders, *And I Cried Too: Confronting Evil in a Small Town,* was published by Meadowlark in Emporia, Kansas. I was with him when he gave his manuscript to the editor, Tracy Simmons, and when we saw her a few hours later she said that she'd read it all in one sitting—couldn't stop reading.

That is the power of the written word when telling an engaging story: to go straight to the heart and to lodge there forever.

# Chapter 14

# *"It's Just So Much More Than a Poetry Class"*

## Visitors

> I was relieved I wasn't found to be an imposter, one just pretending to want to be there because I wanted to gawk at their misfortune and be greedy for their story. The truth is that the opposite is true.
>
> —Katherine Dinsdale, journalist

> Yeah, it's almost like you wait until you get outside to really exhale. Take another deep breath in of free air.
>
> —Shannon Musgrave, hospice nurse and jail volunteer

Recently, I added up the number of visitors who accompanied me to Douglas County Jail writing class during my time there: I counted about fifty. Some of my students and colleagues from the University of Kansas (KU) have joined me. Some of my writing friends have sat in, bringing their poems and stories to read to inmates, listening intently to what inmates have to say. Family members have accompanied me, knowing how much the class means to me and keen to see it for themselves—my father, wife, both daughters, sister, and cousin. My daughter Brenna, a journalist, has been a constant visitor to the class, always making sure she can join us during her visits home. Journalists have come along to write stories. Most always the visits have gone well, and visitors have felt the "rough magic" of the class. Though inmates are sometimes sensitive about being "gawked at," they're usually pleased to be visited by people from "the outs."

It's been revealing indeed for me to work on this chapter, asking certain jail class visitors to give their impressions of their visits. I am so familiar with my jail experience that I miss aspects that seem striking to others. In this chapter, I describe visitors experiencing something close to my own jail visits over the past two decades but seen through fresher eyes than mine. When I talked to these visitors, all sorts of new angles on my experiences emerged—and I had thought that I knew it all so well.

Why were these different people interested in making these visits?

Katherine Dinsdale, the Lawrence journalist who wrote the article "Taking On Life" about the class for *Lawrence Magazine*, said: "The subject interested me on a lot of levels, but the most compelling draw to write the story was my own long-held belief in the healing, clarifying power of even small swaths of silence and free writing, and my own quixotical pursuit of such healing and clarifying. Alongside those noble motives was simple, shallow curiosity."[1] Shannon Musgrave, hospice nurse and poet, said that though she had never been in a jail or prison before, she was excited to visit the class because "I really believe in the work you do there. I think that it's really valuable work, and it's really important work, so I was thrilled to get to be a part of that."[2] She worried that her poems, mostly focused on her nursing career and patients of particular significance to her, would not be appreciated by jail inmates. I assured her that her poems concern essential human experiences that only someone without a heart would not appreciate. I was right.

After hundreds of visits, I am familiar, of course, with the entry process at the jail: sign in to the visitor's log, step through the frame of the Garrett metal detector, raise arms for wanding (a scan with a security wand by the jail entrance security guard), slip "Volunteer" lanyard around my neck, proceed to the double doors, and wait for the first door to clank open. But how does that process appear to others? Dinsdale wrote about being escorted through "several heavy and loud-clanging jail-like (it was a jail after all!) gates and doors. I double checked that I was wearing my coveted visitor's badge on a lanyard around my neck." She eventually arrived at a "non-descript classroom . . . scrubbed free of accidental feng shui," a room of men in color-coded jumpsuits with paper and pencils on the tables in front of them, lit up by buzzing, fluorescent lights. Her overall impression: "This was indeed a classroom in a jail, and jails mean business."

Shannon Musgrave said she felt "disoriented and a little bit claustrophobic" and "off balance" upon entering the jail and glad that she was going to be able to leave in a couple of hours. She said that in the brightly lit corridors, everything looks the same and "there's no landmark to get your bearings," adding to her sense of disorientation. She wondered if the jail architects intended to keep visitors disoriented. "This way," I said to her when we emerged from the elevator, on our way to the classroom.

Ronda Miller, president of the Kansas Authors Club, former police officer, and retired special needs educator, was all nerves when going in for the first time, wondering if the inmates would "see through" her: "Meaning, would they know I am no different, no better or worse, than they? Would they know I was sincere in my respect for what they were going through; that I tried my hardest to understand the varied pathways that took them into incarceration?"[3] Entering the jail, her nervousness increased as she began thinking about "prison riots, being taken hostage, assaulted, killed." Perhaps in some crisis she'd get trapped inside the facility. Then her thoughts calmed somewhat as she checked in through security, heard the banging of steel doors, and walked "numerous corridors," bringing "sobriety," as she called it, and making her wonder "how any of us would survive if faced with a similar situation or sentencing." She thought of stories of injustice and unjust imprisonment, and then her thoughts took a turn to more personal matters that made her visit especially significant:

> I also had personal reasons to feel uneasy. My father had been killed in a homicide decades past, and I was concerned I might have suppressed anxiety or PTSD [post-traumatic stress disorder] arise. I knew I had never come to terms with my personal losses and abuse by males. My visits brought those experiences to the forefront of my mind. Would the men sense that I had once been a police officer? Would they hate me if they knew or found out?

Hearing Miller's reaction to her jail visit, I wondered about all the dark thoughts and memories bubbling up into the minds of inmates when they enter these walls, resulting from their own anxiety and PTSD. No wonder it's referred to as a misery factory.

Vietnam veteran and poet John Musgrave said he thought he'd known what he was getting into when he first came to the jail, after his teaching experience at prisons including the penitentiary in Lansing, Kansas. He was surprised by what the class at Douglas County Jail looked like:

> Nothing was what I thought. But what surprised me was the youth of a lot of the inmates at the County Jail. There were a lot of young kids, and my impression was that they were all in there because of drugs in one

way and another, crimes connected to drugs, possession, or sale of drugs themselves.[4]

John Musgrave found the class much more "interactive and more fluid" than the classes he'd taught at prisons, which had most often been in lecture format. In the Douglas County Jail class, he read what he calls his "combat poems" and talked about how important writing had been to him in his postwar "darkest days," and students asked questions and told him about their own experiences. He has made many visits to the jail class over the years and has come to enjoy them:

> I used to dread sometimes going in for one of those lectures in prison—I've never dreaded going in the jail because it's always a good experience. There's a lot of decent kids in there, and damn near everybody is trying. Some of them are trying real hard; even if they're not gonna be immortal poets, they're still trying hard. They're really serious about writing, they're putting things on paper, they're reading poetry in front of other inmates.

John Musgrave feels he can identify with inmates because of his own military experience as a combat Marine in the Vietnam War, where he often felt completely powerless, a pawn in the game, following orders all the time. There's no running away from tough experience like this because "if you try to run away you just go to a worse place in what's already a pretty bad place":

> 'Cause I remember what that felt like in Boot Camp. I remembered what it felt like in Boot Camp looking four years down the road before I could even think of any other kind of life. So I could understand some of how [inmates] felt, the feeling of being trapped. . . . Someone being in charge of everything you do. Telling you when to eat, when to sleep, where to go, and possibly looking years down the road before you have any hope of it changing. And it made it easier for me to be empathetic. It made it easier for me to connect with them, and I hope I've been successful.

Dinsdale said she felt comfortable in class and "left wanting to come back":

> I was pleased that the men I met seemed glad to have a visitor and pleased that I would participate with them in the class. I was relieved I wasn't found to be an imposter, one just pretending to want to be there

because I wanted to gawk at their misfortune and be greedy for their story. The truth is that the opposite is true. Throughout my two hours in the class, I was overwhelmed at the sincerity and earnestness of the men as they shared their work and commented on one another's writing.

Dinsdale heard the men read about fear of release into a world that has no place for them; about grief for the loss of youth or health or love; about addictions; about happy times too—home cooking, romance, and dreams. She believed that she saw inmates learning to be "authentic in their words and feelings for the first time": "Somehow the words spoken worked to level the field in the room, despite huge differences in language skills and literacy levels. Some of the men struggled to read aloud. Others could scarcely contain the pride and creativity bubbling forth. There seemed to be some renewed dignity and self-worth, as well as concerted efforts toward focused listening and seeing. Words came together to overcome barriers and prejudices." Dinsdale felt like she learned plenty from her experience with inmates struggling to find words that might help describe and contain their too often harsh experiences: "Their work has the potential to heal and help those far beyond the confines of the Douglas County Jail." Like me, she realized that the inmates have a much wider potential audience than just their classmates—that their essential, sincere writing can reach anyone receptive to art.

Shannon Musgrave thought of her visit to the class in terms of her own awakening as a poet, saying that she began writing because of the "burden of memory" loaded onto her in her nursing career. She said that she needed a "safe place" to put those experiences and found that place in writing, and in doing this the experiences "crystalized," giving her a clearer perspective on things that had happened and her reactions to those things and decisions she made based on those events:

> And I thought that maybe that can do the same thing for a prisoner, especially in terms of moving forward and making different life choices or deciding they don't want to live that same life, they want to do something differently. I think that's where the real education is. And that writing is a tool to move into that new place where maybe they've never been before. That place of possibility and change.

As a nurse, she said that she thinks of incarceration in terms of her medical experience, with incarceration as a sort of medical "treatment" that might aid with recovery. When the patient is brought low by illness, or the inmate with incarceration, "a reevaluation process takes place and there's a shift, an internal shift on how to look at my life and how to spend my days, the days I have left that takes them to a different level completely after that shift occurs and they made those decisions that they may not have ever gotten to if they hadn't had to deal with being taken back down by their illness or their circumstances." According to Shannon Musgrave, this reevaluation process helps to break down patterns of negative behavior which inmates often find difficult to break: "If you look at the patterns that people repeat in their own lives, it's the same stuff that happens over and over again. What's that definition of insanity? Doing the same thing over and over and expecting different results." Musgrave believes that when people are incarcerated, they have to pay attention to these negative patterns because the distractions and busyness of life are abruptly halted and they're able to address more fundamental issues.

When Musgrave mentioned this, I realized that for many years I had seen, during free writing in class, inmate writers attempting to come to terms with their experience in the way she describes. Would they have gotten to it without the class? Perhaps. But I would say that writing is all about looking inside in order to write about what troubles us, matters that are too often shunted aside as we carry on with our lives. Seeing people in class doing this vital work encourages others to do it too.

In spite of her fears when entering the jail, *in the classroom* Miller began to appreciate the value of what was happening, understanding how much it meant to inmates. At first in that circle of inmates she'd been nervous, especially because Mike Caron and I were not, in her words, "big, muscular types" who could protect her. But when we got to poetry, Miller was able to "transcend" her fears and "where we were," as she was able to experience

> that the words shared, the haunting, hopeful look in the men's eyes, made me vividly aware of the dire situation and experiences these men were undergoing. Men shared their words, stories, emotions, and tears that some people on the outside would not have believed possible—or not have believed were real. I left with no doubt that they were both. It was refreshing and humbling to see the softer side of what many deem hardened criminals. They are all humans with the variety that that entails for all of us—vastly more similar than they are different from us.

> For those men who either didn't write a poem or care to share their words, it was obvious what a lifeline Brian's class was to them by how in-

tently they soaked up the experience. I suspect Brian may have been the first person to care enough to ask some of them to share their innermost thoughts.

Miller says that the class gives the inmates "purpose, mental acuity, knowledge of craft, expanded vocabulary, understanding of emotions, pride in accomplishments. Mostly, it gives the men a means to mentally escape their situation, if only temporarily." She was able to understand on her visit how important that was for these troubled spirits. Those two Thursday afternoon hours gave "hope to each person that they have something to offer to the world through their words and experiences—and they do."

When John Musgrave visits the class, he spends the first hour talking about his experience in Vietnam from 1967 to 1968, when he was about the same age as some of the youngest members of the class. He says that in looking around at the faces of the inmates, he sees young men similar to the Marines he served with many years ago and feels a strong connection with them. He knows that some of them have been in wars themselves, wars much closer to home, wars in their own neighborhoods, so that there was no place for them to get away from combat: "They're on patrol every day. They're carrying weapons, preparing for violence every fucking day, and they may not realize the toll that can take even if you never get caught or you never get shot, just the toll of having to live like that all the time." He knows that when he speaks to them about the devastating effects of PTSD, there are inmates who know exactly what he's talking about, even though some of them might not have known before that the monster inside them spoiling their lives has a name. He believes in the "commonality of experience" of veterans of war and veterans of street violence, introducing the topic of PTSD in his poetry because

> when I talk about it in that setting, I always see lights go on around the circle, especially when I point out to them, look, I had to go to war to be shot. But if you haven't been shot, then you probably know people who have that got it right in their own neighborhood, and [I] try to make them understand what trauma can do to us and what it makes us do if we don't deal with it.
>
> Since seeing what PTSD has done in my life and in my buddies' lives, to be able to talk to people who maybe have never thought of that at all and whose lives may have been traumatized for as long as they can remember, just been packed with trauma. *Wait a minute*, somebody else

knows about this, and it can be identified, and there are ways to deal with this, that you can take its power away. So it's given me a wonderful soapbox. Not only do I have the privilege of reading my own work, it makes me feel that I'm able to use my work in other ways, even in a more positive way than just educating them about what it's like to live through a firefight. The personal cost of my violence on other people. And maybe there'll be something in a poem that will say, "Holy shit, I know what that's like." Or, "Shit, I never thought of it like that." It's just so much more than a poetry class.

John Musgrave believes that the class gives inmates a forum to record their thinking about things in a different way than they ever have before

because they're locked up and they're much more introspective because they've got no distractions, and this time they have to look at themselves, they have to look at their lives because they're in a fucking jam and how did I get in this jam, what am I going to do to get out of this jam, is this the life I want. . . . That class presents them with an option for being able to record those thoughts, being able to catalogue those thoughts, being able to organize those thoughts and communicate them to someone else if they want to, and if they don't they still have an option that I bet they've never had before. And just to be able to get it on paper. Like I said for me in those darkest years, just the fact that I could get something down on paper and push it away gave me some power, gave me some control of it. And every time I would read it, I would have a new perspective, a new thought.

The most important thing is, I'd captured it, I'd taken control of it, and these guys are having one of the heaviest, most personal thoughts that they've had in a long time, and they're not doing drugs so their mind's more clear, and it can form in their heads and disappear because you just can't keep all those thoughts in your head.

John Musgrave understands well that the inmates too are living through dark days, perhaps their "darkest days," but he believes poetry might be a tool for survival, as it was for him during his desperate postwar years when he wasn't sure if he could survive, when he had put his pistol to his head and wondered if he had the courage to pull the trigger. Poetry was for him an "extraordinary tool" that gave him his best chance of survival, a tool given out in the classroom week after week to men who need it:

But you're giving them an extraordinary tool. What a wonderful toolbox they walk out of that classroom with. With all these different tools of a way to get to know themselves and to present themselves to others.

A lot of people write things that they can't say. That's why lovers give poems to lovers because you're telling them something in a way that you could never say; that way you've found a way that sounds better. When you write it down, you sound better. And if you just try to say it, you might fumble with the words.

John Musgrave likes to think of himself as a sort of modern-day Johnny Appleseed as far as writing is concerned, spreading seeds all around in often fertile soil, never knowing, for the most part, how those seeds will sprout and grow. It doesn't trouble him that he seldom sits in the shade of a tree he has seeded or picks an apple from a branch. To scatter poetic seeds in the Douglas County Jail classroom—that's a great way for a modern-day Johnny Appleseed to spend two hours of a Thursday afternoon.

And how does it feel to get out of the jail after an intense, revelatory experience? According to Shannon Musgrave, "Yeah, it's almost like you wait until you get outside to really exhale. Take another deep breath in of free air."

All of us who emerge from the jail at 3:00 p.m. on Thursday afternoon feel exhilarated by what poetry in a dark, yet well-lit place can achieve. We celebrate with another deep breath of free air and look forward to Thursday afternoon next week, when there will be more important work to be done in a county jail classroom, when we will connect again with the powers of the written word.

## Chapter 15

# "Don't Carry Much with Me No More"

## The Songs of Troubadour Joe Parrish

Programs Director Mike Caron and I agreed that we'd dedicate *Douglas County Jail Blues* (2010) to troubadour Joe Parrish, not an inmate but, in our years working together at the jail, one of the top benefactors to and beneficiaries of the class. Parrish was a local musician who played at cafes and bars downtown, who, in the last months of his truncated life, found his true audience: inmates at Douglas County Jail. I don't think I've been to a better show than Joe Parrish Live at Douglas County Jail. I wish we'd been able to record it to produce our own local version of *Live at Folsom Prison*. Parrish played his signature song each time he performed at the jail—Steve Earle's "Billy Austin," a song of sympathy for the victims of crime but also for the criminal himself.

Inmates took one look at Parrish, listened to his music, and welcomed him to the jail as one of their own.

I first met Parrish at a coffee shop in Lawrence. He was with a poet friend of mine. Parrish was a scrawny guy who looked like he'd done a lot of Woody Guthrie–style rambling. Handsome face chiseled out of hardwood, with a trace of Native American in his high cheekbones ("a quarter Cherokee, I'm told"), dark eyes full of compassion, and on-the-road wisdom. If this guy was a software engineer, then I was Bill Gates. When my young daughter went to see him play at the Luna Café, she watched him sit on the floor, thrash out songs on his guitar, and "shake his head like a buffalo, *like a buffalo!*" In my poem "Blessings," written in 2004, I thanked Parrish (with a reference to David Bowie's "Young Americans") for playing not just one song "to make me break down and cry/but five or six or seven."

Parrish was easygoing, easy to like. He gigged a lot with local musicians, with former Kansas poet laureate Kevin Rabas in particular, who'd play drums while Parrish strummed, picked, and knocked on his big black guitar and sang. Rabas called Parrish "one of the kindest, gentlest souls I may ever know," a "thin, willowy" guy who didn't eat much but laughed a lot, and his laugh was "part cackle, part cough." According to Rabas, Parrish lived frugally, earning just about enough to live by stocking shelves at Dillon's supermarket, involving himself in the local music scene. Rabas describes their gigging: "We played dives. We played outdoor neo-hippie weekend gatherings. We played a barn. We played in people's houses. We played bars with peanut shells or sawdust on the floor. I played brushes on snare drum usually. Sometimes some hand drum, cajon, or djembe. Joe always wore a ratty ballcap and was often smoking, sometimes drinking."[1]

Parrish had done a lot of living and a lot of traveling; he'd even been in Iraq as an entertainer for the troops during Desert Storm. (I often thought that instead of sending in the US Army to defeat our enemies, we should send in American troubadours such as Parrish to win them over.) He'd written great songs about hard travelling, including his "anthem":

**Don't carry much with me no more**
I've got holes in my stomach
got big wings inside my heart
guess I'll just be stumbling on
don't carry much with me no more.

These lines became the epigraph of our jail anthology. A lot of inmates "stumbling on/don't carry much . . . no more."

Parrish's songs were about moving on, taking the train or hitchhiking, carrying his black guitar, and writing songs about it. Parrish was a lot of Guthrie—his guitar killed fascists too—a lot of Jack Kerouac, and chunks of John Townes Van Zandt and Earle (his two favorite songwriters by far). Parrish, who loved Townes Van Zandt in particular, could never quite put his finger on why his songs have something more than others written by the singer-songwriters of his time.[2] How the hell was Townes Van Zandt as good as he was? Parrish identified with him, the gifted musician who didn't quite know what to do with his gift and kept thinking up ways to ruin it that most always included a lot of alcohol and illicit substances—plus some wild rambling. That type of life always has some self-destruction in the mix.

Parrish spent his life drifting around, but as he was getting older and couldn't be so sure of his health, he wanted to settle down at last in Lawrence because he'd been blessed with the love of a good woman, and a man who's lived an itinerant life knows to make the most of blessings that come his way. Gigging with local musicians, Parrish played at coffee shops around Lawrence. Right away I loved his music, his passionate performances, and his choice of songs. When I got to know him and his music a bit better, I'd ask him to play at poetry readings I'd organize. Parrish wasn't going to be famous and end up on the cover of *Rolling Stone* with his double live album selling like crazy, but anyone who wanted their music raw, poetic, and from the heart just had to love what he was doing. No wonder it worked so well to bring him to Douglas County Jail: *raw, poetic, from the heart.* Johnny Cash was unavailable, but Parrish would come each time we asked.

I wanted him to record some songs and wondered if I could do it through the journal I edit, *Coal City Review,* so I gave him a few hundred dollars to go into a local studio to record. Eventually he came up with a CD of about fifteen songs: his own songs and those of Townes Van Zandt, Earle, Guy Clark, and Bruce Springsteen.

Caron and I invited Parrish to come to the jail writing class to play for inmates. His visit was *Live at Folsom Prison,* it was raw and beautiful, it was Parrish, nervous as hell, outside the jail quick-smoking a cigarette, tossing half of it away, stepping through the metal detector, opening his guitar case, no contraband or weapons, just his guitar and songs.

In the classroom, Parrish played his songs to a circle of about twenty inmates, the guys recognizing from the start that he was one of them, that he'd used himself hard but still had a lot left, that he didn't have much in the way of material things like other men of his age, but he did have his songs, and in this way he was living out a great American myth, the troubadour on the road with his music. As Cash would say, a poor man can be rich in music.

*My name is Billy Austin . . .*

Parrish sang Earle's "Billy Austin," about a poor guy who killed a clerk in a store robbery and knows he's done wrong but questions whether he should die for it. (Most all inmates question the severity of their own punishments. Some wits say that if you want to find the densest concentration of men who believe themselves innocent, then you should look inside a prison.) The inmates loved it because they knew he was putting it all on the line for them, knew that even without Parrish saying much, he *was* telling his story in the way he moved, in the songs he sang, and in the way he empathized with hard-luck sinners like Austin.

Parrish played Earle's "My Old Friend the Blues"; first time I'd heard it, and it was so tender-tough and hard won and defiant that I asked him to play it again, you know, like Cash plays his song "San Quentin" a second time and drives his convict audience crazy: "San Quentin, I hate every bit of you" . . .

At the end of Parrish's set, the inmates, Caron, and I applauded, and I remember Parrish, deeply moved, applauding us too, his clapping hands circling round us in a sort of blessing. Here was a man who'd spent a lot of time looking and found at last his audience, guys who *got* exactly what he was saying to them. Then Guitar Dave asked if he could play the guitar—he had earned money busking on Massachusetts Street—and bighearted Parrish passed him his guitar. Dave hunched over the guitar and sang "Knockin' on Heaven's Door."

Parrish came to class three or four times; we all looked forward to it. New guys in class got it right away, got it the first time he walked in, got it from the first note he played, got it from the first word he sang. "He's just like us. And he's fine with that."

We didn't realize how close Parrish was to the end of his road.

In June 2007, shortly after his last gig at the jail, I got a call from his girlfriend that Parrish was in the hospital, and shortly after that I heard that he'd died.

Caron spoke at the memorial service for Parrish, about how he'd given his heart and soul in his performances at the jail and how much the inmates had appreciated it. He'd lifted their spirits a few steps up the ladder, and whoever could do that was welcome.

I'm sure Parrish is still on the proverbial road with his guitar and bag of songs, a travelling man, paying for his food and drink with a song or two, sometimes going on a drunk with his two companions, Earle and Townes Van Zandt. As Rabas said, "Joe loved everyone, and talked with everyone. . . . He gave time. He emptied his pockets. He gave a smile and a handshake." He believed that we should all get along and was ready to step up to try to make things better. Rabas tells this story about him:

One time we had a conflict on the bandstand. Some new guys didn't like how we were playing the gig. We were all in it together, a kind of pick-up band for the night. When Randy stepped back on stage after break, his guitar was badly out of tune. Likely, someone had cranked all of the pegs hard, pretty much ruining the strings. Joe sat down between Randy and the other guys in the pick-up group and ate. No one was getting at anyone. They'd have to go over Joe.[3]

Sometimes I play that first track on his CD, "Billy Austin," and hear him again putting everything into it, his heart full of sympathy for poor Austin, who messes up and has to pay the price for it. Caron and I knew we'd done the right thing in dedicating *Douglas County Jail Blues* to Parrish. In so many ways it was appropriate because his songs captured the spirit of the class, "stumbling on" up the stony road after a few falls. He did something special for those of us who listened to his songs: our lives—and his—would have felt less without them. I can still hear him playing, still see him shaking his head like a buffalo, like a buffalo.

In class on June 22, 2007, shortly after Parrish's death, I wrote this poem for him.

### Travellin' Man

See you when I get there, Maestro.

—Steve Earle to Townes Van Zandt

You always said the highway was your home—

so off you go, Joe, down that highway,

not carrying much with you no more:

bag of songs, pack of cigarettes, and,

of course, your faithful black guitar.

You don't need to carry food—

you can play a few songs for a good meal.

You'll have some new tunes for me, I'm sure,

whenever I get to where you are,

in some honky-tonk or roadside diner,

in a workcamp by the river or striptease bar.

—Brian Daldorph

# Chapter 16
# "The Creativity Faucet Is Still On, and We Are All Drippin' Wet in Poetry!"
## Last Words (for Now)

February 2020, almost two decades after I first started teaching at the jail in December 2001. When I enter the classroom, I find on my desk a packet of seven poems by Shane Crady, one of the most prolific and talented jail class writers of recent years. I glance at the first poem, "The Replacements," and read this marvelous line that seems to sum up our hopes for the class today and into the future: "The creativity faucet is still on, and we are all drippin' wet in poetry!"[1] I'm at my desk, setting up class, when inmate KP bops in. I'd last seen him two years prior, when we had worked closely together on his writing for a few months. I wrote about KP at the end of Chapter 8: he stormed out of class one week because he believed I'd censored one of his poems, only to return the following week with a few new poems—and apologies. In the time in between, he'd realized how much he missed the class. I understand: I hate missing class too.

It's a surprise to see him back. I seem to remember him telling us he was *never* coming back, but I've heard that so many times, I can't quite remember if *he* said it. Anyway, he's back, very skinny, hyper, talking too much, telling us that on the outside he'd kept mainly to himself and worked on his writing and music. Looks like he'd gotten some chemical assistance for his artistic endeavors. He keeps asking me about the poems of his I'd accepted for the *Douglas County Jail Blues,* Volume 2. I explain to him that this anthology is still a work in progress, that I've been working on other things.

He's keen as ever to be a part of the class, breaks my concentration in the writing section by asking me a question about spelling, then proudly reads what he's written—a poem called "Come with Me and Stay Gold"—during Part 3 of the class, the reading section, the poem including the exhortation to "challenge yourself and challenge yourself often!/Challenge Human Authority, for nobody human is perfect." From what I know about him, KP has a long record of challenging "authority." He looks as pleased as any conscientious student when he's done reading his poem. After class, he gives me his mother's address so that I can send him the book when it comes out; he says that his mother's address is a permanent address, whereas he moves around a lot. He says he's been telling everyone about his poetry, how it will be published in a book.

KP's surprising return to class, and his energetic involvement in it, reminds me how important the class has been to inmates over the years—inmates in bad places in their lives, looking at days, weeks, months, or years of incarceration, finding in the bleak circumstances of incarceration something of value, a class that often draws out something good in themselves, something they are keen to hang on to and can return to with some excitement. It often raises their self-esteem and makes them hope for better things. They write, and they are *revivified.* They might even ask me to send a published copy of their poetry to their mothers.

I'm often asked why I have given so much time to jail teaching, over such a long period that I consider it my "shadow career." Most of all, there is the sheer pleasure of being in a dynamic class, with writers keen to tell their stories and listen to what others have to say. With the ever-changing inmate population at a county jail, I never know who will be in class or what good things will happen. Maybe there will be some brilliant new writer in class, like D'A, who came to class for the first time in February 2020, wrote diligently, and then read aloud his words—which thrilled us—read them with the sort of conviction that showed how much they meant to him:

> I'm so different from you
>
> Well I been down, don't get me wrong,
>
> tryna turn a beautiful disaster into a beautiful song
>
> I'm so different from you,
>
> dreams & prayers fill my heart,
>
> giving me hope so I don't tear apart
>
> I'm so different from you.

When D'A finished reading, one inmate in class had only one word for him: "Wow." Inmates need their hearts filled with dreams and prayers like this, need them urgently or else the walls might close in and crush them. The twenty minutes of free writing in class is their chance to get some of these dreams and prayers written down. Much easier to keep what's pinned down in words; much easier to share it with others.

As an instructor at Douglas County Jail for two decades, I have watched inmate writers such as Antonio Sanchez-Day develop week by week, from writers uncertain of their work and reluctant to share it to writers with increased self-confidence and augmented respect in the class because their work was well received. For some writers, this increase in personal and social standing has transferred to their time outside the jail, after reentry, when they were trying to reestablish themselves in society. Postrelease, Sanchez-Day has told us that when he's really struggling to hold his life together and trying to resist the temptations that brought him to near ruin when he was younger, his writing has pulled him through. I'm proud of being a mentor to this former inmate, who was prepared to put in the hard work of making a better life for himself and the people around him. He is now a poet with a first book of poetry, *Taking On Life* (Coal City Press, 2019); he has become an important voice on justice issues in the community and beyond, working with the Criminal Justice Coordinating Council in Lawrence. Sanchez-Day says that at the last council meeting, a judge was "picking his brain" about his experience of incarceration, keen to understand issues of incarceration from the other side. Sanchez-Day was able to enlighten him. The way he sees it, he is giving back and paying it forward.

Sanchez-Day's value to the class and to other inmates was evident in a recent class. Inmate B read his poem—"It's hard to write about dreams and prayers/because when I'm asleep my dreams feel so real,/then I wake up in my cell and I begin to pray"—then talked about his mental health issues. He said he'd been feeling like he's running out of time, running out of space, the jail walls closing in on him. On the outside, he can medicate himself with meth; on the inside, he's supposed to get medications through the jail system, though he's not sure they're giving him the right meds. He said he's been in jail for eight months and can't sleep, can't read anymore in his cell because he's done enough reading. He was angry at the jail administration "because I can't get a Tylenol even though I've got a pounding headache."

Sanchez-Day told B that he knows *all* about mental health issues and incarceration; he said he has "all the good stuff" as far as mental health is concerned: PTSD, bipolar disorder, anxiety. What *he* did when he was incarcerated to stop the walls from closing in was to write, and it's what he still does when he's in his apartment at the bottom of his rabbit hole and the phone weighs about two hundred pounds when he tries to pick it up to call someone who might help. He said he writes when he starts thinking "liquor store, nobody will ever know." Then he remembers that "thinking like that got me here." Listening closely, B nodded energetically. Sanchez-Day speaks with the authority of someone who has done a *lot* of time and thought about what it means and how to live better than that. B's poem and participation in the class led to his interaction with Sanchez-Day, whose own poetry enabled him to turn his life around. Now he wants to help others make the same hard journey of self-reclamation, perhaps to a seat on the Criminal Justice Coordinating Council in town, where a judge will ask him a question and listen closely to his answer.

Whereas Sanchez-Day's story is still being written, one story arc I can complete in this book is that of former inmate Gary Holmes. In class in February 2020, I found out from his nephew that Holmes, "Mayor of North Topeka," had died—one of the first writers I worked with in the program soon after I started in 2001. I remember meeting with him again in summer 2018 at a gritty McDonalds in Topeka when I was working on a chapter about him for this book. He died on August 2, 2019, about a year after I'd last met with him. I think of Holmes hobbling away from me toward his beat-up truck in that McDonalds parking lot. Didn't know that was the last time I'd see him—I was looking forward to giving him a published copy of this book. He told me that meeting up with me at McDonalds had inspired him to start writing again. I wonder if he ever got around to it. He was so proud of his three poems published in *Douglas County Jail Blues*. At McDonalds, Holmes had asked about the class and was pleased to hear that it was still happening, week after week, with inmates keen to write. Holmes knew words can help us to live and sometimes might even save our lives, and he was generous enough to appreciate that inmates still had the opportunity that had meant so much to him at a bad time in his life.

To end the longest short walk of this chapter, of this book, here are a few memories, tattooed on my mind, that will stay with me from my decades of *jail time* in the classroom at Douglas County Jail.

*I remember* an inmate crying as he read his poem about missing his mother and another inmate saying to him, "That's OK, I cry in my cell all the time." I told the class about Jimmy Santiago Baca raging at himself because he couldn't cry after he was told in prison that his father had died, recognizing that his failure to cry meant "life in prison had killed a part of me."[2] The inmate offering consolation in my writing class was trying to keep alive this vital part of his fellow inmate.

*I remember* Big Jae Wae, determined to put his criminal life behind him by serving his time, however long it took, then getting out to make a new start, wrapping his arm around the shoulders of a young, hotheaded inmate and explaining to him that getting angry will only make things harder for him—Wae knew that too well from his own experience, which included too many years of incarceration. He was keen to help a younger version of himself.

*I remember* Sanchez-Day reading to us, for the first time, his poem "Penitentiary Protocol," about what it's like to go to prison—like entering a jungle where you're watched by predators every dangerous step of the way:

When you arrive, read the sign: "Leave all hopes

and dreams behind." Forget all you have or had

in the free world; it no longer matters. It will only

distract you, and you'll become prey to the lions

in this jungle.

After he read this to us, I was so moved by it that I thought: "If this is the *only* poem that came out of my work at the jail, then all my time would have been well worth it." It's one of the best poems I've ever heard.

*I remember* two inmates who'd been provoking each other throughout the class suddenly standing, fists raised, ready to fight, and I stood up between them and said the first thing that came to mind: "Don't ruin this class! It's a good class for all of us!" They stood a moment or two longer, then sat down just as an officer burst in to check on the commotion.

*I remember* one of the two classes my father visited. He sat next to a burly inmate with spectacles repaired with duct tape who boasted to my father that the last time he was arrested it took the entire Lawrence Police Force to restrain him. He also claimed the distinction of being locked up, at one time or another, in every cell in the jail. Everyone knew this inmate as the nicest guy—until he started drinking. He took a liking to my father and described to him the complexities of the cases he was facing and their various stages of progress through the system. Let's just say that my father did not quite comprehend the intricacies of the US justice system as explained by this friendly inmate, but he appreciated the inmate's confidence in him.

*I remember* pausing in my writing in class one day to look around at the ring of inmate writers, heads down, focusing on their work, which for those minutes at least was vital to them, and thinking again of Eldridge Cleaver in his cell trying to save himself by writing, as he told us in *Soul on Ice:*

> That is why I started to write. To save myself. I realized that no one could save me but myself. The prison authorities were both uninterested and unable to help me. I had to seek out the truth and unravel the snarled web of my motivations. I had to find out who I am and what I want to be, what type of man I should be, and what I could do to become the best of which I was capable.[3]

*And I remember* one class that had gone particularly well, and the circle was buzzing with good energy because we'd heard one great poem after another. It was almost time to end when Wae took charge and, bright-eyed, looked around the group: "Has anyone got something else to read? Let's have one more. *One more!*" It was a week until the next class, and he wanted to get the most out of this one. Jason sifted through the papers on his desk and pulled out a sheet. "This one's called 'My Four Best Friends,'" he said with a smirk:

> I have four best friends who
> never do me wrong, they stay there
> and listen to me complain like a broken
> down country song. They never try to
> steal from me, they always keep it
> real with me, and even when they're quiet
> I know they're really feeling me. I've
> only known them for about 2 months,
> but I trust them and they trust me,
> so I think that's enough. They chill
> with me when I wake up, and they
> chill with me before I go to sleep.
> I see them when I lay down and
> even when I'm brushing my teeth.

These are my four friends that I
really want you to meet. They are
my wall, my door, my toilet, and
my floor.

Jason's poem gave us a good laugh even though it's based on the grim reality
of incarceration. If it helped an inmate in the class to get through a tough
afternoon, then the class was a success. It might have helped to disperse a
few black clouds of depression. Instead of staying in his cell and napping
or watching TV in the pod or playing cards or working on a jigsaw puzzle,
Jason had done something more: he'd come out of his cell, joined the class,
and written a poem that meant a lot to others, suggesting that instead of
succumbing to despair it's possible to work at self-improvement, at making
our lives better.

I hope for more years of writing class at Douglas County Jail, where po-
etic thoughts breach cell walls and imagination "knows no cinder blocks."
How else to spend two or three hours every Thursday afternoon of the year?
What could possibly be worth more?

### Jail classroom

Five windows the size of open books,
metal spine down the middle.
In each window after class
an inmate in orange pants, black T-shirt
gazing out at the parking lot,
at blacktop freedom.

> —Brian Daldorph

# Epilogue

I have always said that as long as I'm in town, the jail's still standing, and we have inmates signed up for class, then I will drive out to Douglas County Jail on Thursday afternoons for class. I never considered the possibility of a pandemic.

The year 2020 began with news stories of an outbreak of something like pneumonia in the Chinese city of Wuhan, a place unknown to most of us in the United States. As the weeks went by, these stories multiplied as the number of cases rose, and the dire predictions of public health officials began to be heard through the noise of our lives: something very bad was coming our way—it was just a question of *when* it would come.

On March 12, 2020, in the last jail writing class before the lockdown, Programs Director Sherry Gill wrote a poem about the pandemic.

## 2020

### Covid-19

From the bats across the world

to Kansas, you have made your mark.

You remind us of our mortality

and how frail we humans really are.

Countries and nations unprepared

for your dissemination of particles

in our atmosphere. Hospitals overrun

with sick and dying patients.

Soon it will be here to bend us

into submission.

—Sherry Gill

Prisons and jails have become Covid-19 hot spots in the United States and elsewhere. It's almost impossible to contain a virus outbreak in crowded correctional facilities, with inmates inside most of the time, with very little possibility for social distancing, and with difficulties in establishing other public health measures to contain the spread.

Douglas County Jail, like other jails across the country, quickly introduced safety measures to try to contain the spread of the virus, and one measure was, of course, to prohibit all but essential outsiders coming into the jail. All programs at the jail have been suspended for the foreseeable future.

In November 2020, Kansas exceeded 100,000 Covid-19 cases, with more than 1,000 deaths, as this state along with most all others struggle to deal with a fall spike. According to a front-page report in the *Lawrence Journal-World* on July 18, 2020, "The Kansas Department of Corrections said it is taking precautions against what seems to be an inevitable increase behind bars, keeping restrictions on family visits and continuing to encourage hand-washing and mask-wearing among inmates and staff. 'Increased numbers in communities have us pretty concerned right now,' said Randy Bowman, executive director of public affairs at the Kansas Department of Corrections." The Kansas state penitentiary in Lansing had seen more than 1,000 cases of Covid-19 among staff and inmates by November 2020. Testing at the prison showed that about half of the inmates were positive, with most cases asymptomatic.

On July 25, 2020, the *Lawrence Journal-World* ran the article "Douglas County Jail: Still No Covid-19 cases," in which Jenn Hethcoat, public information officer for the Douglas County Sheriff's Office, reported that there had been no positive Coronavirus cases at the jail among inmates and employees. The jail has been quarantining all inmates for seventy-two hours after they entered or reentered the facility. Inmates have been provided with masks, though they're not required to wear them unless they are in quarantine.

I'm writing this in November 2020. It's almost certain, according to Programs Director Sherry Gill, that the jail will be closed to volunteers for the remainder of this year, and no one really knows what's beyond that because much will depend on the path of the virus. Will it begin to retreat? Will we get it sufficiently under control? Will there be a successful vaccine?

It has been a dry season for Douglas County Jail writing class.

But one Thursday afternoon in the not-too-distant future, we will be back in the classroom, inmates and instructors sitting at desks in a loose circle, heads bowed in prayer to our muses, hands twitching, the creativity faucet turned back on, our pages drippin' wet with new poetry.

# Appendix A.
# Reflections from Former Writing Class Volunteers, Douglas County Jail

**Ryan McCarty, August 2017**

More than ten years out, it's hard for me to really remember writing class. I'm sitting, shoes off and my cuffs rolled way up, watching my kids running through the sprinkler. There's a copy of John Steinbeck's *Cannery Row* on the step next to me, and thinking about Douglas County is like Doc says— it's not too easy to tell somebody the truth about what you're doing and why you're doing it. If you just like wearing a beard, you have to say you have a scar to cover up, or if you're walking across America from one end to the other just to see it, you have to tell people you were doing it on a bet. The jail class was like that. I remember there was this other graduate student who found out I had been spending a couple hours in the writing class every week, and he got excited.

"You could really do something with that—some captivity narrative Leonard Peltier kind of stuff."

I nodded like an idiot, probably. Of course I was trying to score a publication or some research or some standout line on my list of experiences. What else could I have been there for?

But when I think back on why I went out to class, I just keep thinking about lemonade. Before one class I was talking to a guy, and he noticed the warped cover on my notebook where a sweaty glass had been sitting a few days back. I felt bad, like I had brought in some kind of proof that summer afternoons still existed outside. Like the time I had wiped the orange *Dorito* residue on my pantlegs, and the hungriest kid, with no money on his books for commissary, told me I was killing him. Like the times I came in with a little sunburn, and one of the guys noticed.

"You know how lemonade can be in the summer."

What a weird thing for me to say.

"Not in here."

I said something about them not getting lemonade, how that was messed up; at least they should get some of that bullshit powdered Country Time or something like that.

"Drinks don't leave rings like that here. They got no soul."

What the hell do you do with that? You don't frame a theory of human experience around it. It's not even a good blues lyric, like Joe Parrish said when I told him the story on the way out of class one day. He laughed, though neither of us thought it was a little bit funny. The couple of classes Parrish came to run together for me, but I've convinced myself that was the last time I talked to him, with me passing on two of the most serious sentences I've heard.

But that was exactly why I caught a ride with Brian Daldorph every Thursday for a couple years and headed east on K-10 to sit in a room with this bunch of writers. Because I never met anyone else who could notice whether or not a drink had lost its soul, or at least if they had, they'd never admitted it to me. These guys told the truth about things, even when they were lying their asses off. Maybe especially when they were lying their asses off.

Ryan McCarty lives in Ypsilanti, Michigan, where he teaches college writing and adult English as a Second Language classes. He was a regular participant in the jail class from 2004 to 2007, and he hasn't been the same since.

## Limitations: Matthew Porubsky, August 2018

Being confronted by the truth and the reality of actions when inside a jail is inescapable. There is nothing to soften or absorb. Voices in all places are magnified by concrete and metal. Starkness reflects in everything: the clothes, the floor, the walls. Everything bounces back. No matter what demeanor or attitude prisoners affix to themselves, no matter what positive or negative mental energy they stay attuned or addicted to, there's inevitably an instant of self-realization, self-reflection, and admittance of the circumstances that have brought them to their current state. It took me almost two years of volunteering at Douglas County Jail before I had my great moment of realization, and I have never returned since then.

I felt alone inside the jail from the start. I didn't feel the camaraderie I sometimes feel at a dive bar or a greasy spoon. I didn't feel a connection or understanding that I experience at most poetry readings. There is absolutely no sense of the natural world, and all the men in the classroom, myself included, were like a gathering of leftover nails and screws at the bottom of a toolbox. But over time, their voices began to converge.

Singular inmates don't live in my memory as much as the group voice that was demonstrated. As different as they all were, all of the random pieces fit together to arrange a device that could pump out the purest of emotions. These emotions were of intense strain and love and desperation, like most poetry, but with an unbridled vitality. There was no fear of a peer's reaction, no caution of how the audience or editor would receive the work. It was the pit of the tastiest fruit.

Each one of the inmates would shrug off the reading of his poem like it was nothing. Like it wasn't an echo of something burned inside him that he was putting on display. Each one of them was becoming more transparent with each poem, illustrating the access to reams of reality bound by this incarceration. It was a blurry, see-through quality. They were being revealed.

They would line up at the end of class and hand over their pencils, one by one, to be counted and recounted. It was like their insides were in sight. The guts of how things work were on display. I realized how much a prisoner is left to be occupied by clear thoughts. Clear from certain worldly distractions: less drugs and alcohol, the opportunity for regular medications and meals, the overwhelming time of solitude leading to extended moments to simply think and remember. Their capacity for memory became enormous and specific.

Memories bounced around inside the jail and were reflected in their poems. Positive returns in time like eating hotdogs on a beach with sand clinging to skin, childhood bike rides in the old neighborhood, fishing the creek with family. Nurturing memories full of sustenance. Moments that could keep them going on long nights. There were various negative revisits. Spliced mistakes creating explanations and excuses, grandiose played out "what ifs" that turned guilt and grief into a braid of blame and hope. But hope always came, whether responsibility was accepted or not. It was the clarity of the current consequences. Delicate and explorative lines that crept out of the intimidation culture of suggested aggression. All this in a kind of group therapy session of poetry. Each poem shared became an entry point. It was more intimate than a poetry workshop or reading. Their relationship with what was written and read begged the listener for empathy and understanding. There was no business. It was all personal.

The last day I visited the poetry class, these entry points gave me a glimpse that I never paid attention to before. Maybe I had never wanted to until then, or I had just pushed the thoughts away so I could participate with this class the way that I felt I needed to. But that last day, as they handed in their pencils and waited for permission to exit and walk the hallway back to their pods and cells, I asked myself the question that many would have asked the first time they entered a classroom full of inmates: *What had these people done to be here?*

I sat in the parking lot of the jail unable to shake the thoughts. For the past two years, I had been sharing one of the most important aspects of my life with a group of men who were in jail for a reason. I kept saying that to myself: for a reason, for a reason. My thoughts became obsessions; obsessions became fantasies. I had admired them for their honesty and reality, their willingness to accept poetry, their attentiveness and curiosity about the craft in class; but in my mind, minute by minute, these men became the worst of the worst.

I know there are aspects of the criminal justice system that are fractured and broken. I know that a number of those in the class had been in jail for nonviolent offenses and for breaking laws that hurt no one but themselves. That wasn't the case for all of them. The thought of willingly sharing my passion with an inmate who hurt another person or persons in a way that required this type of punishment made me feel anxious and ill. I wasn't going to see them as writers anymore. I was only going to see the crimes I imagined for them on their faces and in their writings. Whether what I created in my mind was near or far from the true crimes they had originally committed didn't matter. I didn't want to know. I wasn't judging them, but, at that moment, I knew that participating in the poetry project at the jail wasn't for me.

I never went back. Those dark thoughts got the best of me. Or those thoughts found a home in me. Nevertheless, my time volunteering at the Douglas County Jail lives in my memory as something good and beneficial, something that I am proud of and I am glad that others have the strength to continue. I think about my reasons, and I'm still torn. I wish I were strong enough in spirit not to think about the hows and whys of their incarceration and think more about the reasons and ways to help them strive toward positivity. Those feelings are paralleled by the idea of someone paying for their deeds in the truest sense of punishment, the absence of the goodness and peace they have taken from others. Then I think, in all honesty, could I have been a few mistakes away from where those inmates were? Could I have been in the same place had I been less fortunate or less lucky with the ways I broke the law? Maybe it was the overwhelming humanity on display that keeps me from returning. I do realize that the only thing that keeps me from participating again is myself.

My family and my creativity are my religion. I can't imagine that is any different than many of the men I shared poetry with in the jail. The hymns and prayers of that religion are poetry. All are allowed to sing. In the case of the Douglas County Jail, I was unable to continue to help others share their voices in something that connects us all.

But still they sing, and they certainly deserve to be heard.

Matthew Porubsky is from Topeka, Kansas. He works for the Union Pacific Railroad and is the author of four collections of poetry, including *Ruled by Pluto* and *John*. He is currently busy with three children and researches the manipulation of vibrations, communication, and Iranian history.

# Appendix B. PERMISSION FORM
# Douglas County Correctional Facility:
# Poetry Anthology

I, [poet], consent to allowing first-time use of my poem(s), titled [poem]

for inclusion in an anthology of poetry from Douglas County Correctional Facility, or in other publications edited by Brian Daldorph and Michael Caron. I verify that my poem(s) was (were) inspired or created in response to class at the Douglas County Jail. If a publication goes into subsequent editions, I grant use in all subsequent editions, so long as I am identified as the author by name or pseudonym. The poem may also be used in materials used to publicize this anthology, on the condition that my name (or pseudonym) be included to identify me as author of this work.

I permit the editors to make minor editorial changes to my work.

I retain the right to submit my poem(s) to literary magazines and use it on my own website or in whatever way I deem appropriate, but I agree to mention that it appears in a Douglas County Correctional Facility publication in any subsequent use.

If, prior to publication, I would like to withdraw my poem(s) from the anthology, I will contact editors Michael Caron (at Douglas County Jail) or Brian Daldorph (at the University of Kansas).

Payment for my poem(s) will be in copies of the anthology only.

---

Signature of Author

---

Pseudonym (if applicable)

---

Name of Author

---

Address of Author

---

Date

_____

Signature of Editor                              Date

I agree to editors using my real name in the anthology:

_____

I would like the editors to use my pseudonym in the anthology:

_____

# Notes

## Preface

1. Michael Tonry, *Thinking about Crime: Sense and Sensibility in American Penal Culture* (New York: Oxford University Press, 2004), vii.

## 1. "Imagination Knows No Cinder Blocks": Education Inside the Walls

1. "Mass Incarceration Costs $182 Billion Every Year," *Equal Justice Initiative*, February 6, 2017.

2. "Correctional Populations in the United States, 2013," US Bureau of Justice Statistics, December 2013.

3. In *The New Jim Crow: Mass Incarceration in the Age of Colorblindness* (New York: New Press, 2011), Michelle Alexander traces the explosion of the prison population in the United States beginning with the "war on drugs" launched by President Ronald Reagan in 1982. She argues that Reagan used the emergence of crack cocaine in US cities in 1985 to support his campaign. She shows that the campaign was waged primarily in poor and minority communities, even though statistics show that people of color use and sell drugs at approximately the same rate as the White population. In the thirty years after the war on drugs was launched, the US prison population grew from 300,000 to more than 2 million, with drug convictions accounting for the majority of the increase. The United States now has the highest incarceration rate in the world, higher than the repressive regimes of China, Iran, and Russia.

4. Jimmy Santiago Baca, *Undoing Time: American Prisoners in Their Own Words* (Boston: Northeastern University Press, 2001), xi.

5. Baca, *Undoing Time,* xi.

6. Baca, xii.

7. Rebecca Vallas, "Disabled Behind Bars," Center for American Progress website, July 18, 2016.

8. "Disabilities among Prison and Jail Inmates, 2011–2012," Bureau of Justice Statistics, https://www.ojp.gov/.

9. The first prison education in the United States was religious instruction in the early nineteenth century; from this, secular prison programs were developed to help inmates read the bible and religious texts. The first major educational program aimed at *rehabilitating* prisoners was launched in 1876 by Zebulon Brockway, superintendent of Elmira Reformatory in New York. By the 1930s, educational programs were established in most US prisons, with courses ranging from basic literacy classes and high school equivalency programs to vocational education and tertiary education. Arts and crafts, including creative writing programs, developed.

10. Patrick Alexander, *From Slave Ship to Supermax: Mass Incarceration, Prisoner Abuse, and the New Neo-Slave Novel* (Philadelphia, PA: Temple University Press, 2018), 30.

11. "Education and Vocational Training in Prisons Reduces Recidivism, Improves Job Outlook," RAND Corporation, August 22, 2013, https://www.rand.org/news/press /2013/08/22.html.

12. Anna Neill, interview with the author, June 2017.

13. Alexander, *From Slave Ship to Supermax*, 16.

14. Alexander, 19.

15. Eldridge Cleaver, *Soul on Ice* (San Francisco: Ramparts, 198), 20.

16. Ken Lamberton, *Wilderness and Razor Wire: A Naturalist's Observations from Prison* (San Francisco: Mercury House, 2000), 33–34.

## 2. "What Truly Matters": Teaching Creative Writing at Douglas County Jail, Lawrence, Kansas

1. Helen Prejean, "Foreword," *Doing Time: 25 Years of Prison Writing* (New York: Arcade, 1999), xi.

2. Prejean, "Foreword," xi.

3. Eldridge Cleaver, *Soul on Ice* (San Francisco: Ramparts, 1968), 15.

4. Jimmy Santiago Baca, *A Place to Stand: The Making of a Poet* (New York: Grove, 2001), 99–100.

5. Baca, *A Place to Stand*, 99.

6. Ken Lamberton, *Wilderness and Razor Wire: A Naturalist's Observations from Prison* (San Francisco: Mercury House, 2000), 101.

7. Michael Caron, interview with the author, July 2018.

8. Caron, interview with the author, July 2018.

9. Brian Daldorph, "'What Truly Matters': Nine Years of Teaching a Creative Writing Class at Douglas County Jail, Lawrence, Kansas," *J Journal* 3, no. 1 (2010): 33–45.

10. In 2017, the jail administration gave permission to one of our best writers, Antonio Sanchez-Day, to return to class as a coinstructor. It's a wonderful tribute to the power of writing that Sanchez-Day was able to transform his life from that of an inmate facing a lot of time to a well-respected coleader of the class. But as we know, "Words is a powerful thing" and might even be transformational in positive ways.

## 3. "Sing Soft, Sing Loud": The Literature of US Jails and Prisons

1. Aleksandr Solzhenitsyn, *One Day in the Life of Ivan Denisovich*, trans. H. T. Willetts (New York: Farrar, Straus & Giroux, 1991), 133.

2. Solzhenitsyn, *One Day in the Life of Ivan Denisovich*, 20.

3. Jimmy Santiago Baca, *Working in the Dark: Reflections of a Poet of the Barrio* (Santa Fe, NM: Red Crane, 1992), 7.

4. Baca, *Working in the Dark*, 7.

5. Jimmy Santiago Baca, *A Place to Stand: The Making of a Poet* (New York: Grove, 1991), 1.

6. Baca, *A Place to Stand*, 5.

7. Baca, 109.

8. Baca, 188.

9. Baca, 257.

10. Baca, *Working in the Dark*, 10.

11. Eldridge Cleaver, *Soul on Ice* (San Francisco: Ramparts, 1968), 45.

12. Joseph Bruchac, ed., *The Light from Another Country: Poetry from American Prisons* (New York: Greenfield, 1984), viii.

13. Bruchac, *Light from Another Country*, 234.

14. Bruchac, 235.

15. Bruchac, xiii.

16. Bruchac, xvii.

17. Bruchac, 26.

18. Bruchac, 32.

19. Bruchac, 35.

20. Bruchac, 50.

21. Bruchac, 94.

22. Bruchac, 257–258.

23. H. Bruce Franklin, ed., *Prison Writing in 20th-Century America* (New York: Penguin, 1998), xii.

24. Franklin, *Prison Writing in 20th-Century America*, 1.

25. Franklin, 12.

26. Franklin, 15.

27. Franklin, 17.

28. Franklin, 199.

29. Franklin, 230.

30. Franklin, 297.

31. Edward Bunker, *The Education of a Felon* (New York: St. Martin's, 2000), 92.

32. Bunker, *Education of a Felon*, 120.

33. Bunker, 115.

34. Bunker, 131.

35. Bunker, 207.

36. Bunker, 215.

37. Bunker, 239.

38. Bunker, 256.

39. Ken Lamberton, *Wilderness and Razor Wire: A Naturalist's Observations from Prison* (San Francisco: Mercury House, 2000), 123.

40. Lamberton, *Wilderness and Razor Wire*, 177.

41. Richard Shelton, *Crossing the Yard: Thirty Years as a Prison Volunteer* (Tucson: University of Arizona Press, 2007), 40.

42. Shelton, *Crossing the Yard*, 9.

43. Judith Tannenbaum, *Disguised as a Poem: My Years Teaching at San Quentin* (Boston: Northeastern University Press, 2000), x.

44. Tannenbaum, *Disguised as a Poem*, xi.

45. Tannenbaum, xi.

46. Tannenbaum, xii.

47. Tannenbaum, 8.

48. Tannenbaum, 19.

49. Tannenbaum, 63.

50. Tannenbaum, 69.

51. Tannenbaum, 199.

52. Alexander draws on Michael Tonry's *Thinking about Crime: Sense and Sensibility in American Penal Culture* (New York: Oxford University Press, 2004), in which Tonry states in the preface that the United States has a punishment system that "no one would knowingly have built from the ground up." He calls it unjust, unduly severe, and wasteful and claims that it does enormous damage to the lives of Black Americans. According to Tonry, imprisonment rates in the United States are five times higher than in other Western countries and seven to twelve times higher than in most. Tonry explores why the US "punishment system" developed into its present state, laying much of the blame at the feet of politicians who saw political advantage in "tough-on-crime" policies even though these policies had disastrous consequences, especially for minority communities.

Alexander also builds on Katherine Beckett's *The Politics of Injustice: Crime and Punishment in America* (Thousand Oaks, CA: Sage, 2004), in which Beckett claims that in response to the civil rights movement and war on poverty programs of the 1960s, conservative politicians highlighted problems of "street crime" caused by what they argued were lenient welfare and justice systems. According to Beckett, "By emphasizing the severity and pervasiveness of 'street crime' and framing the problem in terms of immoral individuals rather than criminogenic (crime-causing) social conditions, these politicians effectively redefined the poor—especially the minority poor—as dangerous and undeserving" (8). Policies proposed and implemented by these politicians emphasized social control rather than social welfare and led to many devastating troubles in the Black community in particular, the focus of Alexander's *The New Jim Crow: Mass Incarceration in the Age of Colorblindness* (New York: New Press, 2011).

53. Alexander, *New Jim Crow*, 2.

54. Alexander, 156.

55. Cleaver, *Soul on Ice*, 15.

56. Cleaver, 15.


## 4. No "Snitches," No "N-Word": Rules of the Class

1. Michael Caron, interview with the author, July 2018.

2. Caron, interview with the author, July 2018.

3. In "Straight Talk about the N-word," on the Teaching Tolerance website, sponsored by the Southern Poverty Law Center, Neal A. Lester claims that the N-word is unique in the English language as the "ultimate insult" used against African Americans but also in recent times used as a term of endearment in Black and some White communities. Lester, dean of humanities at Arizona State University and designer and instructor of the first college-level class exploring the N-word, says that the word evolved from "Negro" in the seventeenth century and was intentionally derogatory. According to Lester, the word has never "shed that baggage" since then, "even when Black people talk about appropriating and reappropriating it. The poison is still there." Lester believes no amount of appropriation can rid the word of its "blood-soaked history." Lester claims that in the use of the word there's a double standard: Blacks can say the word without social consequences,

but Whites cannot. When the word is used in private circumstances, its meaning can be controlled to a great extent, but when it's used in public contexts, the word takes on additional levels of meaning (as we have seen in the Douglas County Jail classroom). Lester argues that some White students in his class were perfectly comfortable with using the word because of their connection to hip-hop: "Much of the commercial hip-hop culture by Black males uses the N-word as a staple." But Black students are often offended by White students using the word, "so this word comes laden with these complicated and contradictory emotional responses to it." In the writing class at Douglas County Jail, Mike Caron and I decided we did not want to try to negotiate these difficulties and therefore banned it. It seemed best in this instance to restrict poets' range of expression in order to lessen the likelihood of tensions in class. In teaching his course on the N-word, Lester is more interested in asking questions than finding easy answers, hoping that the issues raised in his class will lead all students to self-discovery. His description of what he hopes for the class is nicely similar to what we hope the Douglas County Jail class will achieve: "The class strives to teach us all manner of ways to talk about, think about, and to understand ourselves and each other, and why and how we fit in the rest of the world."

4. Jimmy Santiago Baca, *A Place to Stand: The Making of a Poet* (New York: Grove, 2001), 107.

5. Caron, interview with the author, July 2018.

6. Jay-Z, interview with Terri Gross, *Fresh Air*, National Public Radio, November 16, 2010.

7. In writing about gangsta culture in *The New Jim Crow*, Michelle Alexander argues that it is a manifestation of the common occurrence of stigmatized people embracing their stigma. Gangsta rappers embrace the stigma of criminality, attempting to carve out a positive identity. Though she understands why this occurs, she despairs at the celebration of the violence associated with the illegal drug trade: "Black crime cripples the Black community and does no favors to the individual offenders" (172). She claims that rap music tended to be more positive when it started in the 1970s. She argues that it was changed by Ronald Reagan's war on drugs, when young Black men were swept off the streets into prison and began to "embrace their stigma" (174).

8. Caron, interview with the author, July 2018.

## 5. "Self-Expression, Self-Destruction": Creative Writing Class, May 18, 2017

1. Patrick Alexander, *From Slave Ship to Supermax: Mass Incarceration, Prisoner Abuse, and the Neo-Slave Novel* (Philadelphia, PA: Temple University Press, 2018), 92.

2. Johnny Cash, *Hurt*, directed by Mark Romanek, 2003, DVD.

## 6. "In This Circle of Ink and Blood/We Are for Awhile, Brothers": A Poem a Year—Inmate Poetry 2001–2017

1. Ken Lamberton, *Wilderness and Razor Wire: A Naturalist's Observations from Prison* (San Francisco: Mercury House, 2000), 48.

2. Lamberton, *Wilderness and Razor Wire*, 48–49.

3. Judith Tannenbaum, *Disguised as a Poem: My Years Teaching Poetry at San Quentin* (Boston: Northeastern University Press, 2000), 146–161.

4. National Public Radio, *The Two-Way: Breaking News from NPR*, December 7, 2015.

5. Lamberton, *Wilderness and Razor Wire*, 93.

## 7. "My Name Is Methamphetamine": *Douglas County Jail Blues*, Volumes 1 and 2

1. Jimmy Santiago Baca, *Working in the Dark: Reflections of a Poet of the Barrio* (Santa Fe, NM: Red Crane, 1992), 7.

## 8. "[The] Automatic Connection Between Inmates in Class and Mr. Cash": Johnny Cash's *Hurt*

1. Johnny Cash, *Hurt*, directed by Mark Romanek, 2003, DVD.

2. Michael Caron, interview with the author, July 2018.

3. Sherry Gill, interview with the author, July 2018.

4. Antonio Sanchez-Day, interview with the author, April 2019.

5. Johnny Cash, *Cash: The Autobiography* (San Francisco: HarperCollins, 1997), 23.

6. Robert Hilburn, *Johnny Cash: The Life* (New York: Little, Brown, 2013), 17.

7. Cash, *Cash*, 27.

8. Hilburn, *Johnny Cash*, 20.

9. Hilburn, 277.

10. Cash, *Cash*, 255.

11. Cash, 200.

12. Cash, 200.

13. In his autobiography, *Cash*, Cash answers the question he was asked all the time: Why were you in prison?

> I never was. That idea got started because I wrote and sang "Folsom Prison Blues," my 1955 hit, from the perspective of a convicted, unrepentant killer, and twelve years later I made a concert album, *Johnny Cash at Folsom Prison*. In fact, I've never served any time at all in any correctional institution anywhere. During my amphetamine years I spent a few nights in jail, but strictly on an overnight basis: seven incidents in all, different dates in different places where the local law decided we'd all be better off if I were under lock and key. Those weren't very educational experiences, but I do remember learning in Starkville, Mississippi, that trying to kick the bars out of a jail cell isn't a good idea. I broke my toe that night. (56–57)

14. Hilburn, *Johnny Cash*, 633.

15. Hilburn, 549.

16. Hilburn, 550.

17. Hilburn, 603.

18. Hilburn, 601.

19. Hilburn, 602.

20. Hilburn, 603.

21. Jesse James, "Tired and Can't Change," in *Douglas County Jail Blues*, 48.

22. Cash writes in detail about crawling into Nickajack Cave in *Cash*, 169–172. Cash had intended to die in the cave but then felt as though his destiny was in God's hands, not his own, and it was not his time to die. He describes crawling out of the cave to be met by June and his mother, with June telling him: "I knew there was something wrong. . . . I had to come and find you" (171). Cash ends the section: "As we drove back towards Nashville, I told my mother that God had saved me from killing myself. I told her I was ready to commit myself to Him and do whatever it took to get off drugs. I wasn't lying" (172).

23. Hilburn, *Johnny Cash*, 124.

24. Cash, *Cash*, 176.

25. Sanchez-Day, interview with the author, April 2019.

26. Sanchez-Day, interview with the author, April 2019.

27. Sanchez-Day, interview with the author, April 2019.

28. Hilburn, *Johnny Cash*, 175.

29. Gill, interview with the author, July 2018.


## 9. Maine Man: Mike Caron, Programs Director, Douglas County Jail (2001–2015)

1. *Deaths and Entrances* (London: Dent, 1946) is probably Dylan Thomas's best-known collection of poetry. It contains many poems subsequently anthologized.

2. Michael Caron, interview with the author, July 2018. Subsequent quotes are based on this interview.

3. Recondo school is a US military term (from RECONnaissance and commanDO) for highly specialized infantry training or a graduate of a Recondo school who leads small, heavily armed, long-range reconnaissance teams deep into enemy-held territory.

4. Brian Daldorph, "Snake House."


### Snake House

Their new house was all they'd dreamed about.

A bit more than they'd wanted to pay

but they stretched their money and paid

the deposit and first month's payment.

"This is the house I want to live in forever,"

she said and her husband agreed:

"It's our dream house!"

When they found a snake in the basement

he said they shouldn't be alarmed:

the house was out in the country.

"These things happen," he said.

Then there were snakes in the kitchen,
a snake in the laundry, snakes
under the couch, snakes in the heating vents,
snakes in the playroom with their children's toys,
snakes in the garage, snakes in the yard
and once the exterminators had flushed them out
in a few days they were back again.

Snakes in her dreams, snakes in her hair,
snakes in her bed, her legs turning into snakes,
snakes spitting at her, flicking their tongues.

When they moved out, no one moved in,
apart from the snakes, a whole house of snakes,
a writhing twisting house of snakes.

   —Brian Daldorph
(Written in class at Douglas County Jail, December 8, 2011, inspired by snake-catcher Mike Caron)

## 10. "It Don't Get More Real Than That": The Poetry of Antonio Sanchez-Day

1. Katherine Dinsdale, "Taking on Life," *Lawrence Magazine* (Winter 2016): 73–85.

2. Jimmy Santiago Baca, *A Place to Stand: The Making of a Poet* (New York: Grove, 2001), 33.

3. Ken Lamberton, *Wilderness and Razor Wire: A Naturalist's Observations from Prison* (San Francisco: Mercury House, 2000), 185.

4. Antonio Sanchez-Day, interview with the author, June 2017. Subsequent quotes are based on this interview.

5. Langston Hughes, "The Negro Speaks of Rivers," in *The Collected Poems of Langston Hughes*, ed. Arnold Rampersad (New York: Vintage, 1994).

## 11. "Mainly I Just Want to Help People Because No One Helped Me": Sherry Gill, Programs Director, Douglas County Jail (2015–)

1. Sherry Gill, interview with author, July 2018. Subsequent quotes are from this interview.

## 12. "I Done Good and I Done Bad": Topeka's Bad Man from the Badlands, Gary Holmes

1. Gary Holmes, interview with author, June 2018. Subsequent quotes are from this interview.

### 13. "It Really Is a Form of Counseling, in a Sense": Mike Hartnett

1. Michael Hartnett, interview with the author, September 2017. Subsequent quotes are from this interview.

2. Michael Hartnett, *And I Cried Too: Confronting Evil in a Small Town* (Emporia, KS: Meadowlark, 2019).

### 14. "It's Just So Much More Than a Poetry Class": Visitors

1. Katherine Dinsdale, interview with author, April 2019. Subsequent quotes are from this interview.

2. Shannon Musgrave, interview with author, March 2019. Subsequent quotes are from this interview.

3. Ronda Miller, interview with author, March 2019. Subsequent quotes are from this interview.

4. John Musgrave, interview with author, March 2019. Subsequent quotes are from this interview.

### 15. "Don't Carry Much with Me No More": The Songs of Troubadour Joe Parrish

1. Kevin Rabas, letter to the author, November 20, 2019.

2. More than a decade after Joe Parrish's death in 2007, I watched a video of John Townes Van Zandt singing with Nancy Griffith on *American Music Shop* one of his most famous songs, "Tecumseh Valley." My memory played a strange trick on me: it was like I was seeing Parrish again as I watched Townes Van Zandt: his shy shuffle onto stage, his awkwardness, his wiry body, his wary expression, even his gaudy shirt—and when he started singing, that was him too, not much of a singer but giving every little bit of himself to it: "The name she gave was Caroline, daughter of a miner." I'm certain Parrish would not mind at all my confusion.

3. Rabas, letter to the author, November 20, 2019.

### 16. "The Creativity Faucet Is Still On, and We Are All Drippin' Wet in Poetry!": Last Words (for Now)

1. Included with the packet of seven poems by Shane Crady, there's an official form, "Inmate Request for Services/Communications," directed to Programs Director Sherry Gill. Crady was in the work-release pod, going out to a job in town, so he couldn't always come to class. His note said, "Please send me the weekly writing sheet, I'd love to read what's being wrote. hope these are injoyed." Poem titles included, "Such Is life," "Shadows & Dust," "Drippin' Wet," and "The Replacements":

> **The Replacements**
> The Replacements come in
> First one then another
> Some wear this uniform as I do

Some wear the other
Some walk in and the door slams shut
Some stay quiet, others kick and scream
Some post bail and for a time are let out of jail
Others stay where they lay

And if you were to ask, they'd probably tell you
This is the life I chose
But did I choose it or did it choose me

I'm not saying this was my destiny or
even my fortune but maybe it was my fate.
Not that it was meant to be but
this was the hand I was dealt and
I could either rot where I lay or let the
streets carry me away, so I ran from one
to the next with a pocket full of need
and a heart full of greed, it wasn't long, I was
caught in a trap and there was no turning back!
Every time I tried to walk away, the streets they called me back!
The creativity faucet is still on, and we are all drippin' wet in poetry!

I was welcomed with an open heart
and that's how I got my start!

   —Shane Crady

Many inmates could identify with the penultimate line of the third stanza, "Every time
I tried to walk away, the streets they called me back." I hope that in the Douglas County
Jail classroom, and in the cells of incarcerated writers everywhere, "the creativity faucet"
stays on.

   2. Jimmy Santiago Baca, *A Place to Stand: The Making of a Poet* (New York: Grove,
2001), 235.

   3. Eldridge Cleaver, *Soul on Ice* (San Francisco: Ramparts, 1968), 15.